Cosmology
of the Sacred World

Cosmology of the Sacred World

The Vision of the Cosmos of Different Peoples of the World

Edited by

Baidyanath Saraswati
Yolotl González Torres

Decent Books
New Delhi

Published and printed by
Decent Books
D-36/A-1, Mohan Garden
Najafgarh Road
New Delhi - 110 059

Distributed by
D.K. Printworld (P) Ltd.
Regd. office : '*Sri Kunj*', F-52, Bali Nagar
New Delhi - 110 015
Phones: (011) 545-3975, 546-6019; *Fax*: (011) 546-5926
E-mail: dkrpint@4mis.com

ISBN 81-86921-05-2

First Published in India in 1999

Preface

Dr. Yolotle Gonzalez Torres has executed the delicate task of introducing this volume. There was no need to write a Preface after such a worthy Introduction. She happens to be my dearest *guru-bahen* (a student of the same teacher); therefore I obey the command of her affection.

Many scientists will raise their eyebrows on the title of the book *Cosmology of the Sacred World*. What is sacred about the world of matter? How can the cosmic myth be called cosmology? What is the value of myth in the age of scicnce? Such questions, even if presumtuous, need not deter the spirit of anthropologists exploring the store of primal knowledge. Every thoughtful person seeks the meaning of life. Every ancient culture has raised profound questions and sought earnestly for a satisfactory answer to the origin of the world. In the long history of human thought, the Upaniṣads hold an honoured position. Thus we have *Praśna Upaniṣad*, that is, 'Question Upaniṣad', where six questioners seek the highest truth from a teacher. That questioning continues through the ages.

The mystery of the Universe shall remain unresolved, because the question and the questioner are the same. In other words, man himself is the interpretation as well as the interpreter. As a questioning Being, he cannot know the Non-being. Let us, therefore, agree that we don not know. Nevertheless, so long as the question about the world persists among mankind, it is the *dharma* (nature) of every thinking person to explore gracefully the nature of Nature.

The early thinkers started with one thing or the other, but always one particular thing, primal entity, called *Brahman*, God, etc., (having thousand names)' associated with the creation (production) of the Universe. The essays presented in this volume also deal with this problem. Ancient cosmologists have defined the unknown agent of the Universe, using metaphors appropriate for communication at the highest level of understanding. These metaphors are not 'myth' (unreal, in modern sense) but 'reality'. They developed a penetrating insight to discern that entity or power. Modern cosmologists also use metaphors nay of another kind.

Strange as it may appear, there has been no great advance in the fundamentals of cosmological thinking. Take, for example, the recent scientific theory that the Universe has been borrowed from the vacuum. In quantum physics something can come out of nothing. Amazingly, and not so amazingly, the ancient sages have said so precisely in the same language. The concept of zero when applied to *Brahman*, the Absolute principle of the Universe, is identified with both fullness and emptiness. Fullness is the non-dual infinity of *Brahman*. The Universe that is unborn and that which is born is full. The Universe at large has an ontological independence of its own. It is characterized by the term *Brahman*, from the root *brh*, 'to expand'. The sages had thought of an "expanading *Brahman*" long long before the concept of "expanding Universe" was introduced in science. Further, scientists have suggested that at the time of big bang the Universe was infinitesimally small and infinitely dense. It is fitting that the Upaniṣadic sages called it *bindu*, the demensionless point, literally a drop. It consists of a unity of two, one, static and the other, dynamic. It is the dynamic aspect that expresses itself as the Universe of multiplicity but it essentially remains one — the epitome of all. Modern cosmologists are of the opinion that about 100 billion stars, including the Sun, make up the Milky Way Galaxy, a wheel-shaped structure. This galaxy is itself a part of a group of galaxies that form a cluster, while the clusters in turn form the supercluster of many thousands of galaxies. Powerfull telesscopes reveal that this pattern of hierarchical clustering prevails throughout the cosmos. What binds the Universe together are the cosmic strings which are hypothesized to have some bizarre properties. Long long ago, the sage Yājñvalkya (without telescope) had said this to his disciple Aruṇī: "This world and the next world and all beings and all natural phenomena are strung together by the thread, the Inner Controller, the Immortal, the *Brahman*.

Other new paradigms in modern science such as big bang, liberation of matter, gallactic seeds, extraterrestrial life, the living Earth, etc., can be traced back to ancient wisdom traditions. The Hindu notion of the "birth of God" opens a broad front in ocean cosmology, in time biology, in anthropology and zoology, and particularly at the interface of cosmology and theology.

Exploring beyond "New Age" trend the essays included in this volume have brought out important in-depth studies of ancient cosmology, exposing the total range of human experience. Traditional societies are wedded to the memory of their origin, that makes their worldview meaningful. In them, there is no gap between knowledge and existence. They hold the entire heritage of humanity: primal thought, in which are implicit the lessons of life. Their knowledge is transmitted through simple words, (even without words), and followed in the utter simplicity of life.

Baidyanath Saraswati

Contents

Introduction

Cosmology is the term for the study of cosmic view in general and also for images concerning the universe held in a religious or cultural tradition (Bolle, p. 101). All the peoples of the world have conceived the universe according to their own vision but always based on general concepts which have to do with nature and with the mind; with micro and marcrocosm, the individual and the universal spirit. In this volume we are presenting the papers of a symposium which was held in 1995 during the XVIIth International Congress of Anthropological and Ethnological Sciences. As the Congress was held in Mexico City, most of the papers are about different peoples and archaeological horizons of the cultural area called Mesoamerica, but we also have papers on Ancient Rome, India, Colombia and one on the comparative cosmology of India, China and Mesoamerica. Some of the papers about Mexico deal with ancient civilisations and are based largely on archaeological data, while others deal with the beliefs of ethnic groups and their data come mainly from ethnographic sources.

Before referring to the various papers included in this volume I would like to make a brief account of what is meant by Mesoamerica and its general characteristics as it is continuously mentioned in the papers relating to Mexican cultures.

Mesoamerica is a geographical area with almost all types of climate but sharing common cultural traits, where different civilisations developed. In the sixteenth century, when the Spanish invaded the aboriginal kingdoms,

Mesoamerica included most of the present Republic of Mexico (see map), Guatemala, El Salvador, and parts of Honduras, Nicaragua and Costa Rica. Its geographic limits particularly the northern ones changed through history.

The great Mesoamerican cultural area may be divided in five sub-areas: (1) The eastern or Golf coast, (2) the Centre or Plateau, (3) the south-east or Maya, (4) Oaxaca in the south, and (5) the west. In these areas languages of the Zoque-maya, Macro-otomangue, Yuto-aztec, Hokan and other linguistic stocks were spoken.

By 900 BC the general characteristics of the Mesoamerican culture were already present, and even though they evolved through time and were transformed according to regional patterns, the main fundamental characteristics were preserved. The term Mesoamerica is used mainly to refer to the peoples who lived in this part of the world before the coming of the Spanish, but as much of the culture of the prehispanic civilisations survived among the present ethnic groups, one can still say that these share a Mesoamerican culture.

Some of the particular traits of the Mesoamerican culture are maize as its main crop, polytheistic religion with a belief in deities who were associated with natural forces, water, maize, the Sun and Venus being specially important, employing great ceremonial temples with pyramidal bases and human sacrifices by extraction of the heart. The use of two calendars one solar of 365 days formed by 18 months of 20 days and a ritual cycle called the **tonalpohualli** or 'count of days or destinies' of 260 days formed by 20 signs and 13 numerals. The **tonalpohualli** was very important in Mesoamerican cosmovision and its main function was divinatory. Some of the 20 signs had other meanings like designating the quadrants of the universe: east, reed, north, flint, west, house, and south rabbit. There were other signs which had an important meaning like **ollin**, 'movement', which was a symbol of the Sun and of energy

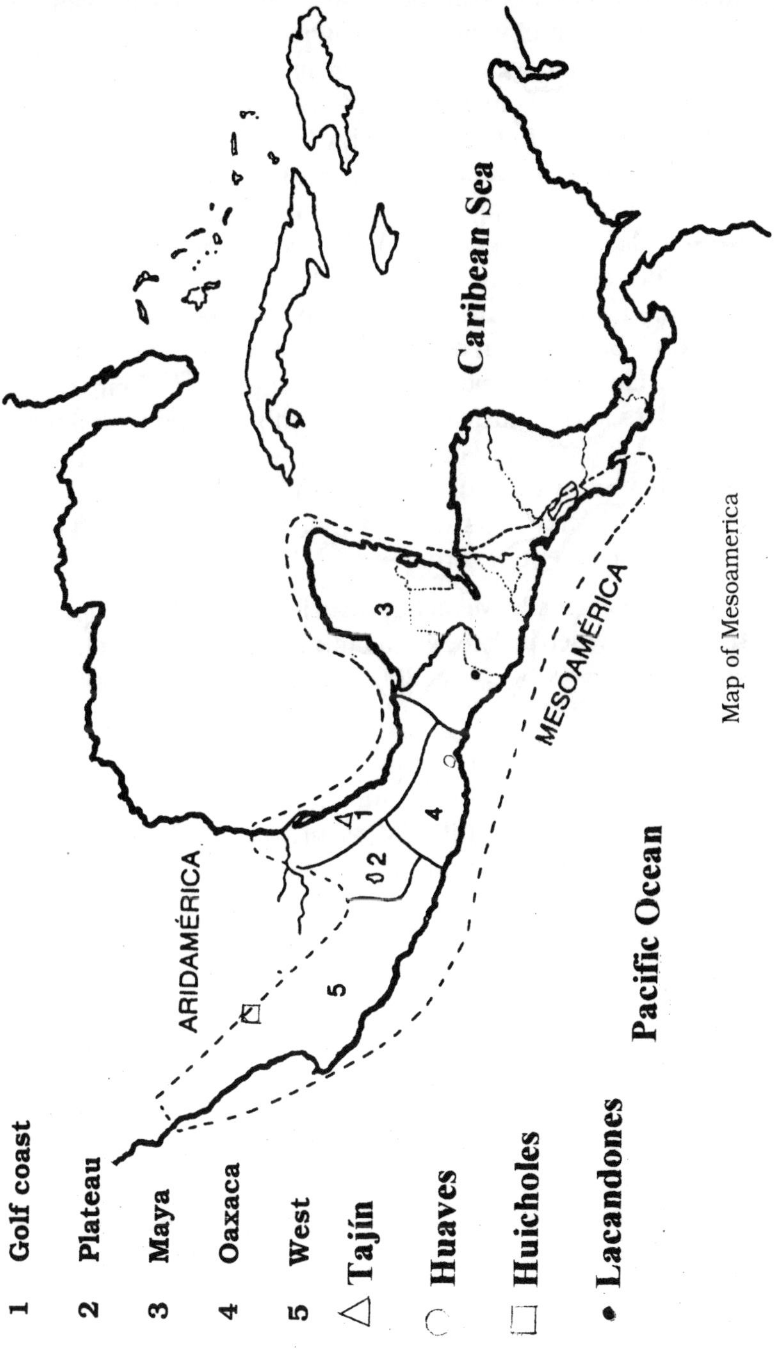

Map of Mesoamerica

in general. Another trait peculiar to Mesoamerica was the ritual 'ball game' which was played with a ball made of rubber (rubber was discovered in America) and played most of the times in a structure which had a ground plan in the form of a double T, which is supposed to have had a symbolic meaning related to the path of the sun during the year. These structures are found in most Mesoamerican archaeological sites with little differences in form. In Tajínl 17 such structures were found. Other Mesoamerican characteristic were the use of books, known as 'codexes', made of bark paper or of fine leather and folded like a screen. In these codexes were registered their ritual calendars and historical events mainly related to dynastic matters. It is an important fact that the Mayans had a complicated system of writing, which has been recently deciphered, they registered astronomical events, and they knew the concept of zero.

Chronologically, Mesoamerican history and development has been divided in three great cultural horizons: Preclassic, *ca.* 1200 or 900 BC to AC 200; Classic AC 200 to 900 and Postclassic 900 to 1521.

The oldest culture found with an urban level and supposedly with a state organisation is the Olmec, which had its centre in the Gulf (of Mexico) area, it is believed that it had a great influence in the development of all the other cultures of Mesoamérica. A very important culture which developed a great metropolis is Teotihuacan, in the centre of Mexico, which was the precursor of the Aztec culture which is the best known because we have the records of the Spanish, who conquered them, and a few of their codexes. The Aztecs, who had come from the north, founded the city of Mexico Tenochtitlan in 1325 and in only two centuries became the lords of almost all the territory of Mesoamerica. Their capital was a flourishing city, greatly admired by the Spanish who came in 1521. In 1525 the Aztecs were defeated by the Spanish and the city was totally destroyed, especially the temples which were considered places of evil by the Catholic Spaniards. Soon the Spanish conquered the rest of Mesoamerica and imposed their religion and their language, but some ethnic groups preserved their culture up to the present. (González Torrres 1991).

We shall present now the papers on cosmology starting with the papers about Mesoamerica, then the comparative paper about Mesoamerican and Asian civilisations and after that the papers on South America, India and Europe.

Sara Ladrón de Guevara's paper deals with a very specific archaeological place called El Tajín, located in the State of Veracruz and dated to about AD 900. As there are no written records she makes an interpretation of the cosmos through a few bas-reliefs of the site stressing the fact that Tajín's culture belongs to a Mesoamerican tradition, especially through the importance of the worship of the Sun, the sign **ollin** and the 'ball game'. She also interprets the depiction of ropes as a communication between the vertical levels of the universe.

Henrik Karol Coscyba's paper on the "Axis Mundi of the Mayas" deals diachronically with the cosmology of the Mayas, especially with the concept of the Axis Mundi, about which he gives a general introduction, including the ideas of several authors. He then proceeds to describe different archaeological objects where he finds illustrated examples of 'the centre of the world', tracing the oldest evidence to about 2000 years ago with the Olmec culture, passing through Izapa and all the Maya archaeological horizons, adding the information of colonial and ethnographic sources. He follows the evolution of the concept of the cosmic tree — Axis Mundi and thinks that the iconographic representation reaches its maximum complexity in the classic horizon.

Marion's article on "Lunar iconography in Lacandón Maya" cosmology is part of her fieldwork among this Maya-speaking ethnic group which lives in the tropical forest of the south of Mexico. She mantains that they share the Mesoamerican belief that they have to sustain the universe through their rituals. Using a structural approach she stresses the parallelism existing between social organisation and cosmic order and tries to prove how a feminine role assumes selenite peculiarities and through an ancient iconography which shows Mesoamerican cosmic dichotomy, is reproduced if not re-semantised by the Lacandons. Through passages of Mayan mythology and ancient texts as well as ethnographic data and the analysis of social ritual and space and its symbols, she reconstructs the apparently hidden importance of women which has been ritually appropriated by men and "allows the Moon to guide the Lacandon with the message it irradiates".

Lupo's article on"The womb that nourishes and devours" is also a product of ethnographic fieldwork, carried out among the Huave, a fishing community of the south Mexico, speaking a language from the Otomangue phylum. He analyses the complex symbolic representations of Earth, playing an important role in the Huave cosmovision as the preferred extra-human interlocutor, and shows how it is, on the one hand, the creator of energy, but, on the other, it needs replenishment. Often the 'spiritual force' of the individual falls to the ground due to some strong emotion and is held in custody by earth and the healer has to perform some rituals to call back the soul. A negative aspect of earth is manifested in the narratives of the **sapcheeb**, 'the bad woman' who appears to men during the dry months of the year when the cosmic order of thunder is absent. In spite of the Huave having many Mesoamerican traits, Lupo emphasises the need to study a system of symbols from within the culture, considering the components synchronically, looking for their meaning exclusively within Huave culture.

Ary Reisbaum's article on "Narratives and pilgrimages" of the Huichol, is also based on his fieldwork among these people who speak a Uto-aztec language, and live in the States of Nayarit and Jalisco in north-central Mexico. He tries to apply Sholem's model of a mystic or prophetic experience to the Huichol who are known for their active participation in these experiences, especially the shamans or **mara'kame** through the ingestion of **peyote**, (*Lophophora williamsi*), an hallucinogenic cactus which plays a crucial part in the cosmovision and the rituals of the Huichol. The maraka'me, through their visions learn how is the cosmos which they then describe in their chants.

Yolotl Gonzalez's paper, "The vertical and horizontal levels of the universe" in India, China and Mesoamerica deals with these conceptions in three of the great cultures of the world. Though these conceptions changed through time, there is a basic model which prevails through all their history. Special importance of the solsticial points is given to the horizontal quatripartite division and to the tripartite vertical division based on the three levels of heaven, the world of men and the infra-world. Through this paper one can visualise the amazing similarities between the conceptions of the universe in the three cultures in question.

Hugo Portela and Herinandy Gómez give us a picture of the cosmology of the Colombian tribe of the Paez who live in a environment of mountains, rivers and lakes, which makes their cosmography very similar to other Andean regions of Colombia and Peru. They divide the vertical level of the universe in three sections: above, below and 'our land' or earth. 'Our land' is divided in tamed or domesticated and wild, sacred or undomesticated. It is also divided in right and left, with a meaning quite distinct from other world vision. The relation betwen the human body and the Paez conception of nature is exemplified in a healing-cleansing ritual which includes a left foot, crown, right foot movement of the shaman over the body of the patient which recovers the relationships with the three worlds and with the right and left sides, removing the 'dirt' which has caused the illness.

Prasad analyses two forms of music and dance, the **don** and the **langré**, and tries to find what they stand for. They are analysed according to their mythico-ritual context through their performance in the Sohrae festival which takes place in December-January after the harvest. Both types of dance and music are also performed during the festivals Baha, Corok and Sohrae. The **don** symbolises union, and is sung mainly in marriages. The words refer to Santal cosmology, such as the primeval condition of the universe, the constitution of the human body and the union between male and female, a union that is also hinted at in the dance that accompanies the song. **Langré** is sung also throughout the year, but it is specifically an invocation to ask for rain, and it may be said that the song and the accompanying drums and dance mean rain. The Earth, Sohrae, daughter of a primordial couple, is sterile after harvest so it has to be propitiated to avoid her dangerousness through the ritual performed by the priests, which includes sacrifice of chickens, followed by the performance first of the **langré**, (rain) and then of the **don**, (union), repeating the marriage of the Sky and Earth mediated by rain.

Saraswati demonstrates how cosmology is illuminated by **Upanisadic** reasoning. In ancient times such issues as origins of man, nature and cosmos were classified under theology; today we place them under science. The paper on "Echoes of the Cosmic Play" highlights the points of congruence between religion and science, and finds evidence for a paradigm shift in anthropology and cosmology. While introducing new concepts such as "soundless universe", "word as world", "sound as element", "time as person", "nature as cuture", and "culture as inverted tree", it challenges the old concepts of social anthropology but strengthens philosophical anthropology by presenting a compelling picture of man in the Universe.

Albert Cook presents an overview of the cosmology of Lucretius, which reflects the beliefs of his time (Republican Rome in the earlier half of the last century BC) and at the same time his personal view of the cosmos. Titus Lucretius Carus was a poet and philosopher who wrote only one very famous poem *De rerum natura*, "On the nature of things", in which he renders in hexameters the atomic theory of Epicurus (341-270 BC), the famous Greek philosopher who was notable for his atomistic theory of physics, which proclaimed that nothing is created, and nothing passes into nothing. The Romans who were politically dominant, acknowledged the syncretic layered nature of their gods, distinguishing the Di novensiles (imported, innovated gods) from the Indigites. Lucretius envisioned a syncretic cosmology by homogenising it according to the system of Epicurus. His declared purpose was to free mankind from religious fears by proving that the soul is material and is born and dead, with the body, and that, though gods exist, they cannot intervene to help or to harm men.

I wish to thank Prof. Baidyanath Saraswati for his help in publishing of this book which may give an idea of the research being done on such an important subject as cosmology by scholars of different parts of the world, and also the National Institute of Anthropology and History of Mexico and Hugo Avila for helping me in editing this book.

Mexico city
April 1999

Yolotl González Torres

References

Bolle Kees W., 1987 "Cosmology" An Overview. *The Enciclopedia of Religion*. Mircea Eliade. Mac Millan Publishing Company. New York, Vol IV, pp. 100-10.

González Torres, Yolotl, 1996 *Diccionario de mitología y Religión Mesoamericana*. Larousse México D.F.

2

Cosmology in Tajín*

Sara Ladrón de Guevara

Tajín is located in the North of the State of Veracruz on the Coast of the Golf of Mexico. It has an abundant and varied vegetation. It is one of the most important ceremonial centres of prehispanic times due to its size and the quality of its architecture and sculpture: It is located in a valley in the slopes of the Eastern Sierra Madre, at a height of 150 meters above sea level, between 20 28'35" North latitude and 90 22'39" West longitude. The extension of the ceremonial area is of 140 hectares where more than 200 pyramidal structures are found.

The archaeological site, has been divided in two zones, the Tajín Chico (Small Tajín), where the residential area was supposed to be located and Ceremonial Tajín, where buildings of civic and religious character were built with a "*talud tablero*" cornice profile using niches as ornament.

Recent explorations date the site between AD 800-1200, which places it in the Mesoamerican Epiclasic, a period which is distinguished by the flowering of urban religious centres along the Mesoamerican area.

It is recognised by scholars that throughout the whole

---

* Translated by Rosanna Dufrane.

area known as Mesoamerica there is a concordance of ideas about the structure of the cosmos, which is confirmed in archaeological inconography as well as in myths from different traditions.

Within the iconographic corpus of Tajín, a piece known as 'the altar', discovered by José García Payon, in particular draws our attention. It is a parallele-piped sandstone split in two parts. It is carved in bas relief on four sides, the upper, the front and the sides. It was undoubtedly embedded, leaving the unworked back and underside surfaces hidden. It also has a circular hole pierced right through the middle, making it the only piece with such characteristics known up to the present in Tajín, where the rest of the bas relief sculptures can be catalogued as slabs, friezes and columns.

This particular piece besides depicting a ceremony, reproduces at the same time in a graphic frame of two dimensions the conception of the cosmos and the order of the symbolic elements: This formal representations' resemblance to other images in the Mesoamerican cultures reveal, the similarity in the ideal representation of the cosmos of the inhabitants of Tajín with the rest of these cultures, even though here, the images are related to the stylistic conventions in vogue. I also believe that the image of the cosmos must have ruled in some way the plan of the city of Tajín as we shall see later.

Iconographically the rectangle in Mesoamerica is comparable to the terrestrial plan and the sculptured upper surface of the 'altar' is rectangular, therefore I think it corresponds to the surface of the earth which is also symbolised by the image of the tortoise found in the lower central section over which is erected an altar or throne.

This altar or seat is similar to those used by important personages in other sculptured representations found on the site. In this case, on top of the altar, the sun is represented by an orifice surrounded by feathers forming a flower with sixteen petals. The sun is represented with a heliocentric conception as the axis of the cosmos, in the centre of the world. The same heliocentric conception is also reflected in the pattern of the city as the pyramid of the niches is at its centre. This pyramid has 365 niches which is a clear evocation of the heavenly body.

The sun's image is represented in the piece we are describing surrounded by two feathered serpents, whose bodies form twice the symbol of **ollin** — the calendrical symbol of the sun — giving the effect of movement, which I think was an obsession in the iconography of Tajín, as is shown in the innumerable interweavings of the architectural ornamentation and also in the numerous structures of ritual 'ball games' which have been found on this site — 17 up to the present. We can surmise that the city was surrounded by places dedicated to the practice of rites which reproduced the concept of the movement of the sun similar to the one depicted in the stone encircled with what we think are opposing elements.

Movement is achieved through the bodies of the snakes erected vertically on the central axis and radiating towards the four directions as if they were paths through which time passes, changes, opposes and resolves in two contrary currents. The feathered serpents are a clear allusion to the god Quetzalcoatl, which is precisely called the 'feathered serpent' and is a god of the planet Venus and of wind, and which according to my interpretation is frequently represented on the site by the repetitious ornament of graded fretwork, which takes an architectural form in the monumental wall, called great **Xicalcoliuhqui**. And if Ezequiel Jaimes Santos's calculations (who was in charge of reinforcing this wall during the Tajín Project) are correct, when this Xicalcoliuhqui is finally freed, we will have 260 niches which constitute a clear allusion to the Mesoamerican ritual calendar.

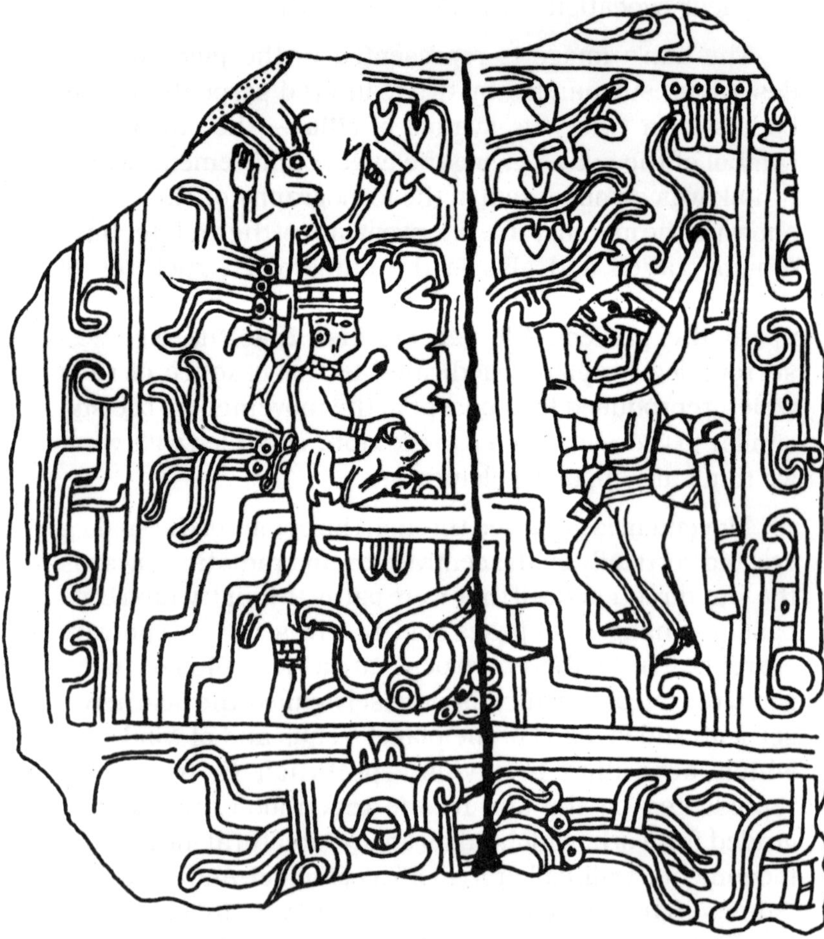

Fig. 1 Cosmic levels and the axis mundi tree, carving on a stone.

Fig. 2 Image of cosmos, Tajín, carved stone altar.

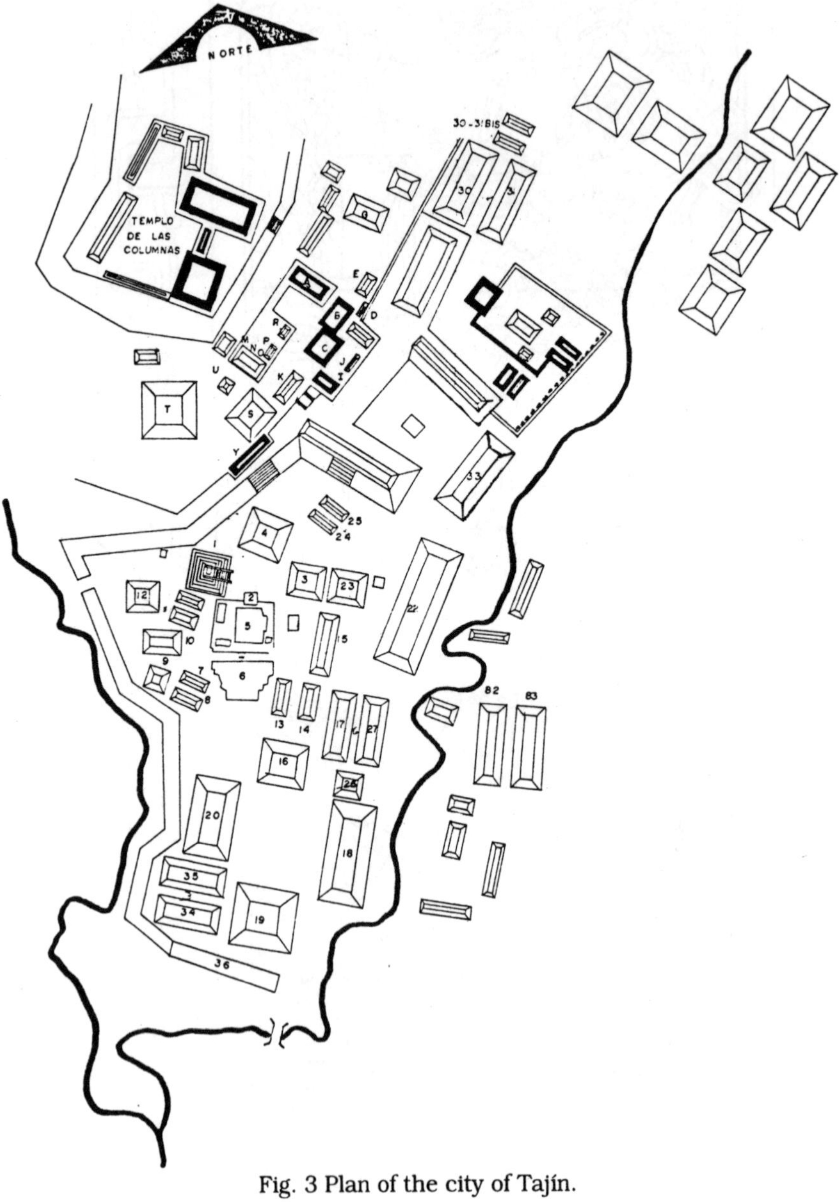

Fig. 3 Plan of the city of Tajín.

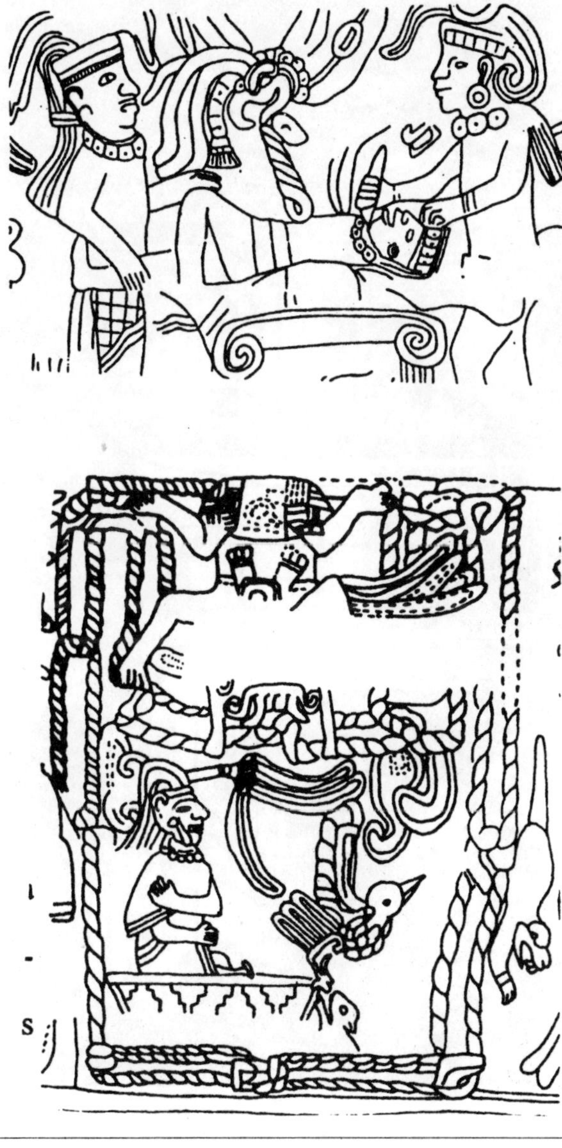

Fig. 4a. Rope coming out of the body of victim
Fig. 4b. Ropes as paths between heaven and earth

Fig. 5 Old engraving of the pyramid of 365 niches.

Another idea which comes to our mind when we see those serpents is the image of the cosmos as intertwining ropes like knots, idea which has been already recognised by scholar like Klein, Rohde and González Torres, all of whom found references to these paths of ropes not only in the chronicles (Mendita, Chilam Balam) but also in the codexes (Vindobonenesis). We find this image of the cosmos in some sculptures of Tajín.

1. The representation of a rope coming out of the belly of a victim at the moment of sacrifice, but it is worth noticing that the rope does not come from the wound as the victim is beheaded, but of the abdominal region which brings to our mind how the umbilical cord was cut at the moment of birth to allow the person to pass from one sphere to another. Passing from the world of the living to the one of the dead is equated to the unleashing of a similar rope. This idea is in accord with the Nahuatl concept of *malinalli*, which besides being a day in the ritual calendar and meaning a grass for making ropes, it also means trausitiou.

2. Thus, we think that in Tajín's cosmology there was a link between the gods with the human level through ropes, as can be seen also in the scene of one column, hinting to this idea of communication between the different levels of the cosmos through a network of twisted ropes which constituted feasible routes.

3. On the South central panel of the South Ball Game, on the sides of a two bodied being, we find the beginning of a basketry weave, a technique which also implies the intertwining of fibbers. These surround a god creator and we suggest that as they show the beginning of a work, it may be the beginning of the cosmic weave, that is: creation.

4. A simple weave forms the glyph of *ollin* which is, without doubt, the most represented motif on the site. I would even add that it is represented obsessively. The numerous ball-games on the site (seventeen) evoke it through their monumental architecture. But, another way of imposing these twists and turns is in the way the city of Tajín has been planned. Here, it is not possible to walk in a straight line which was usual in the urbanistic planning of the Classic sites, one of which is outstanding because of its magnitude: The 'street of the Dead' in Teotihuacan. In Tajín, on the contrary, the visitor is obliged to twist and turn among the buildings. There are no straight roads between one building and another, nor between one area and the next. To move about, one is made to follow the twists and turns, as do the snakes who surround the sun — centre of the cosmos.

That's all there is to say about the twists, turns and knots of Tajín for the moment. Let us return to analysing our piece of stone.

The arrows which pass through this central motif makes one think of the warrior, the necessity of death which permits the sun to survive. We know that the possession of shields and arrows is attributed to the image of the sun and these motives were frequently represented.

Four personages are depicted in the scene. They are priests, and comparable to the four Tlaloques[1] who hold up the sky from the four corners of the earth. The four are wearing headdresses with a scroll eye, emblem of an omnipresent god in Tajín, who we again identify as Quetzalcoatl.

The two central figures seem to be the main ones. They

1. Gods of water of the Central plateau.

are two men, one old and one young, standing face to face, possibly in confrontation for some type of succession of power. The old man is carrying a knife, symbol of sacrifice, of death. On his headdress can be seen a human hand, a symbol which synthesizes opposing meanings of life and death. The young man is carrying a bundle of canes a well-known element in the ceremony of the New Fire which will be burnt on the bonfire in order to renew a cycle of life every fifty-two years.

The personages behind the central ones are standing on the water and carry bags of resin (*copal*). The one on the right has the glyph *ollin*. The waters surge from zoomorphic faces, which are stylized serpents. The fact that there are two more serpents and two more entwined around the sun, undoubtedly, brings to mind the four serpents, who, according to the Ritual of the Bacabs created the world.

As mentioned before, as water is found on both sides of this bas-relief, so it was with the Mesoamerican world which had two oceans as its limits. In the same manner the centre of Tajín was constructed within the limits of two streams. Water, then, flows on both sides of this microcosmos.

We see here, the elements of earth, water, air, fire; where time and movement pass through roads that twist and turn. It is in this ambience that men live and carry out ceremonies to control and reproduce the universe. It is here that they communicate with the gods by twisted paths. It is this image which is reproduced on the altar stone as well as in the urbanistic plan of the city of Tajín, in coherence with the cosmos within its small space boundary.

References

Brueggemann, Juergen, Sara Ladron de Guevara y Juan Sanchez Bonilla 1992, *Tajín*, México, Citibank ed.

Brueggemann *et al.*, 1992, *Tajín*, México, Gobierno del Estado de Veracruz.

Castillo Peña, Patricia 1990, "Catálogo de Escultura del Tajín", *Proyecto Tajín*, Informe Técnico, Temporada 1989-1990, Ms., Tajín, Ver., dos tomos.

Dahlgren, Barbro (Ed.), 1987, *Historia de la Religión en Mesoamérica y Areas Afines*, I Coloquio, México, U.N.A.M. — I.I.A. (Serie Antropólogica: 78).

———, 1990, *Historia de la Religión en Mesoamérica y Areas Afines*, II Coloquio, México, U.N.A.M. — I.I.A.

Goncalves De Lima, Oswaldo, 1978 (1956), *El maguey y el pulque en los códices mexicanos*, México, F.C.E. (Sección de obras de Antropología).

Gonzalez Torres, Yólotl, 1979, *El culto a los astros entre los mexicas*, México, S.E.P., Sep-Setentas Diana: 217.

Klein F., Cecilia, 1982, "Woven Heaven, Tangled Earth. A weaver's paradigm of the Mesoamerican Cosmos", in *Ethnoastronomy and Archaeoastronomy in the American Tropics*, Series of Annals of the New York Academy of Science, v. 385: 1-35, New York.

Rhode, Theresa E., 1987, "Los nudos: apuntes para una investigación iconográfica" en *Dahlgren* 1987: 87-93.

———, 1990, "El tejido del cosmos: residuos de un mito perdido" en *Dahlgren* 1990: 279-82.

Paez, Rubén, 1991, "La cestería como técnica textil", in *Anuario 1989*. Laboratorio de Antropología, Guadalajara, Jal., Universidad de Guadalajara, pp. 54-76.

3

The Maya "Axis Mundi"*

Diachronic Vision of a Cosmological Concept

Henryk Karol Kocyba

The main objective of this paper is to analyze the origin and chronological development of the 'Axis of the Universe' concept amongst pre-Hispanic, colonial, and contemporary Mayas in order to identify the principal ideological components related to this concept during different historical periods.

Before beginning the analysis itself, a theoretical framework is presented which characterizes 'Axis Mundi' symbology in accordance with the comparative history of religions, as well as a possible explanation of the world-wide extension of this symbology, based on the theory of the collective unconscious from Jung's analytical psyschology.

Although this article deals with a diachronic vision, that is to say, one that includes the total history of the Maya People, due to the brevity of this paper, the pre-Hispanic period will be emphasized.

With this in mind, I shall attempt to answer the following specific questions:

---

*Translated by Jean mc Guill

(1) How and at what point was the 'Axis Mundi' concept crystalized amongst the pre-Hispanic Mayas?

(2) How did this concept evolve with time; in other words, what meanings did it have and what were its iconographic representations at different periods during the prehistory and ancient history of the Mayas?

(3) Which elements of the Maya 'Axis Mundi' concept belong solely to that culture and which belong to the 'Axis of the Universe' ideological complex established for the Old World by the comparative history of religion?

Theoretical Aspects

'Axis Mundi' is one of the basic theses of the comparative history of religion since, together with associated symbols, it represents the central part of a 'world system' for traditional societies, both ancient and present. The definition of such a system is attributed to Eliade, who characterizes it as follows:

> (a) a sacred place signifies a rupture in the homogeneity of space; (b) this rupture symbolizes an 'opening', thanks to which it is possible to move from one cosmic religion to another (from Heaven to Earth, and *vice-versa*: from Earth to the lower world); (c) communication with Heaven is expressed through a certain number of images, relative in their totality to the 'Axis mundi': pillar, . . . ladder, . . . mountain, tree, vine, etc. (d) around this cosmic axis the world ('our world') is extended consequently, the center is in the 'middle', in the 'navel of the Earth'; it is the Center of the World.
>
> (Eliade 1988: 38).

The fundamental symbol in this cosmovision is the 'Center of the Universe', and the 'Cosmic Tree' (also called the

'World Tree') and the 'Cosmic Mountain' are its two most frequent manifestations, (Eliade 1981:377-86, 1988:37-47, 1992: 29-59; Chevalier and Cheerbrant 1991:117-29, 272-74, 435-36, 722-26).

Methodologically speaking, it would be best to give the meaning of each of the concepts mentioned above, but due to the reasons already stated, I shall concentrate solely on the symbology of the tree.

According to Eliade, this symbology covers the following sets of ideas:

1. the stone-tree-altar unit,
2. the tree-image of the cosmos,
3. the tree-cosmical theophany,
4. the tree-symbol of life,
5. the tree-center of the world and support of the universe
6. mystical ties between trees and men,
7. the tree-symbol of the resurrection of vegetation

(Eliade: 276).

This wide range of symbolic meanings for the tree is due, on the one hand, to its archetypal character (in the sense of Jung's analytical psychology) and, on the other, to its natural characteristics which are summarized in the *Diccionario de los Simbolos* as follows:

> Thus the tree affords communication between the three levels of the cosmos: the subterranean, because of its roots . . . ; the surface of the earth, due to its trunk . . . ; the heavens, thanks to its branchs . . . Reptiles crawl among its roots; birds fly around its foliage: it connects the earthly and uranian worlds. It brings together all of the elements: water runs through its sap, earth enters its body through its roots, air feeds its leaves, fire results from rubbing it.
>
> (Chevalier and Cherbrant, *op.cit.*,118).

At this point, I should like to open a parenthesis regarding the process of symbolization, which Wierciński defines as the process of codifying information by means of a sign system which is carried out internally in the individual (internal symbolization). Concretely, the process is carried out by means of:

1. a structure of archetypal relations, in other words, biologically determined and genetically hereditary relations which directly connect the centers of emotion located in the limbic system with certain representative centers located in the neocortex. This is archetypal symbolization, and the related symbolic signs have a biologically determined meaning which respond to the adaptive necessities of the human species;

2. a structure of analogous relations, that is to say, relations which identify objects and connect them by means of their visible characteristics, selecting an unifying element. This is symbolization by analogy, and the related symbolic signs have a culturally determined meaning which are based on certain characteristics of the signs themselves;

3. a structure of arbitrary relations, in other words, totally abstract relations which connect objects having no visible similarity. This is arbitrary symbolization and the related symbolic signs have a culturally established meaning, determined by a totally abstract semiotic canon, having no relation with the characteristics of the sign themselves.

(Wierciński: 55).

Here we have a good example of cooperation between different disciplines. The comparative history of religion identifies the universal diffusion of certain symbols and their meaning, analytical psychology explains the reasons for this situation and anthropology clarifies the causative mechanims. Regarding analytical psychology, I refer to the school founded by Carl Gustav Jung and specially to its theory of the collective unconscious. This theory holds that the unconscious is made up of an individual part and a collctive part, the latter composed of archetypes that culturally and consciously are manifested as archaic symbolic images (Jung:352-448, 1984:15-103; Henderson:103-57; 1971: 69-77).

According to Hostie: (*Ibid.*, pp. 73-74)

> . . . archetypes are structures which are unconscious of themselves, common to all men, which direct, in accordance with their own laws, all spontaneous psychic energy, which is neither directed nor governed by the conscious mind . . . they are not innate, since they have been acquired; moreover, they are not individual, since they have been acquired by humanity.

According to this statement, the images of the 'Axis Mundi' and its concrete manifestations are none other than representations of the corresponding archetype, and this fact explains the universal and transhistorical extension of the symbolism of the universal center and axis, as well as clarifies why the pre-Hispanic Mesoamerican is no exception.

Pre-Hispanic Period

In Sotelo's words:

> In the Maya world, the ceiba (Ceiba pataudra) is presented as the 'Axis mundi', as the tree of life, as the world tree and as the center.
>
> (Sotelo, 52).

Thompson, on referring to the subject, says:

> ... a gigant ceiba tree rose up exactly in the center

> of the earth, the sacred tree of the Mayas, the 'yaxchê', the first or 'green' tree. Its roots went down into the lower world; its trunk and branches passed through the different layers of the heavens.
>
> (Thompson 1986:243).

Rivera Dorado,(1986: 44-45) relating the center and the tree, affirms:

> . . . the vertical axis that tied the zenith to the nadir, passing through the very center of the universe, was of great importance since it connected the different cosmic levels and defined the most sacred point, the central place, the navel of the world . . . There the cosmic tree was planted, the ceiba.

All these authors and several more, who concentrated on the meaning of the Cosmic Tree among the pre-Hispanic Maya (Norman: 65-68, Lowe: 269-305, Schele and Freidel: 90, 406-19, Freidel: 119-20, among others) confirm that for the Mayas the tree in question had a very similar meaning to the one established for the Old World. This conclusion, though valid in general terms, is insufficient from the diachronic analysis perspective, since this requires a historical study. Therefore I present here a review of the material evidence of the Maya 'Axis Mundi' concept corresponding to the sequence of archeological periods established for this culture.

PRECLASSIC PERIOD

It is well-known that the Mesoamerican cultural pattern begins to take shape at the end of Early Preclassic period, when the Olmec culture came into being (1300-1200 BC). Given the strong influence received in the Maya Area from the Olmecs, and considering the marked ideological character of this influence, (see Kocyba at the same Congress), it is reasonable to seek the origins of the Maya 'Axis Mundi' among the iconographic material of the 'mother culture'; moreover, as shown by Köhler (1980, Vol. 1: 583-96), the oldest evidence of the concept of the universe with four corners and a central point, come for precisely from La Venta.

From the perspective of the subject of this paper, among the motifs of the Olmec iconography, the crossed bands stand out (motifs 99-104 in Joralemon's catalog), as does the symbol of the five points (motif 177) (Joralemon 1990:13, 16, 21, 32 and 51). The first are very frequent, while the five points motif (four in the corners and one in the center) appear only a few times, for example, in monument 43 at San Lorenzo or on a vessel from Tlapacoya. Of especial interest, is an engraving on an axe from offering 2 from La Venta which appears to be the representation of a cosmic ideogram originating from obsrvations of apparent solar movement throughout the year (*Ibid.*, 23, 25; Köhler *op.cit*; Villa Rojas 1985: 232-33).

Another artistic style that must be included in an analysis of the origins of the 'Axis of the Universe' concept among the Mayas, is the style of Izapa, Chiapas. It is generally accepted that Izapa transmitted several ideological concepts from the Olmec world to the Maya religion (Lowe, Lee and Martinez Espinosa 1982, Norman, Quirarte, Kocyba 1992), and the Izapa material which expresses the concept in question, includes trees appearing on stelae and the crossed bands motif. The trees appear on stelae 2, 5, 10, 25 and 27, and have the following characteristics:

1. on stelae 5 and 27, the trees' branches penetrate the celestial band,
2. all the trees sprout from the grotesque face or entire body of a land dragon,
3. on stelae 2 and 5, the trees have roots that penetrate into the earth,
4. the trees on stelae 2 and 5 are the only ones with

fruit and have two human figures on eithr side of the trunk,

5. the trees on stelae 5 and 25 have a celestial bird at th top part,
6. the trees on stelae 5, 10 and 27 have a line that appears to cut the trunk at its middle portion,
7. the tree on stele 2 has been identified as the gourd cup tree, the one on stele 5 — as the ramon tree, the one on stele 27 as the palm tree and those on stelae 10 and 25 also as ramon trees (Norman *op.cit.*: 65-66) (*Fig.* 1).

Evidently, the most complex symbology of the tree is found on stelae 5 and 25, and although this is not the place for a general interpretation of these stelae (*Ibid.*:132-37, 165-240; Lowe *op.cit.*,299-305; Barba de Piña Chan: 9-59), it is worth making the following preliminary observations:

1. the tree on stele 5 has all the characteristics of the Cosmic Tree as the Tree of Life and Abundance, and is, therefore, an archetypal representation for all images of this kind among later Mesoamerican cultures,
2. stele 25 has two trees (one is a crocodile tree with its head under the ground, the body of which changes into foliage, and the other is a very thin stylized tree), and although both trees have the general characteristics of the Cosmic Tree, it appears that their specific messages are different. The crocodile tree has obvious earthly elements and growth of vegetation and is, therefore, a Tree of Life and Abundance, while the thin tree is similar to a cord or a rope, elements that suggest an interpretation of its being a pillar of the universe and a means of communication between the three cosmic levels.

Besides the characteristics of the Izapa trees already mentioned, these were also interpreted as trees of origin, based on the meaning of the broken trunks on stelae 5, 10 and 27 (Norman *op.cit.*,199-214, Barba de Piña Chan *op.cit.*,23).

As was already pointed out, another aspect of Izapa art related to the concept under analysis is the crossed bands motif. This motif, which appears on several stelae (2, 4, 11, 18, 60, throne 1, among others) and in very different contents, originates in Olmec art and continues in Maya art. In the latter, it appears as the celestial glyph of the crossed bands (T552) or as the 'King' glyph (T544), derived directly from the former glyph (Thompson 1950:142, 274; Rivera Dorado: 71). The general meaning of these two glyphs is related to the concepts of water, sky, sun, and time, but their graphic form has a genetic relationship to the world concept.

The cartouche shape with the crossed bands appearing on stele 18 from Izapa (a cartouche formed by parallel lines with four small circles in the corners), is represented in the headdress of the personage on stele II from Kaminaljuyú, a Maya site from the Late Preclassic period of Guatemala. It must be mentioned here that, according to Norman, stele II from Kaminaljuyú contains an abbreviated symbology of the Cosmic Tree (Norman *op.cit.*, 65, 67) and if it is true, then it can be said that the stele in question expresses the idea of the Maya 'Axis Mundi' through its iconographic characteristics, as well as its epigraphic ones (*Fig.* 2).

A very significant finding from the point of view of the symbology of the center, was a multiple burial from the end of the Middle Preclassic period in Kaminaljuyú, discovered in 1988. It contained 33 craniums, the complete skeleton of a young woman whose hands and feet were tied, 13 ceramic vessels, figurines, a large quantity of potsherds, obsidian chips, lithic tools and mica. The sectional view of the burial is from north to south, and in the center —

dividing the space into two parts — a large ceramic vessel was placed. This vessel has a number of outstanding characteristics. Superior quality, much bigger size — 40 centimeters diameter and inside it a cranium skull had been placed. It was the only container with these characteristics (Velázquez 1991). In a previous text, I presented an ideological and social interpretation of this finding, stating that this vessel symbolizes the center of the universe as a unifying element between the two parts of the burial site, which differ due to the archaeological contents and in their respective ideological meaning (Kocyba 1991b).

Another extremely interesting finding was a set of small, jadeite pendants of the "small head" type, found in Cerros, a Late Preclassic site in nothern Belize. It was made up of four small clay heads with accentuated facial features, and of a mask which was noticeably better made and larger than the small heads. The finding was made in 1975 in the B6 structure, and the distribution of the articles within the structure was quite significant; the large mask was placed in the middle, with the heads distributed in accordance with the cardinal points (Schele and Freidel 1990:121) (*Fig.* 3).

CLASSIC PERIOD

For the Classic period, evidence of the 'Axis Mundi' concept can be grouped as follows:

1. epigraphic data,
2. complex iconographic representations, on mounments as well as ceramics,
3. certain isolated iconographic motifs.

EPIGRAPHIC DATA

As is well-known, the generic name for the Cosmic Tree in Yucatecan Maya is 'yax te (che)', translated as 'green/first central tree' (Freidel 1992:120). Nevertheless, in the Temple of the Cross in Palenque, Schele identified the glyph 'wacah chan' as the name identifying the central part of the panel in other words, the tree, which he translated as 'six heavens' or 'elevated to heaven' (Schele 1987, 1990: 419).

A very interesting epigraphic reference is the 'te tun' glyph, or 'stone tree' which Schele and Stuard reported from Copán as the glyph for the stele (Schele and Stuard 1986). Regarding this we should remember Eliade's words:

> The sacred stele and the tree are symbols that are equivalent to the cosmic pillar supporting the world, which is in the center of the universe.
>
> (Eliade 1986:305).

In conclusion, the phonetic value of the 'te tun' glyph seems to confirm, in the Maya case, the meaning of the stele as a manifestation of the 'Axis Mundi'.

COMPLEX ICONOGRAPHIC REPRESENTATION

The most elaborated classical images of the Cosmic Tree are cosidered to be the representations of panels in the temples of the Cross and the Foliate Cross, and the stone tablet on the sarcophagus of the Temple of the Inscriptions in Palenque.

These images are well-known, and there is, therefore, no reason to repeat again their characteristics; suffice it to say that the Cosmic Tree appears in them as a cross-tree, assompanied by a number of details, such as:

1. the face of the C god (face of a monkey) on its trunk, the phonetic meaning of which is 'k'ul', in other words, 'deity', 'saint' or 'sacred' or indicative of these qualities (Schele and Freidel 1990:410). It is also interpreted as a sign of blood lineage (Schele and Miller 1986:77);
2. the heads of jewelled serpents with square nostrils in which the branches usually end and which symbolize liquid offerings, human blood and tree

sap (Schele and Freidel *op.cit.*,418).

3. the stripe of the bicephalous serpent, located among the branches of the cross-tree, a sign of royal and supernatural power (*Ibid.*,415-16, 418);
4. the celestial bird at the top of the tree, symbol of the center in the directional model of the world (*Ibid.*, 407, 418);
5. one of the heads of the bicephalous cosmic monster at the base of the tree, identified as the quatripartite monster. The latter represents the journey of the sun through the heavens and beneath the earth, while the general significance associated with the bicephalous cosmic monster is that it represents the movement of the stars during the day and throughout the night (*Ibid.*,408, 414-15, 418) (*Fig.* 4).

According to several authors, one of the principal characteristics of the classical Cosmic Tree is that its incarnation is the body of the king, that is to say, that the sovereign is the Cosmic Tree (Rivera Dorado *op.cit.*,60-62, Schele and Freidel *op.cit.*,90, Freidel *op.cit.*,120). This equivalence is iconographically manifested in the juxtaposition of the cross-tree over the figure of the king, in such a way that the trunk of the tree covers the center part of the body and the rod of the bicephalous serpent is held in the king's hands, interlaced with the branches of the tree, while the celestial bird appears as the figure's headdress (Schele and Freidel *op.cit.*) (*Fig.* 5).

The Foliated Cross is recognized as a specific version of the Cosmic Tree, which instead of a celestial bird, has an acuatic bird, instead of the head of the four-legged monster, shows the monster of the 'Kan' cross water lily, and whose branches contain maize grains and leaves, the human heads being metaphors for maize (*Ibid.*,409). Even without a detailed characterization, the conclusion can easily be reached that the foliate cross is a variation of the Cosmic

Tree as the Tree of Life and Abundance.

Closely related to the concept under consideration is the iconographic representation of the so-called "vision serpent". This serpent has been interpreted as symbolizing communication with divine ancestors and the gods invoked in the blood letting rites (*Ibid.*,417). In other words, the vision serpent expresses one of the specific functions of the Cosmic Tree, whose general function is the two-way communication between heaven and the region below the earth. This intimate relationship between the Cosmic Tree and the vision serpent has a beautiful and eloquent manifestation in a tripod dish from the Late Classic period, painted in the 'codex style' and published by Schele and Miller (*op.cit.*,304, 310-11). This dish contains a complex symbolic representation of the Maya cosmos, and the Cosmic Tree:

1. the trunk of thc tree grows out of the head of the god identified as Chac-Xib-Chac, a version of god GI from the Palenque Triad and the prototype of the god Chac from the Postclassic period;
2. the trunk has the head of the god C;
3. the trunk divides into two parts, the left part turning into the vision serpent;
4. the other part continues upward and contains a figure identified as the jaguar-child, a version of the god GIII from the Palenque Triad, associated with the sun;
5. the trunk culminates in the reprsentation of a human face and a large leaf;
6. the celestial bird also appears over the tree, through not directly on it.

This association of the Cosmic Tree with the gods GI and GIII is repeated on another piece from the Late Classic period, on a cylindrical vessel also published by Schele and Miller (*Ibid.*,302, 308).

Fig. 1: Izapa stelae with trees (from Smith 1984:figs.53, 54 and 56).

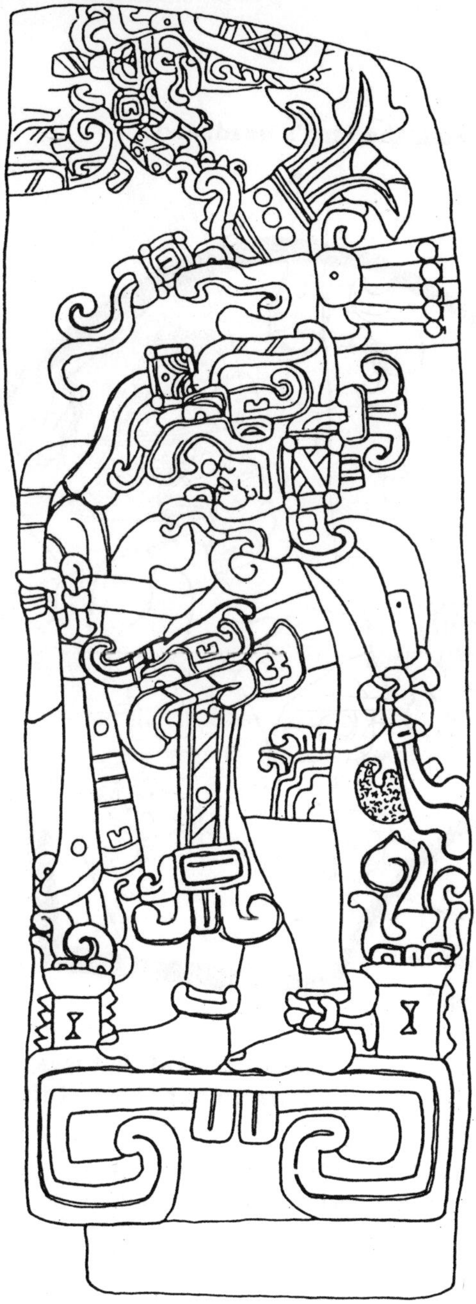

Fig. 2: Stele 11 from Kaminaljuyú
(from Smith 1984: 41).

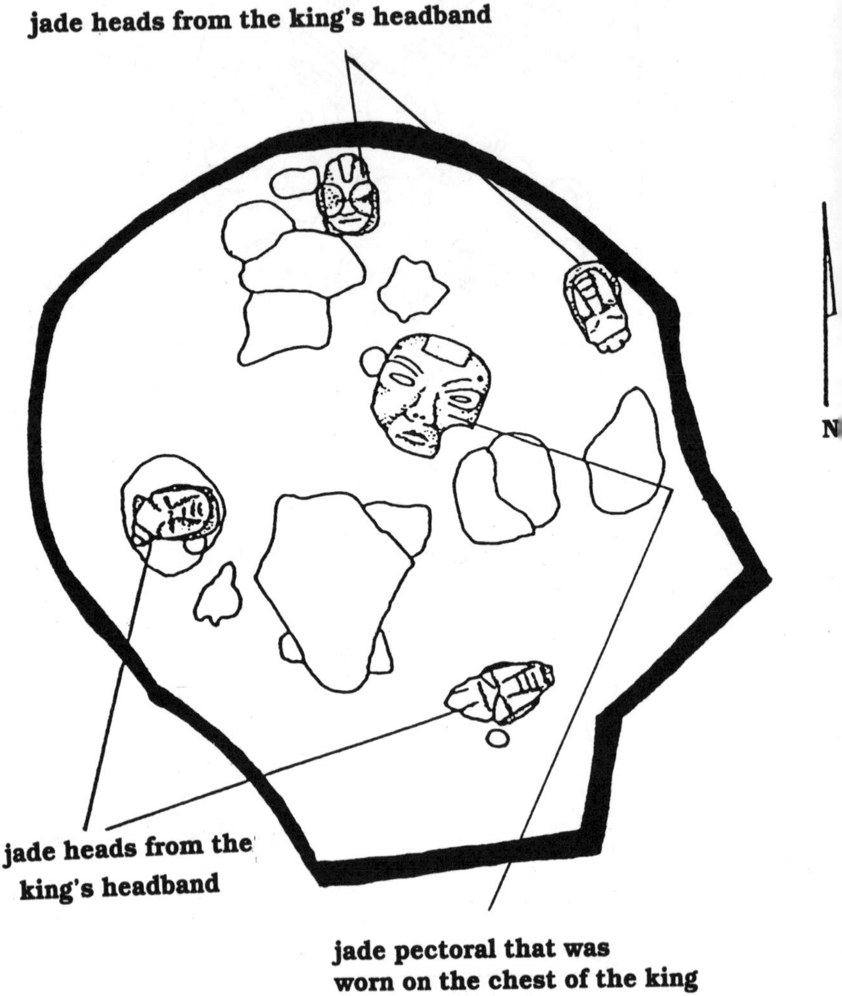

Fig. 3: Distribution of pendents from Cerros in Structure 6B (from Schele and Freidl 1990:121).

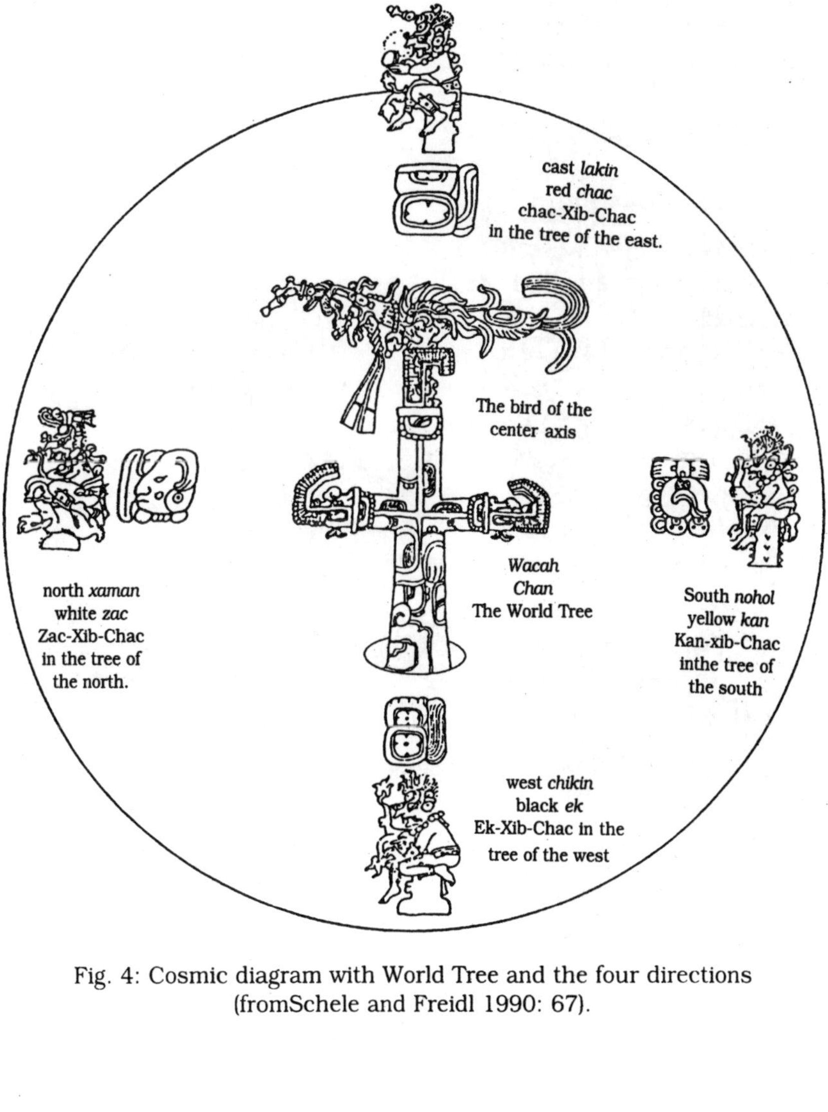

Fig. 4: Cosmic diagram with World Tree and the four directions (fromSchele and Freidl 1990: 67).

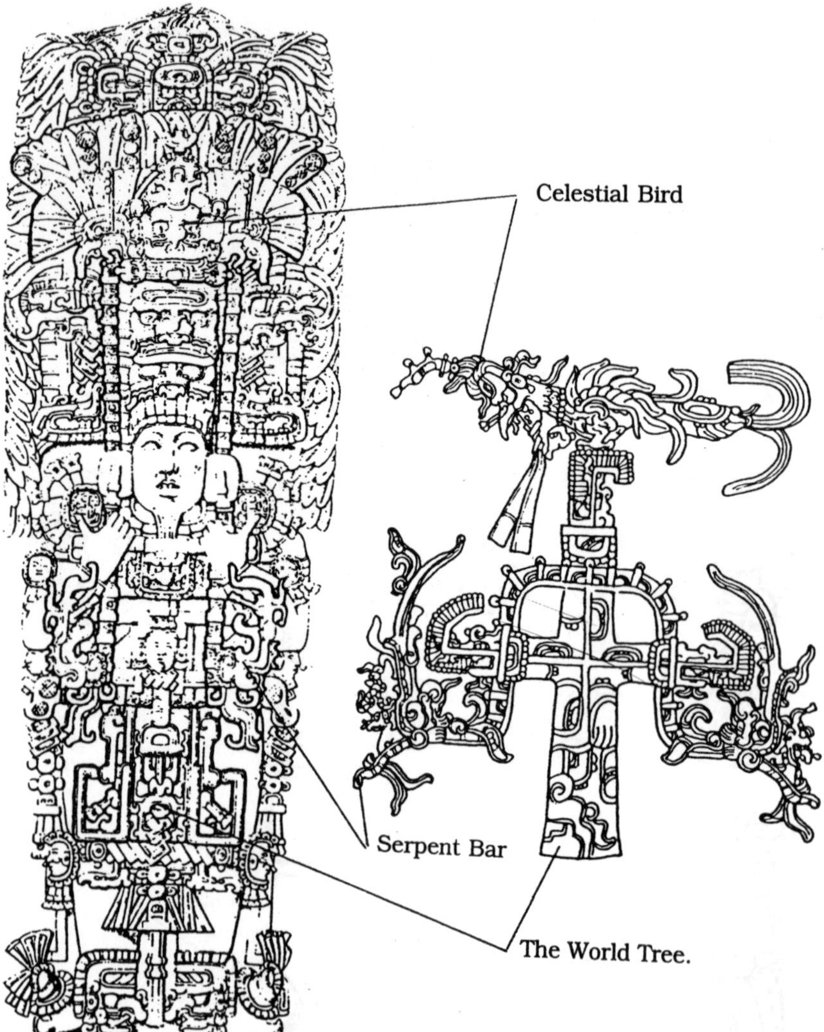

Fig. 5: Identification of Maya king with the Cosmic Tree (from Schele and Freidl 1990: 91).

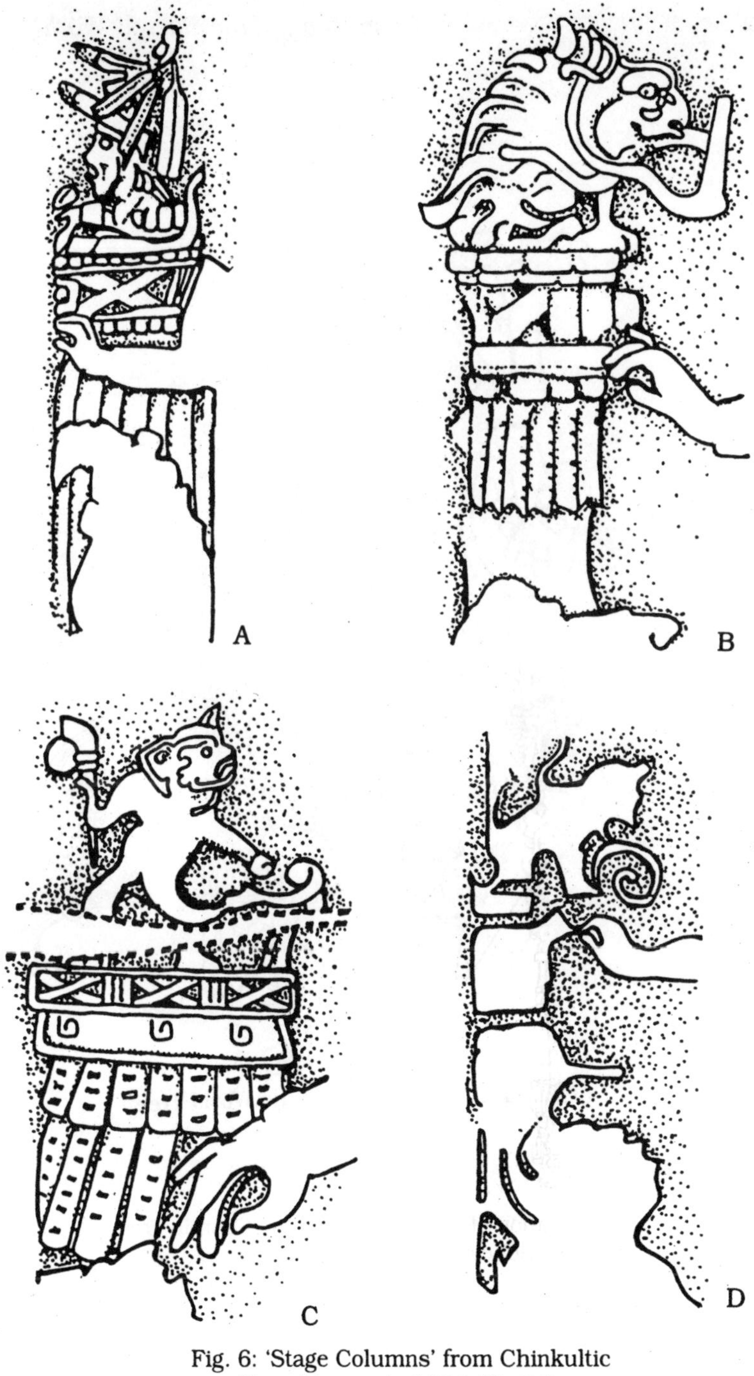

Fig. 6: 'Stage Columns' from Chinkultic
(from Navarrete 1984: Fig.94).

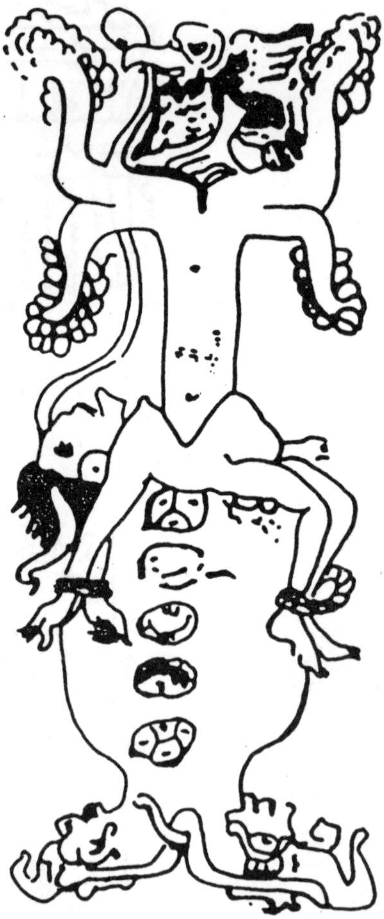

Fig. 7: Cosmic Tree from page 3 of the Dresden Codex (from Montoliu 1989: 27).

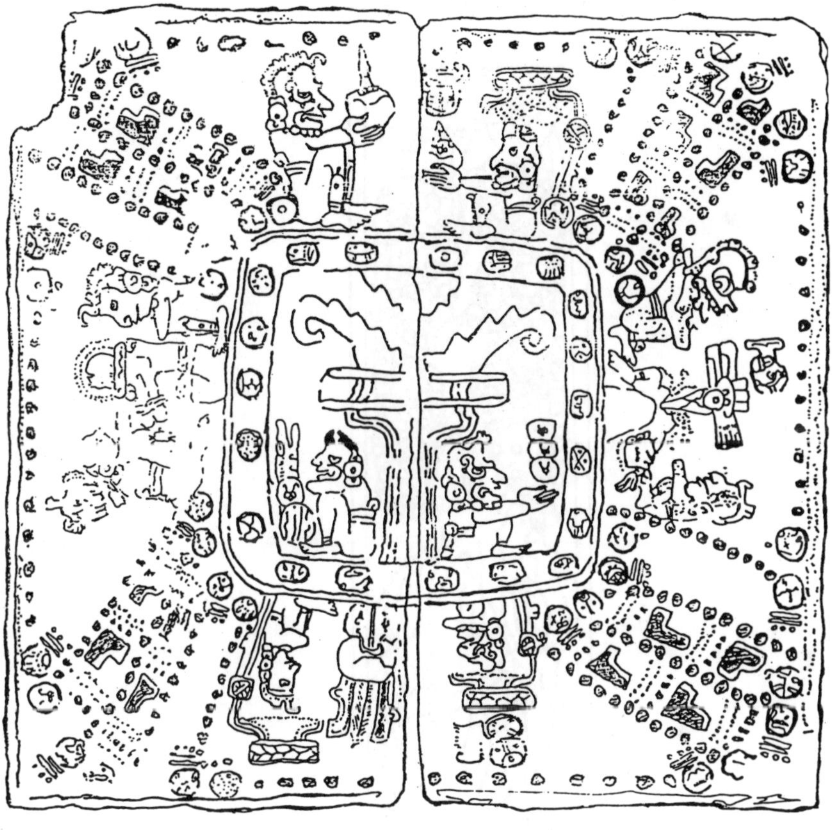

Fig. 8: Cosmic Tree from pages 75-76 of the Madrid Codex
(from Montoliu 1989: 121).

Fig. 9: Cosmic Tree from the balustrades of the North Temple of the ball court in Chichén Itzá (from de la Garza 1984:fig. 41).

Fig. 10: The sacred silkcotton tree according to Cogolludo (from Montoliu 1989: 46).

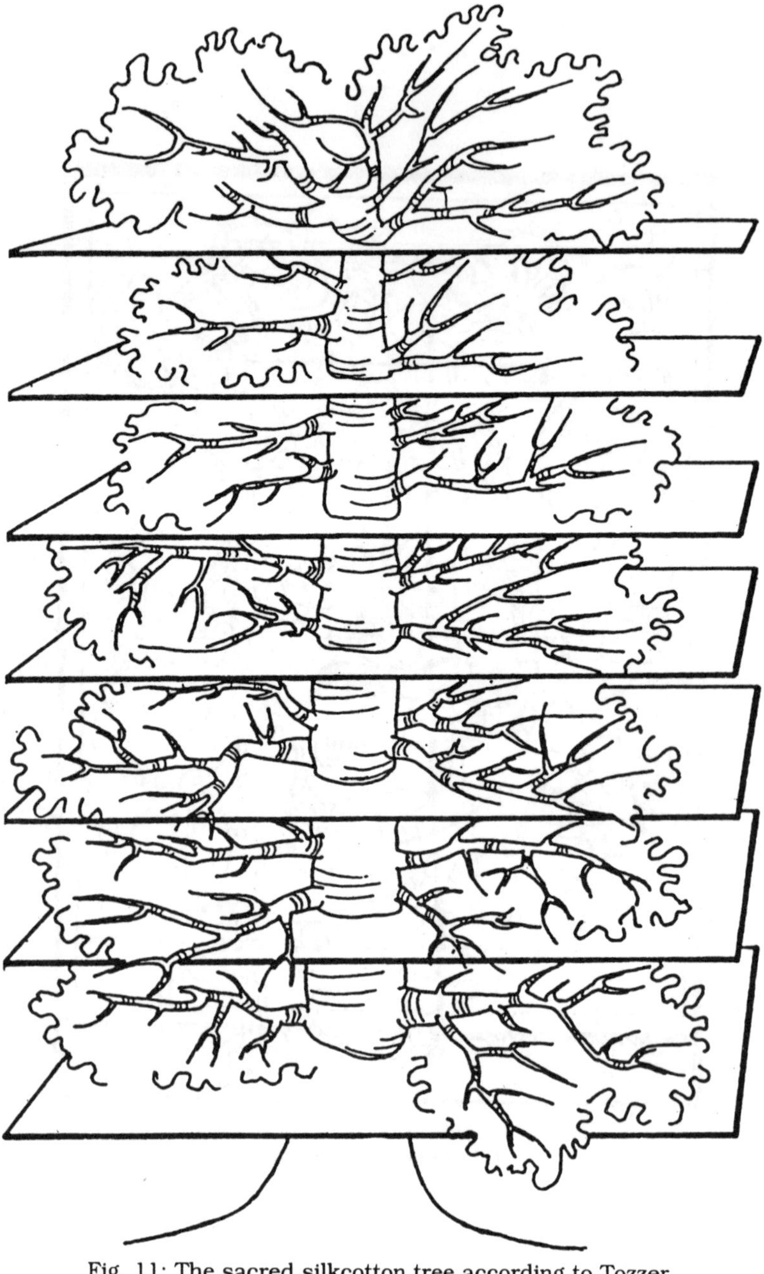

Fig. 11: The sacred silkcotton tree according to Tozzer (from Tozzer 1986:143).

SOME ISOLATED ICONOGRAPHIC MOTIFS

Beides the five points motif (appearing, for example, on the base of a monument in Copán), the crossed bands theme, already mentioned in a celestial context, can be considered as evidence of the concept with which we are dealing. Regarding non-celestial contexts, two cases must be pointed out:

1. several bricks from Comalcalco, Tabasco, contain this motif (Alvarez Aguilar, Landa Landa and Romero Rivera),
2. the crossed bands appear on the top of the so-called 'stage columns' at Chinkultic, Chiapas (Navarrete: 58, fig.94).

The latter are a feature unique to this site in Chiapas, and, as Navarrete assures us, no analogies exist (*Ibid.*). All the 'stage columns' have an animal (bird or monkey) at the top, and together they have been considered as elevated platforms used to show trained animals (*Ibid.*). Based on the crossed bands mentioned and remembering what was said about the symbology of the columns, I favor a different interpretation which is evident from the context of this study; in other words, that the 'stage columns' at Chinkultic are representations of the 'Axis Mundi' (*Fig.* 6).

POSTCLASSIC PERIOD

For this period, there is an extensive series of clues and evidences of the 'Axis of the Universe' concept, of which only the most essential will be mentioned. Most come from the codexs in which a glyph (T663) has been interpreted by Roys as the center'. This glyph is associated with the colour 'yax', green, and its cosmological meaning has been confirmed by (Kelley: 56-57, in Sotelo: 49).

In the *Dresden Codex* there are an endless number of 'crossed bands, but the representation on page 74 merits especial attention. Here the zoomorphic body of Itzam Ná is covered with various planetary signs, all of which have a quadripartite appearance. One of these signs is clearly a manifestation of the five points motif, with the center point being much larger than the other four.

On pages 29a-30a of the same codex, there are four Chacs, each seated on a directional tree of the world. A fifth Chac is seated on an earth sign ('cab') and the affix 'yol', which reads 'yolcab', or 'in the heart of the earth', referring to the fifth direction, that of the cosmic center (Thompson 1986: 244-45, 1988: 227).

On page 3 of the *Dresden Codex*, there is a well-known representation of a human sacrifice; what interests us at this moment is that a tree, with the obvious characteristcs of the Maya Cosmic Tree (the earth monster at the botton and a celestial bird on top) rises from the open chest of the victim (*Fig.* 7). There is an evident similarity between this figure and the representation appearing on the stone tablet from the Temple of the Inscriptions from Palenque. The latter, as we have mentioned, is one of the most complex manifestations of the Cosmic Tree.

Finally, on pages 26c-28c of this Codex, there are trees with the following characteristics:

1. they arise from the 'tun' 'stone' or 'year', glyph, in other words,
2. the trunks are draped with a ceremonial cloak with human footprints on it,
3. the trunks have scales like the earth monster's.

Norman has already suggested that the number of branches may have a symbolic significance; stelae 2 and 27 from Izapa, and the trees on pages 3, 26c-28c of the *Dresden Codex* all have four branches, a fact that may be related to the complex symbology of the number four (Norman 1976: 66-67).

On pages 75-76 of the *Madrid Codex*, there is a scene that is perhaps the best known and the most frequently reproduced in texts on the Maya religion, the famous cosmic diagram with the World Tree in the center and the 'creator' couple on either side of it (*Fig.* 8). Without going into detail on this scene, it is enough to say that the idea of a four-part distribution of time and space, shown on the pendents from Cerros from the Late Preclassic period, found its most perfect manifestation on pages 75-76 of the *Madrid Codex*.

Among postclassic archaeological material, we must mention the balustrades from the stairway of the North Temple of the ball court in Chichén Itzá, Yucatán. Each of these balustrades has a carved tree, the trunk of which arises from a head interpreted as the head of the earth monster. The branches of the tree are full of leaves, fruit and flowers on which birds and butterflies feed (Thompson 1986: 271). Without a doubt, these figures express the version of the Cosmic Tree as the Tree of Life and Abundance.

COLONIAL PERIOD

We have a series of ethnohistoric and historic sources, Maya as well as Spanish from this period (1521-182) that contain various references to the sacred silkcotton trees of the Mayas. The most important, from the point of view of the aspect we are analyzing, is the book *Chilam Balam de Chumayel*, written in Maya language in Roman alphabet mentions twice the directional ceibas. The four ceibas, called the 'Mother ceibas' appear on the first page, associated with different concepts and objects (De la Garza 1980: 220, Rivera Dorado *op.cit.*, 58). Nevertheless, the most significant part of the text is found in the chapter called 'Book of the Ancient Gods' ('Libro de los Antiguos Dioses') where the central ceiba, is described as follows:

And the Great Mother ceiba rose up from the

> memory of the destruction of the earth. It straightened out and raised its top, asking for eternal leaves. And w ith its branches and roots called out to its Lord.
>
> (*Ibid*: 243).

Montoliu, in her exhaustive study of the *Chilam Balam de Chumayel*, based on Roys' translation (1933), mentions the following directional ceibas:

1. 'Chac Imix Che', the Red Food Tree which represents the east,
2. 'Zac Imix Che', the White Food Tree which represents the upward direction,
3. 'Ek Imix Che', the Black Food Tree which represents the west,
4. 'Kan Imix Che', the Yellow Food Tree, which represents the downward direction, (Montoliu 1989:40-41).

As for the central ceiba, Montoliu calls it 'Yax Cheel Cab', 'the First Tree of the World', or 'Yax Imix Che', 'the First Food Tree' attributing to it the following characteristcs:

1. it is born from corn seed germinated as a result of the action of the heat of the sun at its zenith,
2. it is related to the beginning of the counting of years 'tunob',
3. it grows in the center of the earth,
4. its bird is the quetzal, which has green and blue feathers of great value,
5. its fruit causes lust, since it grows in the place of the reproduction of life (*Ibid*., 23, 27, 40).

As Montoliu points out, the same image of the universe, with four ceibas in the corners and one in the center, is repeated in other books of the *Chilam Balam* and in *Ritual de los Bacabes* (*Ibid.*.145).

Regarding non-indigenous colonial sources, the work of Nuñez de la Vega (beginning of the eighteenth century) is interesting. He says about the Mayas of Chiapas:

> . . . they believe that their lineage comes from the roots of that ceiba, and they have it painted on an ancient cloth.
> Nuñez de la Vega 1702:9 in León Portilla 1986:144).

Another important book is that of Cogolludo on the Mayas of Yucatán, he includes graphic image of the sacred central ceiba with the following charactristics:

1. it is born from a rectangular representation of the earth,
2. it has four roots and four branches,
3. it is surrounded by thirteen drawings showing Spanish influence of the lords of the 'katunob' (Díaz Solís 1968:18 in Montoliu *op.cit.*,30) (*Fig.* 10).

Avendaño (end of the seventeenth century, *Ibid.*,30-31) wrote according to the Itzáes of Tayasal, Guatemala, a ceiba called 'yax-chel-cab', which grew in the center of the earth and its branches penetrated the heavens. Landa placed this tree in paradise, stating:

> . . . a tree that is called there yaxché, very cool and providing much shade, which is (a) ceiba, under whose branches and in the shade of which all would rest and take pleasure forever.
>
> (Landa 1978: 60).

The Contemporary Mayas

Ethnological studies carried out among contemporary Maya groups have provided information substantiating that the concept of the central cieba continues to exist.

For the Mayas of Yucatán, we take into especial consideration the study by Tozzer in Valladolid, where he gathered information on:

> a giant ceiba ('vastse') which grows in the exact center of the earth, elevating its branches through successive levels until they reach the seventh heaven, where the 'Great God' of the Spaniards abides.
>
> (Tozzer 1982:180).

The same author states that the ceiba growing in Valladolid had four branches which pointed toward the four cosmic directions (*Ibid.*,191) (*Fig.*11).

To sum up, the ceiba described by Tozzer is a clear manifestation of the Tree of the World, which, on the one hand, brings together the characteristics established by the comparative history of religion for this tree (its po- sition in the center of the world, its role as a central pillar, its function as a channel of communication between the different levels of the universe), and on the other, presents some aspects peculiar to Maya thought on the subject (its orientation towards the four cosmic directions, its vertical division into seven parts, related to the seven heavens).

Villa Rojas presented relevant data on the concept of the 'center', although he did not find evidence of the Cosmic Tree during his research in Quintana Roo (Villa Rojas 1987:443). In Yucatecan Maya, the 'center of the world' is called 'tan yok'ol ka'b' or 'tan yol kab' (Sotelo *op.cit.*, 49). Recalling that in traditional cosmovision the structure of the cosmos has a parallel in the structure of the human body, it is reasonable to think of a central point in the human body as an equivalent to the cosmic center, and it is on this subject that Villa Rojas found his most interesting information. I refer to the 'tipté concept, a special organ found by the Mexican ethnologist among the Mayas of

Yucatán, which he described as;

> . . . a point of reference for the entire system . . . which presents the point at which all the veins of the body start. . .
>
> (Villa Rojas 1980: 36,37).

Its position below the navel establishes four sections or directions in the abdomen, and any change in its position results in an imbalance of the organism (*Ibid.*). This data clearly shows the profound significance in maintaining order that Yucatecan Mayas give the central point and its equivalent in the body.

The symbolism of the cosmic center is also found in the religious life of the Chortis of Guatemala, who keep alive the idea of the four directions of the universe and a central point in a ceremonial cloth with five rings and a ceremonial table with five containers on it (Girard 1962:19, 175, photos 8, 122).

In Chiapas, the Tzotzils of San Andrés Larráinzar express the millenary concept of the center of the world and the four cosmic points through the 'moc' ceremonial platform (Ochiai 1984:189-96). In this case, the four directions are represented by the platform's pillars, and the center is marked by a cross set-up under the platform. In other words, we have here a concrete case of the identification of the Christian cross with the Cosmic Tree, and idea already expressed by Blom as follows:

> For the Indian of today, the cross that we see in his rooms is not the Christian cross, but the direct descendant of this 'yax-ché. . .
>
> (Blom 156: 284 in Girard *op.cit.*, 234).

This idea was later reinforced by Vogt, who informs us that the Tzotzil of Zinacantán consider the cross to be the 'door' leading to the gods (Vogt: 92). In other words, they assign the Christian cross one of the principal qualities of the Cosmic Tree.

Among the Tzotzils of Larráinzar already mentioned, Holland recorded the belief in an enormous silkcotton tree which grows up from the center of the world toward the heavens (Holland 1989: 69). Although the structure of the universe proposed by this scholar, for the Mayas has been recently severly criticized (Köhler: 202), we have here an obvious example of the sacred cieba as the Tree of the World, the same tree mentioned before for the Mopans and Kekchis of Belize (Montoliu: 17). Despite Tozzer and Holland's information about a central ceiba, the most common concept among the modern Maya is of four directional ceibas or four supports of the universe, as is shown in studies from the Highlands of Chiapas carried out by Gossen (43), Vogt (*op.cit.*, 192) and Holmes (220).

General Conclusions

(1) During the Middle and Early Preclassic periods, in the context of the Olmec culture, a concept of the universe with four cardinal points (or inter-cardinal points) and a central point was crystalized. Although a directional pattern with the center as the organizing point appears in the Maya Area at the end of the Middle Preclassic (the pendants from Cerros). The later development of this idea leads to a world concept in which everything has a quatripartite distribution, organized around a central point, as can be appreciate in the cosmic diagram on pages 75-76 of the *Madrid Codex* from the Late Postclassic period. This concept survived the conquest and the colonial period and exists today among some Maya groups in Mexico (the Tzotzils and Yucatecan Mayas), and Guatemala (the Chortis).

(2) The idea of the World Tree as an image of the 'Axis Mundi' first appeared in its fully developed form during the Late Preclassic period in Izapa. Since then, the

Mesoamerican Cosmic Tree rises up from the body of the earth dragon, is crowned by a bird as the symbol of heaven and the center, has roots that penetrate into the earth and branches penetrating the sky. The difference between the Cosmic Tree as the central support and means of communication between the three levels of the universe, and the Cosmic Tree and the Tree of Life and Abundance is established in Izapa.

(3) Since Izapa's time, the World Tree as the central support got the characteristics of a stylized and schematic image (stele 25). During the Classic period, this image progressively evolved, reaching its maximum complexity during the Late Classic period, when its functions were distributed among:

A. the Cosmic Tree itself, as a central support and means of general communication between the three levels of the universe,

B. the vision serpent, symbolizing communication with divine ancestors and the gods invoked in the ceremonies of blood letting rite.

C. the bicephalous cosmic monster, the means of communication between heaven and the grave for the Sun, Venus, and other stars.

During the Postclassic period, the tree in question remains important as a cosmic concept, but loses much of its conceptual and iconographic richness, becoming once again the simplified and stylized image of a tree, as can be seen in the center of the cosmic diagram of the *Madrid Codex* or on page 3 of the *Dresden Codex.* The books of the *Chilam Balam* show that this concept existed among the Yucatecan Mayas of the colonial period, and the ethnological research of Tozzer and Holland also prove the existence of the Cosmic Tree concept itself among today's Yucatecan Mayas and the Tzotzils of Chiapas. At least during the colonial period and among contemporary Mayas, the World

Tree in the version mentioned (as a central pillar and a means of general communication between the three levels) is identified with the ceiba, a tree which has no nutritional qualities but which is impressive because of its strength and size.

(4) The World Tree as the Tree of Life and Abundance has as its prototype the tree on stele 5 from Izapa. In the Classic period it is transformed into the foliate cross-tree, intimately related to corn and strongly pluvial. In the Postclassic period, the tree suffers a process of conceptual and iconographic impoverishment, although it retains the principal features of the Tree of Life and Abundance, as can be seen in the balustrades on the stairway of the North Temple in the ball court of Chichén Itzá. It must be stressed that the Chichén Itzá tree is by no means a silkcotton tree,but a symbolic and metaphoric one. The same tree, as related to food, is still mentioned in colonial sources; however,the World Tree as the Tree of Life and Abundance has disappeared completely among the Mayas of today.

(5) To sum up, the Cosmic Tree as the principle manifestation of the 'Axis Mundi' was presented in Maya religious thought beginning in the Late Preclassic period. It later evolved into two different, but interrelated, currents, reachng us today as the sacred ceiba, the World Tree in its version of central support and union of the different levels of the universe.

References

Adams, Richard E. (Compiler) (1989), *Los origenes de la civilizatión maya*, Fondo de Cultura Económica, México.

Alvarez Aguilar, Luis Fernando, Landa, Landa, María Guadalupe y Romero Rivera, José Luis (1990), *Los ladrillos de Comalcalco*, State Government of Tabasco, Villahermosa, Mexico.

Barba De Piña Chan, Beatriz (1990), "Buscando raíces de mitos mayas en Izapa", in Dahlgren, Barbro, pp. 9-59.

Benson, Elizabeth P. and Griffin, Gilleet G. (Eds) (1988), *Maya*

Inconography, Princeton University Press, Princeton, New Jersey, U.S.A.

Blom, Franz (1956), "La vida precortesiana del indio chiapaneco de hoy", in *Estudios Antropológicos. Homenaje al Doctor Manuel Gamio*, UNAM, Mexico, pp. 277-85.

Chevalier, Jean and Cheerbrant, Alain (1991), *Diccionario de los Símbolos*, Editorial Herder, Barcelona, Spain.

Dahlgren, Barbro (Coordinator) (1990), *Historia de la Religión en Mesoamêrica y áreas afines. II Coloquio*, UNAM, Mexico.

De La Garza, Mercedes (Compilation and Preface) (1990), *Literatura Maya*, Biblioteca Ayacucho, Caracas, Venezula.

De La Garza, Mercedes (1984), *El universo sagrado de la serpiente entre los mayas*, UNAM, Mexico.

Demarest, Arthur A. and Conrad, Geoffrey W. (Editors) (1992), *Ideology and Pre-Columbian Civilizations*, School of American Research Press, Santa Fe, New Mexico, U.S.A.

Diaz Solis, Lucila (1968), *La flor calendárica*, Talleres de Impresión Díaz Mass, Mexico

Eliade, Mircea (1981), *Tratado de Historia de las Religiones*, Ediciones Cristianidad, Madrid, Spain.

——— (1986), *El chamanismo y las técnicas arcáicas del éxtasis*, Fondo de Cultura Económica, Mexico.

——— (1988), *Lo sagrado y lo profano*, Editorial Labor/Punto Omega, Madrid, Spain.

——— (1992), *Imágenes y símbolos*, Taurus Humanidads, Madrid, Spain.

Freidel, David A. (1992), "The Tress of Life: Ahau as Idea and Artifact in Classic Lowland Maya Civilization", in Demarst and Conrad, pp.115-35.

Girard, Rafael (1949) *Los Chortis ante el problema maya*, Antigua Libreía Robredo, 5 vol., Mexico.

——— (1962), *Los mayas eternos*, Libro Mex Editores, Mexico.

Gossen, Gary H., (1979), *Los Chamulas en el mundo del Sol*, Instituto Nacional Indigenista, Mexico.

Henderson, Joseph L. (1984) "Los mitos antiguos y el hombre moderno" in Jung, Carl, G. 1984 pp. 103-57.

Holland, William R. (1989), *Medicina Maya en los Altos de Chiapas*, Instituto Nacional Indigenista y Consejo Nacional para la Cultura y las Artes, Mexico.

Holmes, C. Guiteras (1986), *Los peligros del alma*, Fondo de Cultura Económica, Mexico.

Hostie, Raymond (1971), *Del mito a la religión en la psicología de C.G. Jung*, Amorrortu Editores, Buenos Aires, Argentina.

Joralemon, Peter, David (1990), *Un estudio en iconografía olmeca*, Universidad Veracruzana, Xalapa, Mexico.

Jung, Carl G. (1983), *Los complejos y el inconsciente*, Alianza Editorial, Madrid, Spain.

——— (1984), *El hombre y sus símbolos*, Biblioteca Universal Contemporánea, Barcelona, Spain.

Kelley, David H. (1976), *Deciphering the Maya Script*, University of Texas Press, Austin, U.S.A.

Kocyba, Henryk Karol (1991a), "La religión maya postclásica. Casideraciones teórico-metodológicas", in *Cuicilco*, No.25, Revista de la Escuela Nacional de Antropología e Historia, Mexico, pp.79-91.

———(1991b), "La interpretación socio-religiosa de un entierro múltiple de Kaminaljuyú", in *Memorias del II Coloquio Pedro Bosch Gimpera*, UNAM, Mexico (to be printed).

——— (1992), "La religión maya preclásica: Una visión evolutiva", in *Cuicuilco*, Revistad de la Escuela Nacional de Antroplogía e Historia, Mexico (to be printed).

Kohler, Urlich (1980), "Cosmovisión indígena e interpretación europea en estudios mesoamericanistas. La antropología americanista en la actualidad", in *Homenaje a Rafael Girard*, I t., Editores Unidos, Mexico, pp. 583-96.

———, (1987), "La aportación de los estudios etnográficos en los Altos de Chiapas para la comprensión de las culturas precolombinas de Mesoamérica", in *Anales de Antropología*, vol. XXIV, UNAM, Mexico, pp. 199-215.

Landa, Diegop de (1978), *Relación de las cosas de Yucatán*, Editorial Porrá, Mexico.

Leon Portilla, Miguel (1986), *Tiempo y realidad en el pensamiento maya*, UNAM, Mexico.

Lee, Thomas A. (Introduction and Bibliography) (1985), *Los Códices Mayas*, Universidad Autónoma de Chiapas, Tuxtla Gutiérrez, Mexico.

Lowe, Gareth W., Lee, Thomas A. and Martinez Espinosa, Eduardo (1982), *Izapa: An Introduction to the Ruins and Monuments*, New World Archeological Fundation, Brigham Young University, Provo, Utah, U.S.A.

Montoliu, María (1983), "Reflexiones sobre el concepto de la forma del universo entre los mayas", in *Anales de Antropología* vol.XX, t.II, UNAM, Mexico, pp. 9-39.

——— (1989), *Cuando los Dioses Despertaron. Conceptos cosmológicos de los antiguos mayas de Yucatán estudiados en el Chilam Balam de Chumayel*, UNAM, Mexico.

Navarrete, Carlos (1984), *Guía para el estudio de los monumentos esculpidos de Chinkultic*, Chiapas, UNAM, Mexico.

Norman, Gareth V. (1976), *Izapa Sculpture, Part 2: Text*, New World Archaeological Foundation, Brigham Young University, Provo, Utah, U.S.A.

Nunez De La Vega, F. (1702), *Constituciones diocesanas del Obispo de Chiapas*, Roma.

Ochiai, Kazuyasu and Sanmiguel, Ines (1984), "Moc: El espacio simbólico de la arquitectura ceremonial entre los tzotziles do los Altos de Chiapas", in *Investigacions recientes en el Area Maya. XVII Mesa Redonda de la Sociedad Mexicana de Antropología*, t.II, Sociedad Mexicana de Antropología, Mexico, pp. 189-97.

Quirarte, Jacinto (1989), "Estilos artísticos tempranos de Mesoamérica y arte maya del Clásico Temprano", in ADAMS, Richard E. (Compiler), pp. 275-315.

Roys, Ralph L. (Translation) (1933), *The book of the Chilam Balam de Chumayel*, University of Okahoma Press, Norman, U.S.A.

Rivera Dorado, Miguel (1986), *La religión maya*, Alianza Universidad, Madrid, Spain.

Schele, Linda (1987), *Workbook of the hieroglyphic workshop*, University of Texas, Austin, U.S.A.

——— and Miller Mary Ellen (1986), *The Blood of Kings, Dynasty and Ritual in Maya Art*, George Braziller Inc., New York, U.S.A.

——— and Stuart, David (1986), "Te-tun as the glyph for "stele", in *Copan Notes*, No.1, Copan Mosaics Project and Instituto Hondureño de Antropología e Historia.

——— and Freidel David (1990), *A Forest of Kings. The Untold Story of the Ancient Maya*, William Morrow and Company, Inc., New York, U.S.A.

Smith, Virginia G. (1984), *Izapa Relief Carving: Form, Content, Rules for Design, and Role in Mesoamerican Art History and Archaeology*, Dumbarton Oaks Research Library and Collection, Washington D.C., U.S.A.

Sotelo Santos, Laura Elena (1988), *Las ideas cosmológicas mayas en el siglo XVI*, UNAM, México.

Thompson, Eric S. (1950), *Maya Hieroglyphic Writing: Introduction*, Carnegie Institution, Washington, U.S.A.

——— (1986), *Historia y religión de los mayas*, Siglo XXI, México.

——— (1988), *Un comentario al Códice de Dresde. Libro de jeroglifos mayas*, Fondo de Cultura Económica, México.

Tozzer, Alfred M. (1982), *Mayas y Lacandones. Un estudio comparativo.* Instituto Nacional Indigenista, México.

Wiercinski, Andrzej (1981), *Antropogeneza = evolucia ciwilizacji (Antropogénesis = evolución de la civilización*, University of Warsaw, Warsawm Poland.

——— (1989), *Ewolucja magii i religii (Evolución de la magia y religión)*, Universituy of Warsaw, Warsaw, Poland.

Velazquez, Juan Luis (1992), "Un entierro múltiple del Preclásico Medio en Kaminaljuyú, Guatemala", in *Memorias del I Congreso Internacional de Mayistas*, UNAM, México (to be printed).

Villa Rojas, Alfonso (1980), "La imagen del cuerpo humano según los mayas de Yucatán" in *Anales de Antropología*, Vol. XVII, t.II, NUAM, México, pp.31-47.

——— (1985), "Nociones preliminares sobre la cosmologia maya" in *Anales de Antropología*, Vol.XXII, UNAM, México, pp. 229-51.

——— (1986), "Espacio y tiempo entre los grupos contemporáneos", in Leon Portilla, Miguel, México, pp. 119-69.

——— (1987), *Los Elegidos de Dios. Etnografía de los mayas de Quintana Roo*, Instituto Nacional Indigenista, México.

Vogt, Evon Z. (Editor) (1980), *Los Zinacantecos*, Instituto Nacional Indigenista, México.

4

Some Considerations on the Vertical and Horizontal Levels of the Universe

Yolotl González Torres

The taxonomy of the universe which divides space into a vertical and a horizontal plane has been a common denominator of the symbolic organization of space of ancient civilizations and primitive peoples. In fact the difference between cosmos and chaos was the establishment of an order which implied classification and the setting of limits. Supernatural cosmography places man in a setting of security which points out to him the exact way to move in the world in a specific order of the organization of reality. There was a need to have one or two points of reference, first spacial and then temporal: an individual, on earth, his house, his village, his city . . . , became the center, the main point of interest inserted in a universe more or less wide, in which the most important element was the sun and then the stars.

Cosmology was built through knowledge, natural or supernatural, of what was believed to surround man. This was not only valid for the primitive people or even the old civilizations, as we shall see here, but also for judeochristian thought, as one can see in the cosmography of heaven, which was created by St Augustin, and the maps of Calvino, edited in 1882 (after Di Nola, Vol II, p. 1192), in which the earthly paradise is situated in Babylon, identifying the river Pison and Gibon with the Tigris and the Euphrates.

Many of the cosmological points of reference were influenced by landscape: mountains, rivers, lakes or seas, as well as dreams and altered states of cosciousness of enlightened men, which gave origin to all the complexity of cosmology and religious geography, which was very much linked to the creation myths of the world and to eschatological belief.

The vertical levels and quadrants of the earth's plane suggested taxonomies, not only cosmological, but of natural and social order as Mauss (p. 58) mentioned, "All beings in nature maintain certain relations, with portions of space determined as well". Du Mezil based all his theory of the three functions of the Indo-European peoples, on the vertical planes of the universe, to which were associated respectively: (1) sovereignity, magical and juridical, (2) physical power, mainly war, and (3) abundance, tranquility and fecundity. To this classification he associated the three upper castes of India: brahmana, kshatriya and vaishya, leaving out the shudra.

We have mentioned (1987), with Kirchhoff (1964), that these same functions can be found in Mesoamerican cosmovision. Kirchhoff divides the Mexican Pantheon into three groups, arguing that this division is the result of the diffusion of a great religious system from Asia to America. We do not share his ideas about diffusion, at least not in this case, even though we think that this tripartite division of the universe is found in many aspects of the Mesoamerican cosmovision. We think, on the other hand, that the quatripartite division of the universe based on the four solstitial points and their derivation, is fundamental to practically all the ancient civilizations, perhaps even more to the societies we shall talk about.

Independently of all the factors which are implicit in the

conception of a vertical axis, as well as on horizontal levels, the sun is the most important reference point of all these conceptions. A myth of the *Rigveda* explains it: the God Vishnu, or the sun, with three steps marked space: from the horizon to the zenith, from this to the horizon and then in a retrograde stage, as his duration as a fish, he passed from the west to the east through the waters, again to the place of birth of the sun (*Matsya Purana,* p. 3).

But where the presence of the sun is more definitive is in the division of the four quadrants of the universe. It is for this reason that generally the names of the main directions are given by the position of the sun associated to his daily movement: the place where it rises, the place where it sets and his right or his left side, according to where it is believed his face is. If he looks towards the west, as in India and Mesoamerica, the north is the right of the sun and the south is the left. In China the central and most important region is the place where the Polar star is, therefore east is left and west is right (Granet 1952, I. p. 114). Besides there are names attached to the quadrants which have to do with geographical features, or mythological thoughts, for instance *Mictlampa,* 'the place of the dead', for the north, and *Cihuatlampa,* the place of women for the west, in the nahua language.

The *Matsya Purana* (p. 332) says that the sun goes regularly to his habitations: *Udaya* or birth and *Attaramaya* setting: "the sunset and the sunrise create the east and the west respectively".

It is highly probable that the solstitial points had greater importance among the ancient peoples than the cardinal ones, and that when they talked about the east or other direction, they were referring to the space between the solstitial points.

It seems that the space covered by the sunlight is equivalent to the demarcation of the universe. Since 1963, we showed a map which proved that at least for the Mexicas — if not for all the Mesoamerican peoples — the solstitial points at the most extreme points towards the north and the south, in the yearly sojourn of the sun, marked the extremes of the universe; further on, there was no light or heat and darkness ruled. That is why the north and south quadrants overlapped with the region of death in many cosmovisions. Hindu tradition says that after the mountain Lokaloka which surrounds the 7th island of the mythical continents, there is a sea and after that, the shell of Brahma's egg which is the limit of the universe; after that there is the no-world, eternal darkness. In the same way, the Chinese say in the book *Shu chun* of the VI c. that the emperor Yao sent four brothers who were magicians to take care of the four corners of the world, to prevent the sun from going on without stopping, on his journey to the south or to the north, because if this would happen the nights or the days would be eternal and people would die of cold or heat.

It was believed in China that the earth was a quadrangular space or that it had the form of a pyramid, and that there were columns in the periphery, but there is no agreement whether there were four or eight columns. Only the column of the north-west, Mount Kun lun was well-known and was concieved, like Mount Meru for the Hindus. It was also believed that the sky was sustained by the four legs of a turtle. The quatripartite division of the universe, as a taxonomic system in China, was so important, that from it was derived the octagram of which, number one, *khien*, heaven, masculine, was situated in the south and number eight, *kikun*, feminine, was in the north. But they also had, as we mentioned, a fifth direction or center, associated to the pole star. All these are associated with animals, with the planets, with the elements and with colors and with the 28 *hsiu* or asteriscs divided by seven and placed in each quadrant. The following are the directions and the elements associated:

EAST	water, Jupiter, green, blue dragon, spring.
SOUTH	fire, Mars, red, red or bermillion bird, summer
CENTER	earth, Saturn, yellow
WEST	metal, Venus, white, white tiger, fall.
NORTH	wood, Mercury, black and black turtle and winter.

All this is combined with Jupiter's 60 years calendar with cycles of 10 trunks and 12 branches, to create a very complicated adivinatory system.

The Chinese also believed that there were two trees in the eastern and western axis: the sun climbs through the Fu san or K'ong sang tree when it raises in the East, then goes up the sky, and comes to the earth through a western tree. In these two directions there are also the so-called 'feather mountains' which are inhabited by supernatural beings. They also said that there was an altar in the centre and four others in different directions of confederate China, each one of them with the color corresponding to its direction and in each of them there should be also a particular tree (Granet 1981, p. 61).

Granet (1959:I,244-57)transcribes very interesting paragraphs which gives us a clear idea of the cosmology of Virtue or Tao, associated to the dynastic changes in which the quatripartite division played a fundamental role. Virtue or Tao is situated at the centre and on its four corners there are four mountains and their respective guardians, beings who had been punished for breaking the spatial and temporal order, but after performing certain rites, they were reborn as the guardians of the Central Virtue. Each of the four sectors of the square space takes the name of a cardinal mountain. The Empire was called the space between the four mountains and the four regions, and the four doors was a reference to the capital. When the new emperor was appointed and a virtuous kingdom was established, he had to take a round of the four mountains to assure the possession of his domains. It seems that the only real mountain is the T'ai shan, which is located in the East and which has had a sacred character from time immemorial. It was said that in the Kun lun mountain in the West lived Hsin Wan mu, an ogress with tiger claws who later became the goddess of medicinal plants and of immortality. The west was also one of the Buddhist heavens.

Even if the quatripartite division is not as obvious in the cosmovision of India as it is in that of China, it also plays a very important role from which classificatory systems are derived, like the *varnas* or 'colors', which are not only used to designate the classical divisions of castes in the Indian society, but also types of earth, temples, gods, and even the stars which are classified in four orders (Bose, p. 237). In the same manner there were four Vedas, four *ashramas* or ways of life, four forms of life: infernal, animal, divine and human, four are the eras: *krita*, *treta*, *dvapara*, and *kali*, four are the *pitris* with corporeal forms and so on. On the other hand number nine is also associated to the earthly level and to the quadrants: four are the solstitial points, four the intermediate and one central. From here, that the nine Jain *lokantikas*, which take care of these points and the nine or ten Hindu *lokapalas* which are the following: Indra, who rides an elephant and rules the east; Isha or Ishamina, a form of Shiva, rides a bull and is situated in the north-east; Kubera, the god of wealth rides on a horse and stays in the north; in the north-east is found Vayu, god of wind who rides a deer; to the west is Varuna, god of water who rides a fish or the mythical *makara*; to the south-west is Nirrita, a minor deity who rides a buffalo and to the south-east Agni, god of fire riding on a sheep. At the center, the zenith is presided by Brahma and at the nadir is the serpent Sesha who holds the sleeping Vishnu. There are also different types of trees associated to the quadrants:

east, banian; south, fig; west, pipal; and north, *plaksha* (*Matysa Purana*, p. 268).

We have to add also that to each of the quadrants a season and a group of *nakshatras* are associated, even if in India the seasons are in different number. The *nakshatras* are kept in four palaces as in China.

In a ritual described in the *Matsya Purana* (p. 246) the planets are associated with the quadrants and with different deities: Shiva with the sun, with red color and his place is the center; Venus with the east, associated to Indra; to the north-east is Mercury, associated with Hari and the color yellow; to the north is Jupiter with Brahma and his color is also yellow; to the north-west Ketu and Dritagupta with smoke color; to the west, Saturn with Yama and black and to the south, Skanda with red.

By the time of the Puranas, the universe and earth in India were conceived as a disk surrounded by seven concentric rings or islands. We have mentioned that at the periphery there was the shell of the egg of Brahma which divided the world from the non-world. In the central island called Jambudvipa, lived beings who were under the law of *karma*. In the center of Jambudvipa was Mount Meru, with four sides of different colors: east, white with brahmanical properties; south, yellow with vaishya properties; west, the color of a black bee with shudra properties; and north , red with kshatriya properties (*Matsya Purana*, p. 301). At the top of Mount Meru was the jambu tree. The Jambudvipa land was divided by parallel mountains into nine regions or *varsas*.

At the four sides of Mount Meru are four different mountains, and four cities: to the east Mansotara, Sastvekasas, Mahendra's city; to the north of Meru is Vibhani, city of the moon; to the west, north of the Manasa mountain is Susha, the city of Varuna; and to the south is the city of Dharmaraja, called Samyamana (*Matsya Purana*, pp. 338, 339). To the north of the Manasa mountain are the *lokapalas*, 'caretakers of the world' in the four directions for the "propagation of virtue and the protection of the universe" (*ibid.*, p. 338). It is also said that the *lokapalas* are situated in the center of the mountain Loka *loka* occupying each of the quadrants and that their names are: Vairaja Sudhama, Prajapati Kardama, Hiranyaroma Prajanya and Rajasa Ketumana, all free from the sensation of pain (*ibid.*, p. 342). We can see in these guardians of the limits of the universe a great similarity between India and China as in both places they establish order and duty. We can also see that both north and south are places of death. One is the city of the moon and the *pitris* are supposed to dwell in the moon. Dharmaraja who lives in the south is also the lord of dead, a conception which is shared with Mesoamerica.

In the four cardinal points of the Jain map of the universe (Caillat, p. 11), there are four mountains called of antimon, at the top of which there are sanctuaries of the *siddhas* of the cardinal directions.

Prof. Villarojas (1968) and myself (1963), in separate works pointed out the importance of the solstitial and the equinoccial points of the sun, in the cosmovision of the Mesoamerican peoples; studies published later, as well as archaeoastronomical researches have confirmed this idea, which implies of course, the importance of the quatripartite division of the universe, which can be seen in calendars, codexes, archaeological representations, buildings, and so on. Taking as the core, the quatripartite division, we can construct almost all the important symbolic numbers having the rectangle as a model: four plus the center = five; the four corners of the three levels, plus the center = 13, the four solstitial points, plus the four cardinal directions, plus the center = 9, etc.

The solstitial points in ancient Mexico seem to coincide with the places where the sustainers of the sky, trees, columns, men or gods, are and which can be identified in the Borgia and Vatican B codexes, as the gods Quetzalcoatl, Tezcatlipoca, Tlahuizcapantecuhtli and Mictlantecuhtli, mentioned in the *Historia de los Mexicanos por sus pinturas* as the men named Cotemuc, Itzcoatl, Izmalli and Tenesuche, who helped Tezcatlipoca hold the sky after it fell. On the other hand, in the Fejervary Codex, the god of fire is placed in the center and in the four quadrants are four trees with a bird at the top; two gods at their side and some other objects. In the corners there are trees surrounded by calendrical signs. Every figure had a meaning which must have related to their position in the four quadrants of the universe.

The pages 48, 49, 50, and 51 of the *Codex Borgia* are also famous for their multiple iconographic meanings. Especially important seem to be the temples of each direction: of the sun in the east, of the moon in the north, of germination in the west and of the dead in the south. Several pages of the *Borgia Codex* also show tlaloques or gods of water and quetzalcoatls, or gods of wind, in the four quadrants of the universe. According to the Mexica tradition the tlaloques were placed in each of the corners of the world holding pitchers full of different types of water. The Jains also believe that there are receptacles with water in the corners of the world and that they will be filled or emptied according to the season of the year.

On page LXXV of the Maya Trocortesian Codex, the world and its quadrants are illustrated and in that culture it is also believed that the gods of water were located in the four quadrants.

In Mexico in the Nahua and Maya areas the quadrants were associated with four of the 20 signs of the *tonalpohualli*,[1] the so-called 'year markers' and with an element and a color: *acatl*, 'reed', east, water and red; *técpatl*, 'flint', north,

1. See introduction.

wind and black; *calli*, 'house', west, earth and white; *tochtli*, 'rabbit', south, fire and blue. They were also associated with a color, a deity and a season as Carrasco (p. 52) has shown. According to him north was equivalent to the summer solstice in the month of *etzalqualiztli*; south, to the winter solstice ending in the month of *panquetzaliztli*; east to the spring equinox in the month of *tlacaxipehualiztli* and west to the autumn equinox in the month of *ochpaniztli*. In the same manner the quadrants were also associated with provinces of the State.

The *Popol Vuh*, the sacred book of the Mayas, mentions the existence of the four corners of the world, and the four 'angels' which are located there and which must have been the *bacabs*, and in the Chilam Balam, mention is made of four trees of different colors and a bird at their top. Sosa (pp. 195, 196) has studied the present-day Maya culture of Yucatan where the *h'men* specialists on divination still preserve the conception of the quadrants of the universe, and they believe in four trees and four gods of water located in each 'corner' of the universe. In each corner there is a cloud of different color: white, black, yellow and green. They also believe that there are four guardians of the town, village or even field, who are located in each of its corners.

Besides the four quadrants, and the four corners of the world there is a fifth, the *omphalos*, the most sacred point, where communication with the other worlds, with the supernatural, is established. It is a pivotal point in the sphere of time and space where all the opposites are united. In China the Polar Star which is equaled to the emperor is located in the fifth place. In this center, fire and water are united, metal and wood, movement and immobility, sky and earth. Generally this place is occupied by a mountain or a tree, or perhaps a hole, like the one the Mexica had at the center of the Ball game, which is also a map of the cosmos. López Austin suggests that the terrestrial surface was divided as a cross, and the navel was represented as a green stone in the center. We already saw that the Indian Sesha, the cosmic snake holding Vishnu, stays in the center of the underworld.

Usually this *axis mundi* extends vertically upward to the pole star and downwards to the underworld. Iconographically, the *axis mundi* can also be expressed as a tree or a mountain. In the *Katha Upanishad*, an inverted tree is described with its roots upward towards eternity (Campbell, p.192):

> Root above, branches below, this primal fig tree!
> Pure indeed is its root: it is brahman, known
>   as the immortal.
> In it rest all the worlds:
> No one soever goes beyond it.
> All this, verily is that tree.

The present-day Maya of Mesoamerica believe that, in the center of the world there is a huge ceiba tree, which has its roots in the underworld and its foliage in heaven.

We have seen that in Mexico the Fire god is represented in the center of the world, but also the god of death is located in the center of the underworld.

We have mentioned how the most important direction for the Chinese was the center, where the Pole star, the Tao and its earthly representative , the Emperor, were situated, and around which everything revolved.

The center can also have a mystic meaning, as it is given in the tantric doctrine in India: the point, or *bindu*, in the center indicates the first visible principle, the androgenous man, the seed of being and consciousness, which can actually never be visible or imaginable. From the side of man, it is the point of final dissolution. From the point of view of creation it is the first act of projection which consists of dividing itself into masculine and feminine.

Fig. 1: The quadrants of the universe, its gods, trees and animals.
(Fejervary Codex p.1)

Fig. 2: The city of Mexico — Tenochtitlan and its division in four quadrants. (Mendoza Codex p. 1)

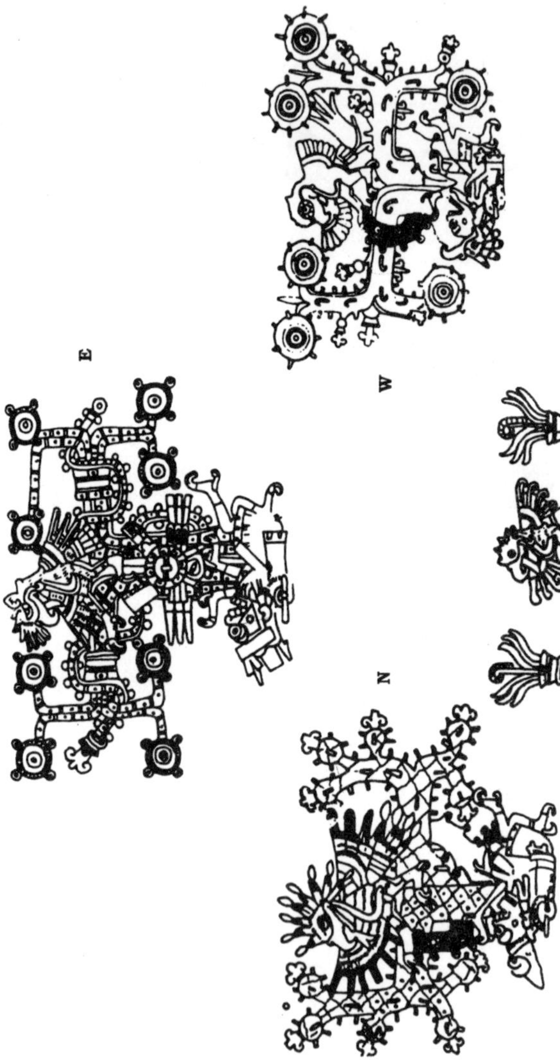

Fig. 3: The trees of the four quadrants of the universe. (Borgia Codex pp. 49-52)

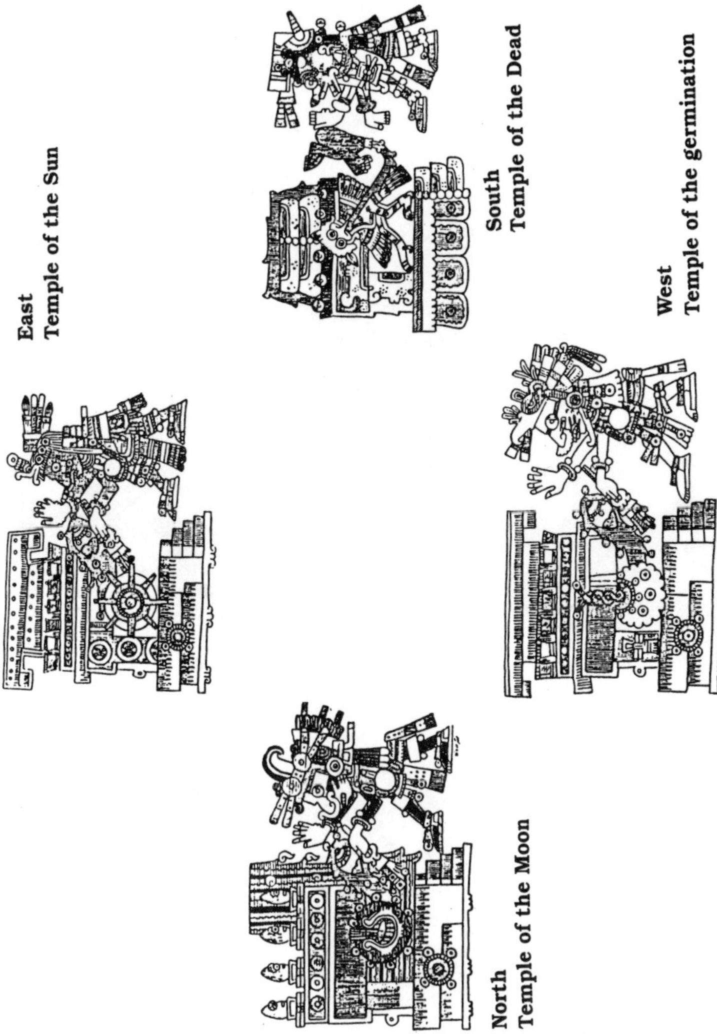

Fig. 4: The temples and gods of the four quadrants of the universe.
(Borgia Codex pp. 49-51)

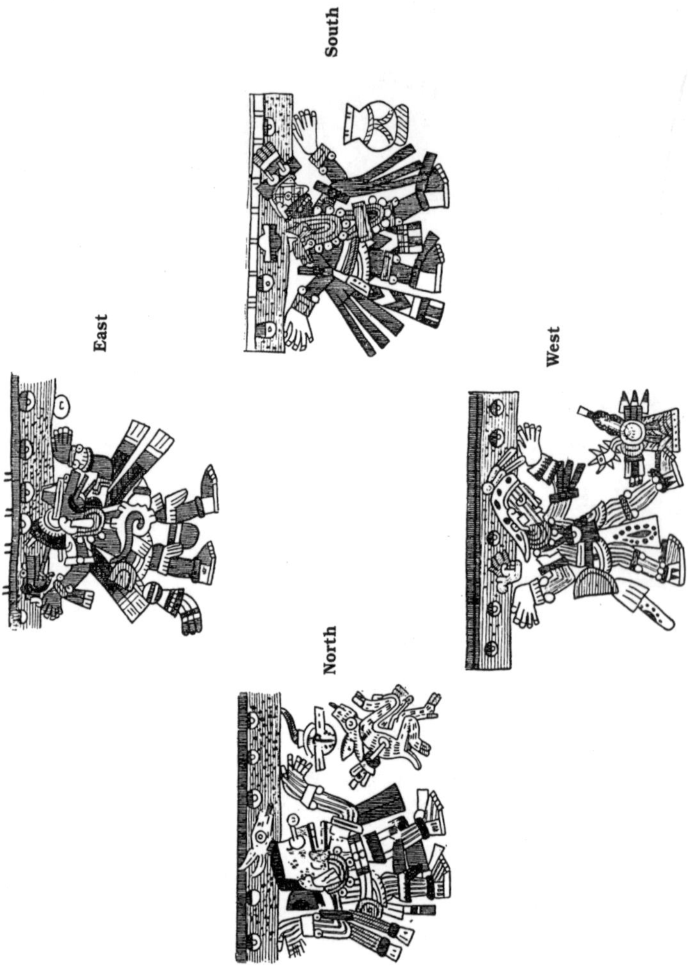

Fig. 5: The four gods bearers of the sky.(Codex Vaticano 3773)

Fig. 6: The five 'unsurpassable gods' (*Pañcānuttaras*), [Gouache on paper, XVIIIth century, Rajasthan].

Fig. 7: Guardians of the universe
[Jouveau-Dubreuil, *Archéologie du sud de l'Inde*].

North: Kuber on horse. **N.E.**: Iśāna (Śiva) on bull. **E.**: Indra on elephant. **S.E.**: Agni on ram. **S.** Yama on buffalo. **S.W.**: Nirṛti on man. **W.**: Varuṇa on fish. **N.W.**: Vāyu on deer.

Fig. 8: The five sacred tigers, simbolizing the divinities corresponding to the five directions, China.

Fig. 9: King of the mountain of the East, China popular engraving

Fig. 10: Thai Shou, the mountain of the East. Ming Dynasty, engraving, China.

Fig. 11: Green dragon of the East, spring. China.

Fig. 12: White Tiger of the West, Autum, China.

Fig. 13: Phenix of the South, summer, China.

Fig. 14: Black Warrior of the North, winter, China.

The northern and southern limits of the middle or earth level of the universe seem to merge or become fused with the vertical levels which are usually seven or nine or thirteen, according to the different traditions. We have seen that north and south which are somehow places of darkness, are inhabited by nocturnal and deadly beings: the moon, the ancestors, the gods of death. While the eastern and western directions are more related to heavens connected with the sun, even though the west, as we have seen in China, and also in Mexico is the place of women, and of germination.

We have already mentioned the importance of the three vertical levels of the universe: the level of the earth where human and animal life takes place and the *infra* and *supra* world inhabited by supernatural beings. These last are also divided in several strata as already mentioned, which vary according to traditions: for instance in India seven are the regions of the *devas*: *Bhuh, Bhuvah, Svah, Mahah, Tapah, Tupah, Satyam* (*Matsya Purana*, p. 185), and out of the seven groups of *pitris* which are "a race of divine beings who inhabit the celestial regions and who receive in their society the spirits of the dead people for whom the adequate mortuary rites have been performed" (*Matsya Purana*), three, the Manasa *pitris* have corporeal form and inhabit the inferior levels in the Jyotisokhasa along with the stars and planets and four don't have it and inhabit the upper levels. The Hanismana *pitris* live in the region of the sun and the Susvada and Ajyapa *pitris* live in the Kamagudha in the region of Prajapati Pardama. The residence of the Somapa *pitris* is the Manasa region in the Upper Brahmananda, and they are eternal, the same incarnation of *dharma*.

The lower region also has seven levels, inhabited by all the infernal beings — certain demons, the titans, etc., and each of these regions is darker according to its depth.

The Jain vertical levels of the universe are seven. The

inferior are called *narakas* which are places of punishment; the upper levels of the infraworld are Ratnaprabha and Sarakaraprabha and they are under Mount Meru. In these places live 'extremely unjust deities'. On the second level there are the *kumaras* (young and beautiful) who are of ten classes and have their own *rajas* and are divided into northern and southern. Above the *kumaras* live the gods and spirits who are in the mountains and forests and are called Vyantaras. They stay in the Ratnaprabha infraworld which is located in the surface of the earth and live in wonderful towns with a life without worry, full of music and dance. They are divided in eight groups: *Pisacha, Bhuta, Yaksha, Rakshasha, Kinnara, Kimpurusha, Mahoraga* and *Gandharva* (Caillat, p. 84). These are actually supernatural beings which are in a category between gods and demons, sort of malign and benign geniuses, some of which are mixed up with non-Aryan ethnic groups. We could suppose that they were situated in the four corners of the world and the four dircctions, like the *lokantikas*.

In the upper levels (*ibid.*, p. 86), the third world is inhabited by the gods of light, and still higher, in the fourth group, are "those who inhabit the palaces of the paradise of the Vaimanikas, (and) are distributed from the middle heaven to the umbrella of perfection".

In the upper world, each one of the 12 levels is symbolized by an animal: antelope, buffalo, boar, lion, *slura* (frog), or leopard, horse, elephant, snake, rhinoceros, bull and another type of antelope. We could guess that these animals are somehow related to the 12 zodiacal signs.

Even if in China the infraworld does not seem to count, there is the belief in a hell with several levels, where the souls of the dead are punished, and the deeper the level the worst are the punishments. Needham (p. 198) says that during Han times there was a belief that heaven had several levels, perhaps based on the idea of the astronomer Chang hu who believed that heaven had nine positions and earth seven continents. It was also believed that the immortal Saints inhabited the different heavens and the Emperor of Tao was in the highest heaven (Di Nola, pp.16-36). In modern China there are ten hells ruled by ten personages called the ten kings.

If we turn to Central Mexico we can see that there are two or three traditions of stratified heavens of eight, eleven and thirteen levels.

In pages one and two of the Vaticano Ríos Codex A3783 — which even if drawn in colonial style contain prehispanic ideas — the different levels of heaven and earth are illustrated. In the upper part of a 12th heaven there are three strata which are called by the interpreter *teotl* which means god or sacred. The illustration has only colors, and symbols of rays of light, then follow other skies of different colors. The sun is placed in the third sky, and in the second is the goddess 'skirt of stars', or the 'Milky way', and in the first the moon and the god of water. In other versions the strata are 13: in the upper one stays the god Ometeotl, Sacred Duality, then follow different gods, on the fifth there are 'five gods of different colors' and the sun is located in the fourth strata, while the moon doesn't appear here. There are, of course, one or two more versions and it has been proposed that the so-called 'thirteen gods of the days' of the sacred calendar are the same gods who inhabit the 13 layers of heaven. There are also a group of nine gods called 'the lords of the night', which could be the masters of the different layers of the infraworld and who could be associated to the different phases of the moon.

There are also several versions about the number of infraworlds, which coincide with the stages through which the soul has to pass on its way to its final destiny, which we may briefly describe, according to Sahagún (pp. 204-05): first, the soul had to pass through two mountains which were crushing against each other, then by a big snake, then by a lizard called *xochitonal*, then through eight deserts, then the eight mountains, then through the wind of obsidian razors, then a river which had to be crossed with the aid of a red dog which had been killed at the time of the funeral, and only then, the soul could face the Lord of death.

It is worth mentioning that many of these traditions, in a simpler or distorted way, are still prevalent among many of the Indian communities in Mexico.

The apparently universal idea, of a supra- and infra-world divided in strata, could be explained by the observation of the celestial phenomena. That is why in several traditions sun and moon circulate in inferior strata, while the stars, or the constellations, are placed in higher levels. It can also be explained by the number of planets to each of which a particular path was given. If heaven was divided in strata, then it could easily be populated with supernatural beings, the planets themselves or celestial or supernatural beings related to them.

As the concepts of time and space were so imbricated, with the planets serving as markers, as we have already seen, the sun established the limits of the terrestrial and aquatic plane. But the limits, could not be very precise, and were mingled or merged with water and space (*akash*).

But also the number and names of strata of heavens and hell corresponded and coincided in several traditions with the stages through which the soul had to pass to reach the highest plane, like the stages mentioned by the mystical St. Teresa or Dante's heavens and hells, or even the stages through which the soul of a shaman has to travel.

We could have here, apart from an example of similar solutions of the observation of nature in different cultures, a search for a basic order within the human mind, striving to organize their universe according to certain patterns taken from nature itself, order which was distorted with the discovery of things which go beyond what nature shows us, but which on the other hand, we may realize in the near future to be just one.

References

Bose, Nirmal Kumar, 1977, *Culture and Society*, Asia Publishing House. Ranchi.

Caillat, Colett and Kumar Devi, 1983, *The Jain Cosmology*, Harmony Books. New York.

Campbell, Joseph, 1974, *The Mythic Image*, Bollingen Series C: Princeton University Press, Princeton, New Jersey.

Carrasco, Pedro, 1979, "Las fiestas de los meses mexicanos" en *Homenaje a Paul Kirchhoff*, INAH, México, pp. 51-60.

Chilam Balam de Chumayel, Libro de, 1988, (tr.) del maya al castellano Antonio Diaz Bolio, Prolog, introduction and notes by Merdedes de la Garza, S.E.P. México.

Di Nola, 1970, "Cosmologia", in *Enciclopedia delli religioni, Vol. II.* Vallechi Editore, Roma.

Du Mezil, George, 1977, *Mito y Epopeya*, Seix Barral Editores, Barcelona.

González Torres, Yolotl, 1963, *El culto a los astros entre los mexica*, Master Thesis, Typewritten copy, ENAH, México.

——— 1974, *El culto a los astros entre los mexicas*, SEP Setentas, México.

——— 1987, "Taxonomía mesoamericana" in *Historia de las Religiones en Mesoamérica y áras afines*, I, Coloquio, Ed. by Bárbara Dahlgren, UNAM. México.

Granet, Marcel, 1959, *Danses et Légendes de la Chine Ancienne*, T. I Annales du Museé Guimet, Biblioteque d'etudes T. LXVI: Presses Universitaires de France, Paris.

———1989, *La religion des Chinoises*, Imago, Paris

Historia de los Mexicanos por sus pinturas, 1941 in Nueva colección de documentos para la Historia de México, ed. by Chávez Hayhoe. México.

Kirchhoff, Paul, 1962, "The diffusion of a Great Religious System from India to Mexico", in *Proceedings of the 35th International Congress of americanists*, Mexico Vol. I, p. 73.

López Austin, Alfredo, 1980, *Cuerpo Humano e Ideología*, Unam, México

Maspero, Henri, nd., "The Mythology of Modern China", Asiatic Religion, in *Encyclopedia of Mythology*, Crescent Books, New York, pp. 252-384.

Matsya Purana, The, 1972 ed. by por Jamna Das Akhtar, Oriental Publishers. Delhi.

Mauss, Marcel, 1971, *Institucion y Culto. Obras II*, Barral Eds. Barcelona.

Needham, Joseph, 1959, *Science and Civilization in China*, Vol. III. Cambridge University Press, Cambridge.

Ou-ita, 1952, "Chinese Mythology", *Enciclopeadia of Mythology*", Paul Hamlyn, London and New York, pp.179-402.

Popol Vuh, *Las antigus historias del quiché.* 1947 Notes and Introduction by Andres Recinos.F.C.E. México

Rawson, Philip, 1982, *The Art of Tantra*, Thames and Hudson. London.

Sosa, John R., 1991, "Las cuatro esquinas del mundo: análisis simbólico de la cosmologia maya yucateca" en *Arqueoastronomía y Etnoastronomía en Mesoamérica.* Eds. Johanna Broda, Stanislaw Iwanisewski y Lucrecia Mopomé, UNAM, México, pp.193-202.

Soustelle, Jacques, 1940, *Le pensée cosmologique des anciennes mexicaincs*, Paris.

Teogonía e Historia de los Mexicas, Tres Opúsculos del siglo XVI, 1973, Ed. by Angel María Garibay, Porrua, México.

Villa Rojas, Alfonso, 1968, "Los conceptos del espacio y tiempo entre los grupos mayas contemporáneos" en Miguel Leon Portilla. *Tiempo y realidad en el pensamiento maya*, UNAM, Mexico, pp. 119-169.

5

Lunar Iconography in Lacandon Mayan Cosmology[1]

Marie-Odile Marion

The Lacandones,a handful of Mayan families in their refuge in the heart of the tropical jungle in Southern Chiapas, have managed to maintain up until the present, the logic of their social system, whose symbolic dimensions explain and legitimise the set of institutions by which they reproduce themselves. Immersed in a world of perpetual movement and based on the cyclical pattern inherited from their pre-Hispanic past, the Lacandones are responsible for assuring, through rituals, the perpetuity of the cosmos, and consequently of human society and the universe.

Their history is tied to the course of the heavenly bodies, particularly to that of the sun and the moon. They live in constant anticipation of the predicted cataclysm that will end their era of humanity, as happened to previous generations of Mayans from whom they inherited their destiny and knowledge. This notion of a history impregnated with millennium fatalism is the main axis around which their social, environmental, and astral space revolves.

The interpretative pattern of the forms of Mesomerican

---

1. The English translation of this text was done by Ramon Cervantes Martínez.

thought as proposed by Graulich[2] have been very useful for reconstructing the conceptual model through which the Lacandones organise their univese. The opposing and complementary relationships that connect the heavenly bodies in their perpetual movement of ascent-descent from a celestial position to the subterranean world explain the link between the phases from light to darkness, dry season to rainy reason, and from sun to rain. This same logic applied to the organisation of their cosmos allows the Lacandones to structure their social system. They have done this fundamentally following an old but not archaic model, and so in this way they demonstrate that the logic of their organisation conceals that of their thoughts.

The constant parallelism existing between the social organisation and the cosmic order repeatedly highlights the roles, statutes, attributes and responsibilities of the men and women in the control of their society. Patterns of cosmic origin are culturally assumed, assuring through their complement and opposition the reproduction of the social universe. Therefore, these patterns are the contextualisation within the human order of the mythical representations with which they conceive the heavenly bodies. In this way, the men assume solar roles and attributes, while the women are covered with selenite insignia. The objective of this paper is to show how such feminine peculiarity is expressed, in other words, the social extent of the cosmic configuration of women and how an ancient iconography has been reproduced and elegantly reinserted, or 're-semanticised' by the Lacandones within their conceptual system. Consequently, we attempt to highlight this culture's great capacity for resistance and its ability to retain and recontextualise the most reliable and significant elements of their conceptual system, in order to

---

2. Michel Graulich, *Mythes et rituels du Mexique ancien préhispanique:* Académie Royale de Belgique, Bruxellers, Palais des académies, 1987.

keep their logic from being altered in spite of the constant and strong pressure resulting from the invasion of Western emissaries.

In the interest of simplifying this paper, it has been developed based on four great spaces, where the multifaceted personality of the moon will shine to guide our steps. These four spaces include: the astral space, based on a journey through mythology; the environmental space, using mythology, the colonial chronicles, and iconography; the social space, through kinship terminology and ethnographical data. All of the aforementioned elements will acquire real significance from a holistic perspective in the fourth and final space: the ritual space.

The Astral Space

Lacandon mythology notes the fundamental role the lunar divinity plays in the process of creation, the apocalyptic phases of cyclical destruction (caused by the creator's fits of anger), and restoration of the universal equilibrium. Ak Na' (lit. Our Mother) is the common name given to the moon. It is also the name of the wife of the omnipotent god who created the forest to give it to the Lacandones only after hanging a sun in the sky to assure growth of the corn. Frequently designated by the esoteric name of X-k'ale'ox,[3] the moon goddess is the principle of complementarity and opposition that moderates the strong and irritable personality of the creator. Even though she is apparently subject to the decisions of her powerful spouse, she recurs to multiple measures to overcome his authority in order to put off, modify, or annul his whims which are contrary to the well-being of her creatures.

The moon goddess was entrusted with creating women and teaching them the art of weaving. She is the protectress

3. "Sacred leaves of the ramon" (Brosimium alicastrum), according to Bruce, 1965: 97.

of procreation, childbirth, and fertility in general. These aspects connect her to the ancient goddess Ixchel, whose cult was intensely venerated in the peninsular lowlands as a result of the penetration of the Putun Itza culture, of which Ixchel was one of the main divinities. Both celestial and earthly, Ak Na' is a wealth of great power of which Lacandon women must be considered the rightful heirs in virtue of traditional uterine transmission of female belongings and privileges. The bond they weave with their lunar mother during the process of gestation is nothing more than one of the varied expressions of the intense complicity that binds women and whose original skein is patiently unrolled by Ak Na' from the highest heavens.

After having lived in her earthly abode in Yaxchilan, Ak Na' went to live in heaven along with the other gods of native theogony. At her spouse's side, she supervises the transition of the seasons, and the propagation of nocturnal shadows after a day of solar irradiation. On one occasion, she had to abandon her husband in order to force him to renounce his plans for destroying humanity.[4] Afterwards she took refuge on an island on the Usumacinta River. For this reason, the Lacandones insist that all islands that rise from the heart of lakes have a small stone structure of pre-Hispanic origin. These plinths of earth in the midst of the waters are the earthly refuges of the moon goddess, underscoring the affinity of this deity with the earthly and aqueous elements of the indigenous universe.[5]

---

4. See Bruce 1974: 183 and Boremanse 1986: 277-81. The Tzutuhils of San Pedro la Laguna affirm that the lunar eclipses are provoked by the moon's lies, which are aimed at angering her husband. To punish men, the Sun then hides his face. The inverse happens among the Lacandones, since in their mythology the Moon seeks to avoid the destruction of the universe provoked by a solar eclipse. In reference see Thompson, 1975, as quoted by Marion, 1992: 366.

5. Marion, 1992: 366.

Ak Na' is suspected of having had sexual relations with her husband's brother and such an affair — which the Lacandones conceive to be common inside the family residence unit — is widely commented upon in Mayan myths referring to the moon goddess since the dawn of history. A Kekchi myth analysed by Thompson[6] tells of the double adultery of the Moon, first with her brother-in-law (which Thompson identifies as Venus) and then with the Prince Vulture. At the end of this second affair, the Sun manages to recover his mate. In the Dresden Codex the representation of the moon goddess copulating with a creature identified as a vulture[7] seems to confirm the authenticity of the contemporary myth.

It is useful to combine the mythical evocation of Ixchel's adultery and the chapter from the Popol Vuh that refers to Ixquic's escape from Xibalba. After having conceived Hun Hunahpu, this princess of darkness (and therefore both earthly and lunar, since she gave birth to the heavenly bodies) was saved from death by four nocturnal birds of prey (identified in the text as owls). They were given the task of sacrificing her and taking her heart to Ixquic's father. She manages to convince the birds of prey to spare her life and in place of her heart to take a gourd filled with coagulated red resin. The birds of prey allow her to escape from Xibalba and they deliver the sacrificial vessel to Hun-Came. After having done so, they abandon the world of darkness and choose the path of the earth, where they become the helpers of their protectress. Although the text refers to 'owls', they were actually four nocturnal rapacious birds — since they lived in the world of darkness — who afterwards changed into celestial rapacious birds. They

6. Thompson, 1939.

7. Thompson, J.E., *A Commentary on the Dresden Codex, a Maya Hieroglyhic Book*; American Philosophical Society, Philadeplhia, 1972, p. 48. See also Gonzalez, Y. 1991: 96, Ixchel copulating with a Chac (Dresden Codex).

became the protégés of the hevenly bodies and received their own cosmic space for having helped Ixquic give birth to the twins who would become the Sun and the Moon at the end of their terrestrial stay. Such an hypothesis would explain why vultures enjoy a privileged space in the Mayan sky, despite their association with the world of the dead since the dawn of history. The Lacandones associate them indirectly with death. When the creator decides to cause an intense drought in order to intimidate man and oblige him to make offerings, he hangs the sun from the sky of the vultures, causing the forest and cornfields to burn, the lakes and streams to dry up, and causing panic among the people of the forest. The vulture, a symbol of death associated with the world of darkness and a celestial being because of its nature of flight, highlights by having sexual intercourse with the Moon, the Moon's dichotomous relationship. As the Sun's wife, she is the patroness of life, but as the Prince Vulture's lover, she becomes the princess of darkness and bestows death and affliction.

It is not by chance that the Moon chose Venus and Prince Vulture as her lovers. Venus is the morning star. It anticipates the return of the Sun,[8] and represents life's hope. The vulture is a creature of the night and death, who reigns where life ends. By choosing them as lovers, the Moon affirms the plenitude of her cosmic functions: as legitimate wife of the Sun she assures the reproduction of the world and the multiplication of life, while as mistress of liminal space and time she bestows death, anguish, disorder, and chaos. If the Moon is an adulteress, then it is conceivable that her daughters are too. Women reproduce their power by seducing men, just as their mother did.[9]

The conflicts arising between the Moon and her husband as a result of her extramarital affairs cause eclipses. The

8. It is also the twilight star and as such accompanies the declining descent of his younger brother in the west.

9. Marion, 1992: 370.

Mayans unanimously affirm that during the course of one of these conjugal quarrels, the Sun hit his spouse so hard that she lost one of her eyes. This explains why the Moon now shines less, for before she outshone the sun in heat and light.[10]

The Natural Space

We have seen, based on certain mythological references, that the Moon is related to aquatic and subterranean spaces. A careful analysis of the climatic cycles and their representation in the Lacandon conceptual system will specify the position that these cycles hold in the ecological field of the universe for its capacity to control atmospheric clements.

In a myth about the origin of the rains[11] the Lacandones introduce some fantastic characters in charge of distributing the rain, wind, clouds, thunder and lightning in the Four Corners of the world. These "bearers of atmospheric phenomena" are closely related to the three characters in the myth that Bruce identifies as the Chäk Xib (lit. the Red Sons of the Creator). A conflict turned those three men against their younger brother, and therefore they were punished by their father who condemned them to return to a natural state and to remain from that point on in the forest of men instead of living by his side in the astral space of the gods.[12] Related to the rains as well as death — called

10. According to the Chujs, Cakchiquels, Yucatecans, Jacaltecs, and other Mayan groups.

11. Bruce, 1974: 63-67, Cline, H., "Lore and Deities of the Lacandon Indians, Chiapas, Mexico", in *Journal of American Folklore*, Vol. 57, No. 224, Boremanse, 1986: 54-56. See also Marion, 1992: 661.

12. This fratricidal struggle between elder and younger brothers is accounted for in the Popol Vuh in the myth of origin of the Chols, and the rift resulting from the confrontaion explains the difference between nature and culture and the coming of the heavenly bodies. Marion 1992: 372, Poul Vuh, 1953: 135, Morales, 1984: 76.

Wayantekoob — in the mythology of the Southern Lacandones, they are close to Menzabäk[13] as well as to Ak Na'- X-k'ale' ox because they are her sons. Their name 'Chäk Xib' associates them closely colour red which identifies them. One of the figurative characteristics of the ancient Mayan pre-Hispanic goddess. Ix Chebel Yax, wife of the creator Itzam Na',[14] is precisely her association with the colour red when, at her spouse's side, she is responsible for flooding the earth.[15] Nevertheless, in other aspects this polymorphic goddess is associated with weaving and childbirth, under the name of Ixchel, and is then represented by the colour white. In the Chilam Balam of Chumayel[16] she is also associated with food, in particular with maize, under the esoteric name of Colel Cab (Owner of the Earth). Among the Lacandones, she is associated with the fruit of the ramon[17] and called by her ceremonial name of X-k'ale'ox. Together with her three sons, the "Red Boys", she is related to the rain and wind. The Yucatecan lunar goddess, Ixchel, is also distinguished as the chief of the Chacs, those wind and rain spirits of post-classic Mayan and contemporary mythology. López de Cogolludo even states that she is

13. Guardian of the rains and of the place where the souls of the dead are concentrated, after having been judged and punished by K' isin upon entering the subterranean world.

14. The meaning being Itzam: iguana and Na': house, in other words 'house of the iguana'. This great Mayan god of the classic period is considered by archaeologists to be the creator of the universe represented with the body of a saurian, upon which the world rests. Different Mesoamerican versions of the original monster, (half earthly — half celestial) confirm this cosmogonic interpretation of the origin of the earth and was shared by pre-Hispanic cultures. See: Graulich, 1987, Thompson, 1975: 574 and 257.

15. Thompson, 1975: 257.

16. Quoted by Thompson, 1975: 258.

17. (Brosimium alicastrum or Trophis racemosa) which is used to substitute the corn (maize) in case of shortage. In Maya the term is 'Ox' or 'Hach ox'.

related to the Chac of the South.[18] In Mayan cosmology, the south is represented by yellow, as well as the name of X-k'ale'ox.

In the Dreden and Madrid Codices this goddess appears associated with the rains, the colour yellow, and surrounded by Chacs. Cascades of water flow between her open legs as well as from the containers which the personages tilt towards the earth.

A Chol myth from the region of Palenque tells of a character called Chahc who sent one of his helpers to his house to ask his wife to weave a cloth. The couple's offspring were frogs that guarded their home. The wife of Chahc spun much cotton, which was changed into clouds. with these clouds, Chahc was able to control the rainfall.[19] There is also an analogy between the wife of the rain deity and the cotton and cloud carriers of water, highlightining the homology between a feminine divinity of water and the lunar goddess.

If all this archaeological and ethnographical information seems to confirm the bond linking X-k'ale'ox (X-Kan Le Ox, in Yucatec) to the Chacs and therefore to the origin of the rains, its comparison with the Lacandon myth reveals however, not only a certain analogy, but also a series of ambiguities. X-k'ale'ox and her sons are associated with the colour red because apart from being responsible for the celestial waters, they are also responsible for the East and for life. The red colour represents the return of the sun to the East.[20] In the rain myth, Menzabäk shares the soot

18. López de Cogolludo *Historia de Yucatan, escrita en el siglo XVII*, Merida, 1867-8, quoted by Thompson, 1975: 258.

19. Aulie, W. and E. Aulie, *Palencano-Chol Vocabulary and Folktales with English Translation*, 1951. Manuscript quoted by Thompson, 1975: 306-07.

20. In Mayan cosmology the colour red is associated with the East, white with the North, black with the West and yellow with the South.

between his helpers, in such a way that they are able to pour over the forest the water-filled winds. It just so happens that the South does not receive any soot: in effect it is said that the South "is a dry wind, without rain. South returns the clouds to North. . . ." North is associated with the colour white and according to Thompson, white (zac) is the other colour attributed to the lunar goddess, for she is also the patroness of the art of weaving (zacal: weaving).[21] Undoubtedly the text refers to the double personality of the lunar goddess, wife of the creator (white/weaving/birth) and mother and chief of the bearers of winds (yellow/dry wind/death). Under this last aspect of southern wind — wind of drought and death — it could also refer to the ill-fated or even mortal aspect of this multifaceted divinity.

> A text of the Chilam Balam of Chumayel highlights the association of the Moon with the colour white, the rains and cotton: The moon shall have white circles of rain. The skies will be full of rains; and they will resound of the downpours; the rains will invade the skies, the celestial rains, celestial rains of cotton. . . . [22]

As a mother of the wind-bearers (among the Lacandones) and chief of the rain carriers (in the majority of other Mayan cultures),[23] the lunar goddess imposes a feminine principle among the symbolic representations of the rains. Her presence in the underworld is highlighted by the existence of the X-Tabay, the last representations of the ancient Mayan Ix Tab.

The X-Tabay are female divinities of the forest who

---

21. Thompson, 1975: 257 and 1972:47. In Mesoamerican thought, the North is also associated with the underworld (Mictlan), Duverger, 1979: 125; night and the rainy season (personal message from M. Graulich, March, 1992).

22. Chilam Balam of Chumayel, 1979: 165.

23. See Thompson, 1975: 297-337.

usually appear and seduce men travelling through the woods, especially when these men are subjected to a period of sexual abstinence for ritual reasons. In a Lacadon myth it is said that X-Tabay was excluded from human society after having killed her father because he sexually molested her. As a result, these women became divinities of the otherworld who have intercourse with beings of nature or become the companions of the souls of the dead in the world of Menzabäk. They represent the archetype of women's seductive power. They are dangerous, attractive, coveted and feared. At the limit of reality where they appear to men and at the limit of the imaginary universe of souls, they are the personification of female ambivalence, because they provoke the death of the living whom they seduce, and they assure the well-being and pleasure of the dead they have forsaken in the beyond.

An ancient Mayan divinity identified as Ix Tab is represented in the Dresden Codex with a cord knotted around her neck. Associated with the lunar goddess (because she appears in the table of representations of the lunar eclipses),[24] she also signifies death. In this aspect, some have attempted to portrary Ix Tab as the protectress of those who commit suicide by hanging, but other elements indicate that she could be considered one of the manifestations of the moon power applied to transmit death instead of life. In fact, in the Madrid Codex one of the evocations of the god of death is a character represented with a waist loom.[25]

Because of its unmistakable female character, this piece of art in Mesoamerican thought undoubtedly remits to a lunar goddess of death adorned with the same accessories as her homologous patroness of weaving and of childbirth. The cord that Ix Tab wears around her neck

---

24. Thompson, 1975: 365.

25. Madrid Codex, (4th edition) cited by Thompson, 1975: 268.

probably represents the umbilical cord. Lacandon women wear a woven cotton thread during their pregnancy. These cords refer to the principles of symbolic filiation, aspects that will be analysed further on.

The analogy between the cave of Menzabäk and the Tlalocan is highlighted by the fact that the lunar goddess is liable to be living there,[26] and its Mayan equivalent is undoubtedly the X-Tabay of Lacandon mythology.

Landa mentions that a giant ceiba (yaaxche'[27]) grew in the centre of the world of souls. A Tzotzil myth[28] tells that dead chidren were retrieved by the ceiba and that the tree fed them with its multiple breasts.[29] The ceiba is closely related to the X-Tabay. It is said (in the Yucatan and among the Lacandones) that these marvellous women come forth from the trunk of the ceiba to seduce men. Both the ceiba and the women who pass through its trunk are associated with the principles of life and death. This act is confirmed by the image portrayed by the mythological tree which, since ancient Mayan times has been considered a link between different spaces of the universe and the support of an axial symbolism characteristic of Mesoamerican thought. It is conceivable that this tree was used by the X-Tabay to enter the underworld because they emerge from its trunk to seduce Lacandon men in order to drag them to their deaths, to later become their companions.

If the Lacandon X-Tabay are the current reference of the

---

26. Thompson, J.E., "The Moon Goddess in Middle Aamerica with Notes on Elated Deities", C.I.W. Pub. 509, Contib. 29, Washinton, 1939, p. 144. Gonzalez refers to the X-Tabay as the wife of K' isin, among the Lacandones, 1991: 205.

27. Ceiba petandra.

28. Studied by Thompson, 1975: 364-65.

29. **See** in reference the Lacandon myth of origin of childbirth. The women traditionally bury newborns in the trunk of a tree and fear that a child will disappear in the branches of a ceiba.

ancient Mayan Ix-Tab, then we must deduce the permanence of the life-death dichotomy surrounding these female characters related to the moon and darkness, childbirth and death, but also with the norms of kinship. The Moon-Ak Na' is the original mother of the True Men. According to her celestial aspect she represents a principle of consanguinity and symbolic filiation with the women who are her descendants. On the other hand, the X-Tabay, victims of incest, guilty of patricide , and excluded from the circles of exchange, become the wives of the souls in the world of the dead. Since death inverts the principles of organisation established in the Lacandon world,[30] it is not surprising that these beings linked to the female principle of consanguinity (Ak Na': maternity) once in Metlan[31] should become the objects of matrimony.[32]

The Social Space

The term Na', which means "mother" is, out of all the kinship terms, the one which translates the greatest polysemous variation. In effect Na' also designates the house, specifically the place where the Lacandones sleep and engender. The maize storehouse constructed in the centre of the milpa (u na' i nar: the maize house) is where sexual encounters take place, especially in the case of men who maintain a polygamous home. The term is also the name for the moon, the lunar month (and therefore by extension the menstrual cycle), and the temple (u na' i ku': the god's house) where the men reproduce their alliances with the divinities and insure the fertility of the soil, the healing of the sick, the reproduction of fire, the return of the

30. Marion, 1992: 647.

31. The universe of the dead in Mayan mythology.

32. In their earthly aspect these lunar goddesses could evoke the transgression of the incestuous taboo: marriage with one's mother, since in her celestial aspect, Ak Na' is the symbol of maternity and symbolic filiation.

rains, the end of an eclipse, the initiation of their sons to community life.

It is a term that defines and reproduces the universe of women although paradoxically it is situated in the middle of masculine spaces, such as in the case of the milpa or the god's house, in the heart of a social space determined by belonging to a group of agnate descent, characterised by the recognition of patrilineal filiation. Based on the perspective of native kinship terminology, a family is identified by the presence of a woman inside a material structure, which then becomes a social structure. The man builds the house, the woman administers and reproduces the home. Na' is a concept closely linked to the idea of human fertility and family created by a man in relation to a woman.

Like the human body, the home is also a living being that gives its dwellers shelter and allows their reproduction. The house has arms (the main beams: kab), a head (the roof ho'or), a vulva (the door: hoor), feet (the four secondary posts ok), a penis (the posts of the main structure: che'), a back (the back wall: patch), etc. In this manner the home is born with the birth of the first child, (prior to this the couple lived in the home of the woman's father) and in turn it also dies with the original procreator, at which time the house is abandoned.

The house is a feminine concept representing a polysemous variation of mother and of lunar fertility and it elucidates the logic of a kinship system based on matrilocal residence with patrilineal descent.

In Lacandon Maya, the uterus is called 'u kuch i mehen'. It originates from the verb 'kuchik' which means 'to carry'. It also refers to the cotton cord women use to weave fabric on their waist looms. It is not the cotton (taman) nor is it the piece of cloth (nok); 'Kuch' is simply the raw material of human life. It is in the uterus, that little cotton bag women have in their womb, where they patiently weave the texture of their children. It would suffice to remember the vocation of Ak Na', the universal mother, the first child-bearer, the patroness of weaving, the protectress of pregnancy and childbirth in order to understand the logic of the representation of intrauterine life. Placed under the protection of Mother-Moon, the women weave within themselves the offspring that they will bear and the uterus is nothing more than an allegoric expression of this process. As weavers of human life, they reproduce on earth the historic vocation of their lunar protectress. A native custom emphasises the importance of this allegoric image of the Mother-Moon during the process of gestation.

Among the Lacandones there is a custom of tying a cotton thread around a newborn's neck. This cord has been spun by the newborn's mother during her pregnancy and tied to her own neck or wrist during the process of gestation. After childbirth the cord is placed on the neck of the newborn and in this manner the virtues of protection which are supposedly transmissible are passed on at this moment from mother to child. In the Dresden Codex, the lunar goddess appears as the protectress of weaving and of childbirth. The colonial chroniclers comment that women who desired to procreate implored protection from this divinity. This belief has persisted among the Lacandones and the symbolic gesture of spinning and weaving cotton are associated with the process of gestation and provides evidence for the endurance of a symbol of this magnitude.

On his day of initiation, the child is taken from the world of women, and therefore from the Moon's protection, and enters the world of men, becoming another element in the social chain involved in the reproduction of the solar course. The men will offer copal (vegetable blood) to the heavenly bodies in his honour. This brutal rupture between the shadows and light, between the domestic space of women and the public domain of men, is done when the cotton cord tied around the young one's neck on the day of birth, is now cut by his mother and saved for possible future use.[33] For obvious reasons of time we cannot go into depth concerning the symbolism arising from the cotton cord, although there are many incidents in the ethnography, iconography, and colonial chronicles allowing us to explore an area still not thoroughly analysed.[34] We shall only stress the validity of an interpretation of symbolic filiation which exists between the 'Moon', the women and their children, transmitted from the beginning of Mayan time, through the cotton cords that women have continuously spun to ensure the transmission of life. Once the cord has been cut, the child should be able to survive without being threatened by the lethal dangers imminent at childbirth, since birth in itself is an irruption from the world of the dead.[35] Upon separating the child from the Moon's protection and placing him under the care of men and the Sun for the long journey of his human existence, a second birth is observed, a definitive emergence to community life and a complete scission from neonatal life.

The Ritual Space

In the Lacandon communities that have not yet ceded to the logic of missionaries, the temple (u na' i ki, or 'the abode of the gods') is the space where men meet in order to carry out divinatory, therapeutic, or propitiatory practices that are intended to re-establish the cosmic order, the health of a

---

33. Marion, 1992: 569-70.

34. Fore more details, **see**: Marta Ilia Najera: *El don de la sangre en el equilibrio cósmico*, UNAM, Mexico 1987, pp. 63-70; *El Libro de Chilam Balam*, 1979: 166; Thompson, 1975: Tozzer, 1982; Nordike, 1973: Marion and Dichtl, 1988; Marion, 1990 and 1992.

35. According to the myth which referring to the second apocalypse, says that from the soul of the dead the men of the last creation will be born.

sick person, or thwart the threat of drought, eclipses, etc. . . . Women are completely kept away from this space, although their symbolic presence is maintained through a series of elements which, when listed, allow us to reconstruct the logic of the Lacandon conceptual system.

Since remote time, the lunar deity holds a predominant place in the ritual complex of the Mayans. In order to define the permanence of these functions we shall once again turn to the iconography of the classic period. The goddess Ixchel, just as she is represented in the Dresden Codex, carries a glyph on her back. The iconographic representations are diverse, but the symbolic burden in the majority of the cases is an animal, frequently a bird, or to be exact, a parrot. The parrot continues to be an omen of sickness among the Lacandones, for whom it announces infections of the respiratory system. The goddess's burden ('kuch') also signifies luck, prophecy and enigma.[36] Ixchel is also associated with the dramas and dangers that threaten humanity. The interpretation of glyphs, associated with each of those days on which they appeared, allowed the soothsayers to foretell the destiny of men and to counteract their bad luck.

The Motul dictionary specifies that Kuch also means labour, scarcity, and epidemics. The importance of this term has been highlighted when it designates the uterus and the cotton cord, both of which are associated with the beginnings of life and birth. Consequently, the result is the reunion, within the term, of contradictory aspects related to the lunar goddess in process of childbirth and destruction. By carrying the child on her back, Ixchel reproduces life, and by sustaining misfortune in her 'mecapal'[37] she dispenses calamity and disaster.

---

36. Thompson, "The Moon Goddess in Middle America", *op. cit.*, p. 48.

37. Porter's cotton strap.

It is sufficient to observe the awesome representation of the lunar goddess reproduced in the Dresden Codex,[38] to be seduced by the powerful evocation of this dichotomy. Naked and with swollen breasts full of milk, the goddess carries in her 'mecapal' a small being who looks like her son. In reality it is the god of death, whose face is stripped of flesh and whose spinal cord looks like that of an iguana or saurian, a figurative characteristic of Ah Puch, the god of Metlan during the classic period. As patroness of childbirth, the lunar goddess is also associated with death, which she dispenses alternatively. Here we have, intimately mixed with the life-cycle from its beginnings to its end, the divinatory protectress and creator of women who transmits to them through the umbilical cord (the cotton thread uniting them) the power of life and death over the beings whom they will bear. The female principle dominates from the origins of the world (universe of water and semi-dearkness, process of intrauterine gestation . . .) and appears associated with death and the end of the solar cycle (floods, the victory of darkness over light, the irruption of the apocalyptic jaguars . . .).

In the temple monopolised exclusively by men, women with their moon power appear to be absent. However, even though they are physically excluded, they invade the ritual space once more by means of certain elements of the cult, and precisely those related to the process of conception.

Together in the House of the Gods (Na'), the men cremate vegetable blood in ceramic pots that act as the protective wrapping of their gods. The essence of the deities is contextualised by some stones gathered in places that are considered sacred (because it is the earthly dwelling place of the deities). Submerged in copal ashes, the gods are fed during these ceremonies, with vegetable offerings

38. *Dresden Codex*, p. 17.

made of annotto,[39] copal,[40] rubber,[41] tobacco, and also with corn and balché, the ritual drink. After a certain amount of use, the gods' pots are replaced, the old incense burners are buried and new ones substitute them, after a long ceremony that usually lasts several weeks.

In the midst of the sacred space, an incense burner prevails over the renovation practices, which demarcate the cycle of gestation and birth of the new incense burners. It is a ceramic pot with a long arm that the Lacandones designate with the term of Ak Na'.[42] Unlike the others, this incense burner never dies and invariably presides over the most important stages of this unusual ritual, which is intended to give life anew to the wrapping of the gods.

Likewise, the celebrant of the ritual, the most knowledgeable and wise man in charge of personally addressing and feeding the gods, draws some circles on his chest, which become his 'breasts' (u yim u nok: lit. the breasts of his tunic). In this manner, he highlights his ritual personality of 'male midwife' of the deities, during the birthing process.[43] In the enclosure that shares her name, Ak Na' dominates by her sole presence, the incense burners of the main gods of native theogony. She imposes her power of life and death over the old clay bodies that will be buried and over the new pots that start their life-cycle, to ensure the perennation of the cosmos and the reproduction of the ethnic group.

In order to reactivate the course of the cosmos, to revitalise the Sun on its journey, the men feminise themselves ritually, by taking away from the women their attributes

39. Bixa Orellana, Maya: Cuxu.

40. Bursera sp. Pom.

41. Hevea brasiliensis, Maya: K'iik.

42. Marion, 1992: 760; Tozzer, 1982: 129.

43. Marion, 1992: 773.

and powers and appropriating them, just the time necessary to keep away lethal dangers and to correct some atmospheric, biological, or social disorder. When they sing to their gods, the Lacandones tattoo themselves with feminine marks, covering their bodies with the spots of the great American feline, an animal linked to earthly forces and an apocalyptic companion of solar eclipses. When the men ritually appropriate the powers held by women in an everyday context, they seek to put into effect the reproduction of the cosmos by endeavours similar to those of their wives who reproduce society. Social and cosmic spaces are found closely linked, mixed, and mutually overlaid in order to ensure the stability of the historic logic of the Lacandones.

Through their mythology, in the ritual phases that mark the most important moments of their lives, the protective image of their lunar goddess countinues to illuminate the thoughts of the Mayans. Such has been the case for centuries, through the reproduction of an iconography that shows the perennation of Mesoamerican cosmic dichotomy; giving us tangible proof of the capacity for intellectual retention of the societies which have conceived this dichotomy, and allowing the moon to guide them with the messages she irradiates.

6

The Womb that Nourishes and Devours

Representations of the Earth in the Cosmology of the Huave of the Isthmus of Tehuantepec (Mexico)

Alessandro Lupo

> The study of narration in myth is only one part of the study of myth; and the search for its meaningful elements should not be limited to the terms of the narration. To find the proper codes of a myth one must delve deeply into the religious tradition underlying it. It is not sufficient to start from the hypothesis that certain symbols are obvious and clear to anyone who merely wants to identify universal oppositions and convergences.
>
> ***López Austin*** (1990: 464)

> If almost anything can remind the Hawaiians of sex is it not because, at least as a condition of possibility, the universe of persons and objects is already charged with immense forces of semantic attraction? The universe is a genealogy, which is to say a total cosmological project of sexual reproduction.
>
> ***Sahlins*** (1985: 12-13)

This study is an attempt to analyze the complex symbolic representations of Earth elaborated by the Huave of San

Mateo del Mar, a fishing people who live on the Isthmus of Tehuantepec in the state of Oaxaca, Mexico.[1] This ethnic group, which speaks an isolated language of the Oto-Mangue phylum (Kaufman 1974), occupies a narrow strip of coastal land around the brackish lagoons east of the Tehuantepec river, an inhospitable region which until recently was very isolated. Most of the land is arid and sandy and unsuitable for cultivation. The climate is hot and dry and subject to extreme seasonal variations. During the summer (June-September) there are often torrential rains that flood the entire Huave territory and repopulate the large brackish pools with fish and crayfish. This is followed by several months (November-February) when there is a violent north wind, and then by a period (March-May) of calm and torrid drought when the pools of water dry up almost completely.

Before the large increase in population of recent decades (Lupo, n.d.), which has profoundly changed their way of life (v. Cuturi 1990), the Huave managed to get all they needed to live from lagoons abounding in fish; and they sold the excess fish to buy other food and items they could not produce.[2] Today even though there is a serious commitment to agriculture, especially in the more fertile western part of the territory, it cannot satisfy the population's needs,

1. The Huave have been studied since 1973 by the Italian Ethnological Mission in Mexico, directed by Italo Signorini (for further information, v. Signorini 1979, 1981, 1990, n.d.; Lupo 1981, 1992, n.d.; Cuturi 1981, 1990).

2. An increase in population and unfavorable weather conditions have greatly depleted the fish resources, thus making fishing less remunerative and driving many people to turn to agriculture even though it is not very profitable. Furthermore, improvement in transportation has spurred many Huave to take salaried jobs in the nearby oil refinery at Salina Cruz. Since the beliefs that we are analyzing here do not yet reflect these recent socio-economic changes, we shall refer to the Huave means of subsistence as it was prior to the last twenty-five years.

particularly for maize, the staple of the native diet. Stock farming on the barren eastern pasture lands also gives meagre returns, so the Huave economy rests mainly on fishing, especially for crayfish, which is a valuable commercial product.

However, this activity is carried out exclusively in the internal waters: shallow lagoons connected to the ocean by only one inlet and pools of rainwater periodically flooded with sea water. The delicate ecosystem the Huave depend on is, therefore, completely subject to the rainfall, which determines the volume and the salinity of the lagoons and thus the abundance of their yield. This explains why the entire cosmologial system, including public rituals and sacred narrative, is centered around weather themes.[3]

For the peoples of Mesoamerica — and the Huave are no exception — it is impossible to separate beliefs about the regime of the waters, whether celestial or cthonic, from those about Earth, on whose surface lakes and seas rest and in whose bowels rivers and springs and rain-bearing clouds originate. In iconography, mythology and ritual, terrestrial divinities are very often associated with the vivifying water element. It is enough to recall that Earth was often conceived of as an immense being (very often a saurian reptile) floating on cosmic waters and was associated with the cold, dark, fertile and humid aspects of the universe, as opposed to the warm, luminous and dry ones typical of the complementary celestial and daytime elements (v. López Austin 1984, I: 58-68). Beings belonging to the latter category were generally considered masculine, while Earth was feminine.

Nevertheless, in Mesoamerican thinking the components of the cosmos are often viewed and represented as embodying dualistic principles, albeit in unequal proportions. Therefore

3. This theme was dealt with in another section of the congress by Italo Signorini (v. Signorini n.d.).

Earth haș been, and sometimes still is, represented as a divinity incorporating a masculine aspect in addition to its principal female one. (cfr. Caso 1973: 72; Nicholson 1971: 406, 420-22; Signorini and Lupo 1989: 226-28), though most often this masculine aspect is less important. The prevalently female connotation of Earth symbolizes its creative energy as generator and sustainer of plants and animals and thus, more or less indirectly, of humans. However, as we know from the depletion of agricultural soil, this energy is not boundless; and it is not believed to be created from nothing. Its incessant output requires constant replenishment. Indeed, in addition to being the procreator, Earth is the final repository of everything ephemeral. Since all dead things decompose and are transformed into new life in its bowels, Earth is envisioned as a voracious being, ready to seize and swallow up any source of energy (material or spiritual) within its grasp. This may occur by chance or intentionally for 'nourishment', and explains the pre-Hispanic representation of the earth monster with immense gaping jaws and other fanged mouths at the elbow and knee joints. It also explains the belief, still held in a large part of Mesoamerica, that Earth is ready to swallow up not only the bodies of the deceased but also spiritual elements that are separated from the body as a result of a violent emotion (we are referring here to the widespread belief that a *susto* 'fright' causes the 'loss of soul', and to recover it one must pray and give offerings to Earth).

For the Huave Earth (*nangah iüt* 'sacred earth')[4] is like

---

4. To simplify transcription of the Huave language, the criteria used in the other writings of the Italian group have been slightly modified (v. Signorini 1979: 15): 'ü' represents a sound similar to 'eu' in the French *feu*; 'ch' is pronounced as in Spanish and English; 'x' is the same as the 'sh' in the English *shoe*; and '̤' corresponds to the sound ṫs̩ in the International Phonetic Alphabet.

an enormous disk[5] inside the solid vault of heaven; the ocean waters rest on it and define its boundaries all around (v. Lupo 1981: 268-69; 1991: 219-20). It is the support of everything, the theater of all events and — since it is a sentient, animate being — the omnipresent witness to everything that happens in the universe. Nothing occurring on its surface eludes it; nothing is forgotten (it is 'like a tape recorder', Signorini and Tranfo 1979: 225) so that the most solemn oaths are sworn on it and 'confession' of the presumed causes of sicknesses is addressed to it during healing rites (*ibid.*).[6]

Huave women always give birth on the ground, so the newborn is welcomed by Earth; and the placenta and umbilical cord are buried in the earthen floor of the dwelling (Rita 1979: 288-92). Immediately after the birth, during the rite presenting the infant on the household altar, the midwife exclaims: "*Nqanüy landoh, latahkiay presentar wüx mundo; ahmiük tiül nangah iüt monopoo¢ . . . lahlüy, lamataaq recibir* 'Now it is over (the birth), (the newborn) has presented itself to the world; it fell on the holy blessed earth . . . is already here, now has been received' ".[7] Inherent in

5. This belief is like that represented on a smaller scale by the Nahuas and Totonacs of the Sierra of Puebla, who liken it to the clay disk (*comal*) used to toast food (Ichon 1969: 36, 131; Lok 1987: 218-19).

6. This custom brings to mind the purifying role that in ancient times the Aztecs attributed to the earth goddess Tlazolteotl who, "inasmuch as she is the devourer of filth, devours men's sins and so purifies them. The rite of confession as it was practiced before her priests comes from this" (Caso 1973: 75).

7. The ritual expression *nangah iüt monopoo* which we have translated as 'holy blessed earth', expresses the utmost respect for the deity mentioned by associating with the term *nangah* 'sacred' that of *monopoo*, which usually designates the highest positions in the religious hierarchy. An informant suggests: " 'this earth is like a church', it is very sacred"; indeed, *teampoo* means 'in church' (v. Stairs and Stairs 1981).

Earth's 'reception' of the newborn is the idea that, in a certain sense, it is appropriating the new creature and extending its control over it. The informant J.O. comments on this passage as follows: "when the newborn comes down to earth, the earth has received it *for its own use*; and that's why the earth knows everything about a man's life". In addition to expressing concepts such as the fragility of man and his total dependence on divine will, which are generally in keeping with Catholic belief, these words reveal concepts that are clearly indigenous. The most important is that man comes into the world to 'serve' the gods. This idea can be found in the principal cosmogonical myths of Mesoamerica (v. "Leyenda de los soles" 1975: 120-21; "Historia de los Mexicanos . . ." 1985; Tedlock 1985: 79) and is the basis for maintaining that certain rituals (prayers, offerings, sacrifices) are intended to 'sustain' the gods by giving back to them the energy received. For the Huave, Earth is undoubtedly an emanation of the Christian God, but it also has its own role, functions and attributes. It is subordinate to the Christian God but retains a margin of independence that will be pointed out in the course of this paper. During a supplication for healing, the ritualist A.M. uses figurative language for the relationship between God and Earth: "*Dios Padre, Cristo Redentor, ik indeaand, ilihkimb intere meawan, intere mundo, intere ningüy tiül ileah tiül iwix, ike indeaand, ike ihaw* . . . 'God Father, Christ Redeemer, you hold in your hand, you hold everything in your arms, the whole world, everything is here in your hands and at your feet,[8] you hold it in your hand, you see it . . .' "; and later says: "*Teat Dios Padre Eterno que nahlüy tiül santa Gloria omeaa¢ mbasaka¢ nelihkimb nangah iüt monopoo¢ querida tierra* 'Lord God

8. It is interesting to note how this metaphoric expression in the Huave ritual language ('in your hands, at your feet') is also used today by the ritual specialists of other groups like the Nahuas of the Sierra of Puebla (Lupo 1993: 89) and the Quiché of Guatemala, and it can even be found in the Popol Vuh (Tedlock 1985: 259).

Eternal Father who is in holy paradise in the heart of the sky (and) holds in His arms the holy blessed earth, beloved earth'." Thus Earth is 'in the arms' and 'in the hands' of God, just as men — "*mikwal nangah iüt monopoo¢* 'children of holy blessed Earth" — are 'in the hands' of Earth. The subordination of Earth to God is also expressed in the clear separation into opposite spaces: the terrestrial disk below, God above, superior, in the 'heart of the sky'.

Since Earth is the space in close proximity and thus witness to all human events and keeper of all human secrets, it becomes the preferred extra-human interlocutor. Not only does it 'see' everything, but, as we shall see, its very substance is readily available for the necessary rituals. Indeed, in the case of strong emotions like fear, shame, and anger, the Huave believe that the *omeaa¢* inside', heart', in this case the 'spiritual force' of the individual, falls to the ground and that this loss seriously weakens the organism and brings on illness. To recover, it is necessary first of all to establish what event caused the detachment (bear in mind that many years may have passed between the traumatic experience and the onset of the illness), then gather earth from the place where the emotion occurred, and finally carry out the rituals to bring back the patient's *omeaa¢*. For the intervention to succeed it is essential that Earth itself be disposed to give back what it is holding in custody. Indeed, even though the Huave do not explicitly express, as other Mexican populations do, the conviction that Earth 'nourishes itself' on the souls it captures, they do believe that with the passage of time the soul penetrates deeper and deeper into the ground — almost as if it were 'digested' — so that if the emotion causing the illness occurred in the distant past one must dig more deeply (Signorini and Tranfo 1979).

The healing rite — variously called *delehes* (from the Spanish 'diligencia') or *apah omeaa¢* 'call the soul' — centers completely on involvement with Earth. The healer dedicates to it two of the three candles lighted before the household altar (one of these candles is planted directly in the sand floor of the house; the other in the bowl containing soil from the place where the loss of *omeaa¢* was assumed to have occurred; and the third in front of the sacred images on the altar). The sick person is laid directly on the Earth (to be precise, on a shawl spread on the ground and carefully sprinkled with soil which is taken from the bowl and collected at the end of the rite). The healer picks up the soil left in the bowl, 'warms it' over the smoke from the copal, and puts it back into the bowl; he then touches the forehead, chest and extremities of the patient in order to restore to the body the spiritual essence with which Earth is thought to be imbued. Moreover, during these acts the ritualist repeatedly invokes Earth, dedicating prayers and making offerings to it, and declaring among other things that "*nahmiük tiül oleah tiül owix nangah iüt monopoo¢ nataag confesar nüüch cuenta . . . niüng akweat omal niüng akweat omeaa¢* 'I kneel at the feet and hands of the holy blessed earth (and) confess (and) give account . . . of where (the sick person) has left his head, where he has left his heart' ". He asks Earth to join forces ("*metaag anaag responder* 'that they answer each other' ") with the water (that he vaporizes by blowing on the patient's body) so that together the two element-forces "*maxaingiw tiüt hijo de Dios* 'raise from the ground the child of God (the sick person)' ". He himself does the same thing by calling the *omeaa¢* by name: "*Fulano de tal! witiür hijo de Dios! tawar! naxaing ik tiül nangah iüt monopoo¢* 'John Doe! stand up! child of God! let's go! I raise you from the holy blessed earth' ".

The concept of Earth we have seen thus far emerges from answers given during ethnographic interviews, from prayers, and from several important household rites (birth and healing). It is a concept of a ubiquitous, omniscient extrahuman entity, generally inclined to be neutral towards humans, from whom it does sometimes detain the spiritual component, but who, if properly invoked and humored, proves to be extremely well-disposed and helpful to them. Since there is constant concern about arousing the hostility of the supernatural, euphemisms are used when speaking with any supernatural being who might be hostile or evil. This euphemistic language is even more evident in prayer, which is the basic instrument of *captatio benevolentiae* and must follow strict rules in form. Huave culture also forbids very justifiable complaints in everyday speech because they might sound disrespectful to the divinities.[9]

Nevertheless, despite their extreme caution, the Huave do give some very negative interpretations to certain emanations of Earth. However, this does not happen explicitly in colloquial speech or in prayer but through allegory and myth. We shall combine and briefly summarize here various versions of the stories about the *sapcheeb* (also called *malamujer* 'evil woman'), a feared creature who is said to be exhaling from the earth when a few drops of rain from occasional 'passing clouds' (*tiiüd oik* 'clouds on the road') come in contact with the parched ground during the dry season. The name of this anthropomorphic 'vapor', which can be translated roughly as 'shark that seizes', perfectly captures her perverse voracity.[10]

9. The only exception is the north wind (*iiünd*) which, though violent and extremely unpleasant, is considered incapable of inflicting punishments as harsh as those inflicted by lightning (*monteok*) and the south-east wind (*ncharrek*) (v. Lupo 1981: 303).

10. The image of the sharp teeth in 'shark that seizes' is probably intended to evoke (but in a 'metallic' image) a concept like that of another telluric figure of Mesoamerican mythology, who is known by the Nahuatl name of *Tepusilam* 'old lady of copper (or iron)'. For the Nahuas of Durango, she is a terrestrial woman-monster who lures and devours men (Preuss 1982: 81-85, 91). As Ziehm (1982: 14) points out in her introduction, the word 'copper' "evidently is intended to represent something which is hard, which bites and cuts and corresponds to the 'obsidian' component in the name Itzpapalotl (butterfly of obsidian)", one

→

1. One night during the hot season, a young man named *Anchay* ('lazy') is walking along the shore of the ocean looking for turtle eggs[11] when he comes upon an attractive woman who makes amorous advances toward him. The young man accepts and lies down with her on the sand, but at the very moment of penetrating her she disappears and his penis is stuck in the ground and cannot be extracted. The next day some fishermen find him and tell his family, who try in all possible ways to dig him free. In the end they have to cut off his penis and he dies.

2. Later on, two fishermen, a young man and an old one, who have not caught anything, decide to sleep on the shore. They plant a stick in the ground to spread their net as a tent to sleep under. Shortly after, a breeze stirs the net and two female figures appear. The younger one, who is headless, wants to approach the sleeping young man and touch him. She says she is curious about his reputation as a womanizer. The older woman tries in vain to dissuade her. The headless *sapcheeb* reaches out and gets her fingers caught in the net. After vain efforts to free herself, she is abandoned by her companion. At sunrise the terrified fishermen notice that the creature that disturbed them during the night is a

---

→ of the ancient earth goddesses of the Nahuas of the central plateau. For the cult of a terrestrial divinity called *Jantepusi ilama* in regions closer to the Huave area, see the historical research by Aramoni (1992) on the Zoque of Chiapas, who still tell tales about a terrestrial goddess with a toothed vagina (v. Báez-Jorge 1988: 291-321).

11. It seems relevant to note that when night hunters of marine turtle eggs (of the species *Chelonia mydas* and *Eretmochelys imbricata*) think they have found a 'nest', they probe the ground with a thin stick and then dig out the find with their hands.

bird (a pelican in one version, an *ech* in another)[12] with its beak caught in the casting net. They kill the bird with a stick and then burn it.[13]

3. One night a friend of the unfortunate Anchay named *Kangeen* ('penis of stone')[14] is on his way to Tehuantepec when he meets a woman who looks like his sweetheart. She suggests she go with him; and after some hesitation, he agrees. He also agrees

---

12. The *ech* is an imaginary bird believed to kill people who sleep in the open-air — especially along the ocean shore — by pecking at their anus and navel and eating their intestines, so that they die from lack of nourishment. According to an informant who gives another version, the *ech* comes close to the sleeper and sticks its beak into the ground. Soon after the person dies from atrocious abdominal pains.

13. Some elements of this and the other stories are reminiscent of the passage in the "Leyenda de los solcs" (1975: 123-24) in which — according to the revised translation by Graulich (1988: 92-93) — two hunters, who are brothers, are approached by two two-headed deer which are soon transformed into women. The older brother lies with one of the women, who kills him (by biting him and 'piercing him': *qualcoyonia*); the younger one, having fled and escaped the other woman's dangerous advances, makes her fall on thorns and then, with the help of the fire divinities, burns her. This woman-monster (*tzitzimitl*) is none other than the earth goddess Itzpapalotl (v. note 10).

14. Even though the informants seem to have no doubt about the meaning of the name, it should be noted that *kang* 'stone' is also a euphemistic term for the vagina (otherwise called *chit*). Thus *Kangeen* could also mean 'vagina-penis', an oxymoron that is not altogether unjustifiable, as we shall see in the rest of the tale. It should also be noted that *Kangeen* appears in another story — in a farcical vein — as the brother of *Anchay*. A bachelor eager to have sexual relations with as many women as possible, *Kangeen* furnishes himself with the penis of a skunk. This magically guarantees him great success. To insure an even greater erection, he licks the talisman; but this arouses such a tremendous erotic frenzy that he runs through the streets grabbing whomever he meets until he dies of exhaustion and starvation.

to lie down with her to rest for a moment. Overcome by sexual desire, he wants to satisfy it, but just as he is at the point of possessing her he realizes he no longer has a penis but an enormous vagina dripping an evil-smelling liquid and causing him tremendous itching (*la¢amb* 'it bites', 'it itches'). At the same moment the woman disappears. Terrified, the young man goes to an old man for advice. The old man scolds him for his naiveté and suggests how he can recover his penis. He must get the skin of a black sheep and stick four pins into it in the form of a cross (or thorns of *ok* 'coyol', *Acrocomia mexicana*). After that, wearing a neckband that has been blessed (*nangah xiüt*) and carrying the sheepskin and a horsehair whip, he must scour the seashore at night to find the *sapcheeb*. *Kangeen* follows the old man's advice and finally the woman appears and makes amorous advances. *Kangeen* pretends to accept them and convinces her to lie down on his sheepskin rather than directly on the ground as she wants to. At this point he takes out his whip and begins to lash her vigorously. The woman is trapped by the magic sheepskin and cannot get up or flee. *Kangeen* orders her to give him back his penis. The *sapcheeb* resists for a while by changing herself into a cow, a mule and other animals; but eventually she is overcome by the beating and gives in. *Kangeen* feels he has his male sexual attributes again, so he pulls the sheepskin out from under the *sapcheeb*, who makes a strange sound and disappears immediately.[15]

4. On the Thursday night before Easter a man is keeping watch in the church over the image of

15. Gossen (1979: 349) has found a very similar tale among the Tzotzil of Chamula, only the man whose penis has been changed into a vagina must mate with a cow in order to become normal again; and at the end the cow is transformed into a woman.

Christ in chains[16] when he sees a woman he knows pass and nod to him. Attracted by the prospect of an amorous adventure, he chases her as far as the southern end of the village; but, even though she is only walking, he does not catch up. The woman continues on towards the ocean shore and he follows until he is thrown to the ground by a violent blow on the head. He has hit against one of the crosses that are put up to protect the village during Holy Week. At this point, unharmed, the man realizes the risk he has run and hurriedly retraces his steps (the comment of the narrator J.C. was: "She's the *malamujer*, that one. But it isn't true she's a woman; she's a man, a man").

5. A woman who has just given birth falls asleep. When she awakes the baby is gone and she cannot find it anywhere. In her desperation she falls asleep again, and when she wakes up the baby has reappeared. However, since the baby was taken away by the *malamujer*, who took advantage of the inattention of the parents 'to play with it', it dies after three days.[17]

At this point let's try to understand what these stories mean for the Huave and what ideas they convey about Earth besides the usual ones about ethics and rules that are found in the stories of the *sapcheeb* and many other Meso-American female figures believed to trap men in search of amorous adventures (the *Llorona* 'Weeper', *Matlalcihuatl*,

---

16. In the church of San Mateo del Mar, there is an image of Jesus bleeding from his beatings (strangely named "San Nicolás Penitencia"). During Holy Week it is used to represent Christ's imprisonment before the crucifixion.

17. Appropriation of the newborn is one of the tendencies the *sapcheeb* shares with a similar character among the Nahuas of Durango, *Tepusilam* (v. note 10), who "also ate newborn babies left alone by their parents. When the parents returned the baby was missing" (Preuss 1982: 97).

etc.).[18] First of all the *sapcheeb* is explicitly recognized as a manifestation of Earth. She is "*omeaa ṇangah iüt* 'interior, heart of the holy earth' ", an ethereal projection of it, in the same way that mysterious animals in the vicinity of certain large old trees are believed to be emanations of the trees, which "*ahiür omeaa¢* 'have heart' ". Apparitions of the *sapcheeb* are limited in time and space: they occur at night, almost always along the ocean shore, and only in the very hot months; they are aroused by scarce drops from passing clouds ("it is not normal rain" and "they are the very rain itself") and are seen only by men.

The *sapcheeb* is sexually attracted to men, but as soon as her desire is satisfied it changes into 'capture' of the victim's sexual organ. The informants' comments reveal a conviction that the *sapcheeb* does not necessarily mean any harm, but since the act is so unnatural the outcome is very dramatic: "she does not want to kill; she wants him as a friend, to screw with; this is impossible because he is a man, of flesh and blood, while she is a spirit, like the Siren", the other Huave extrahuman female figure, who has a constant desire to mate with man (the only one who can give her offspring). Contact between the *sapcheeb* and the newborn is also involuntary and just as tragic. The motivation to take the child is the same dissatisfaction that drives her to seek the impossible contact with man. Her incomplete female nature induces her to carry off — temporarily and with no evil intent — the offspring she cannot have, so that

18. A vast literature on these female characters demonstrates obvious connections with ancient, pre-Hispanic terrestrial divinities like Cihuacoatl, Xochiquetzal, Itzpapalotl and the *cihuateteo* (v. Caso 1973, Correa 1960, Nicholson 1971, Báez-Jorge 1988). Hunt (1977: 103) reports the belief that the men seduced by Matlalcihuatl show signs of pregnancy, but at the moment of birth expel feces. This idea, with its inauspicious olfactory effects, brings to mind the sexual change undergone by *Kangeen*.

she can 'play' with them; but in this case too unnatural contact between a human being, especially a very fragile one like a newborn baby, and a creature from another ontological order, provokes irreparable damage.

There are also other situations, not, however, directly involving the *sapcheeb*, where the carnal union of creatures belonging to different dimensions of reality is believed to cause sexual mutilation. In commenting on a comic story where a lecherous old man convinces a naïve young bridegroom to let him 'break' the imaginary teeth of his wife's vagina, Rita (1979: 265-67) reports another story in which a man is emasculated while embracing a female crocodile to which he is attracted because its sexual organs are like human ones.[19] In this example of 'zoophile perversion', where the main sexual drive is the man's, as well as in the tales of the *sapcheeb*, where the situation is reversed, mutilation is caused by copulation that is strongly desired but unattainable, or rather desired because it is unattainable ("because she can't"): "the [*sapcheeb*] wants. But she is not a human being. How can she have sex if she is not human? She can't."

Another aspect of the *sapcheeb* that should be taken into consideration is her changing appearance and ambiguous identity (including her sexuality). In order to lure men she must borrow the features of flesh-and-blood women because she herself is "without a face" (without a head in the second story).[20] However, her true form is not

19. It should be noted that for the Huave the crocodile is one of the recurrent animal alter egos for women (Tranfo 1979: 198-99). Moreover, we should not overlook the possible connection — albeit weak — between this story and those of the *sapcheeb*. Indeed, in the pre-Hispanic period, the crocodile was often used to represent Earth: there are examples in the Aztec *cipactli* and the *Zipacna* of the Popol Vuh (Nicholson 1971: 406; Tedlock 1985: 94-98, 372).

20. Very often the Llorona too is seen as a very beautiful woman

→

human. This is clear from her metamorphosis into a bird when she is entangled in the net and from the transformations she goes through when she is magically trapped by *Kangeen.* Even her sexuality is ambiguous; she is not as unequivocally female as she appears at first sight.[21] Aside from the narrator's explicit comment at the end of the fourth story, this is revealed in the appropriation-substitution of the victim's penis and in the phallic symbolism underlying her behavior in the second story, where her finger-beak is caught in the net. This is the same beak that the bird *ech* (her '*avatar*') sticks into the body (navel, anus) of its prey or into the ground; and the movement is exactly the same as the one used by those who tried to copulate with Earth-*sapcheeb* and thereby lost their penis.

The *sapcheeb*, therefore, seems to represent a dangerous transgression of Earth from the natural order of fixed identity and roles. This transgression is seen in actions such as the attempt to take over the space (the seashore) and prerogatives (masculinity) of men. And all of this occurs at the time of the year when there is no lightning, the heavenly phenomenon which the Huave believe keeps things running smoothly. Indeed, a flash of lightning is the greatest manifestation there is of the power of the divinities (*monteok*, literally 'those who perform miracles', or, broadly speaking, 'lightning'), who not

→ from far off but from close by has a horrible, skeleton-like face (v. Correa 1960: 71-75; Ingham 1986: 110-11; Signorini and Lupo 1989: 85). At times the *sapcheeb* appears headless (in which case she is also called *toko* n̤ik 'cropped neck') and is reminiscent of the colossal statue of the earth goddess Coatlicue, from whose headless trunk sprout two serpent heads, and of the two-headed deer, which is a metamorphosis of Itzpapalotl in the "Leyenda de los soles" (1975: 123; v. note 13).

21. Bear in mind that in Mesoamerica Earth is both masculine and feminine, although in most cases the latter aspect is more apparent than the former (cf. Signorini and Lupo 1989: 228; Lupo 1990).

only produce and control the rains but also strike down all things (humans, animals and plants) that 'are not respectful' and commit the sin of *hubris* by overstepping their boundaries.[22] The hot months when there are no *monteok* are also the months when ominous forces manage to venture beyond their usual domains. Lent and Holy Week, which commemorates the greatest victory of the forces of cosmic disorder, fall in this period; and every year the Huave put on a display representing the passion of Christ and the advent of the champions of caos.[23] It is no coincidence, therefore, that the only appearance of the *sapcheeb* in the village happens on the Thursday before Easter.

The instruments used to counteract or thwart the action of the *sapcheeb* have a strong male connotation and are closely associated with water, sea water in one case and rainwater in the other (but never chthonic waters). In the second story the net protecting the fishermen is the instrument of male labor *par excellence*; and it is strongly tabu for women to have any contact with it (a woman who

---

22. Huave narrative is dominated by the theme of lightning striking in order to restore cosmic order. It decapitates the serpent about to unleash cthonic .waters and submerge man, or more simply, it burns up those who are disrespectful in words or deeds (v. Tranfo 1979: 200-201; Lupo 1981: 295-302). Every year the municipal authorities turn to the *monteok* to ask for the rains that are so essential to the community's well-being; and this takes place in the month of April on the shore of the ocean (Signorini 1979: 102-103).

23. From Thursday to Saturday before Easter, the village is taken over by ritual anarchy. All work stops and the municipal authorities are 'replaced' by *repotada* 'deputies', who go around the village on a rampage, putting anyone who works or laughs into jail, hitting anyone who is found sleeping in church, etc.; they act this way "because they belong to *nimeech* the devil".

touches or walks on her husband's net brings bad luck to his fishing).[24] Moreover, since the net is in constant contact with sea water it is permeated with salt, which has a very strong sacred connotation (indeed, it is called "*nangah kiniük* 'sacred salt' ") and a widespread apotropaic use;[25] but, above all, the net is made up of 'thousands of crosses', each of which evokes the regulative power of God.[26]

The second object used to combat the *sapcheeb* is the skin of a black sheep ('everything that is black is medicine') because it has a cross (made of pins or thorns)[27] and is also

24. This comes from the sexual division of roles, and can also be found, for example, among the Guayakí of Amazonia, where the woman is strictly forbidden to touch her husband's bow because it is bad luck for the hunt and the man to touch the basket she uses for gathering. The bow and the basket are obvious phallic and uterine sexual symbols (Clastres 1977: 79-99). Among the Huave the symbolism is less obvious: the net seems to have a female connotation (for example, 'catching' the finger of the *sapcheeb*); and the stick the fishermen use to probe the sand when they search for turtle eggs probably has a male connotation (as does the stick used by the few who farm to dig up the land; cfr López Austin 1990: 224).

25. Probably because of its use in baptism, salt is widely believed to 'keep away' the spirits. In a Sierra Popoluca tale a man is ensnared by an extrahuman seductress who very carefully washes him before coupling with him in order to clean away the salt he has ingested with his food (Foster 1945: 202).

26. The casting net is also used as protection in the healing rite intended to save the alter ego of a sick person (v. Signorini and Tranfo 1979: 254); and rolled-up net is used to make the handle of the *machete* that the *monteok* brandish to unleash lightning.

27. There is a phallic connotation (obviously of European origin) to the pointed metal objects universally used to resist the snares of femininity by 'penetrating it'. In some versions of the tale thorns of the *ok* (a type of palm with very sweet fruit) are used. It should be noted that for the Huave the *ok* has very strong sexual implications. The signs left by the juice of its tender fruit so resemble those of male and female secretions during sexual intercourse that the verb *aok* means 'to copulate'. In →

the garment fishermen once used to protect themselves from the rain 'when there was no nylon'. The sheepskin in the third story harks back to Huave mythology where lightning is used as a sort of flying carpet to move around in the sky. The skin of the black sheep represents rainclouds lightning rides as it does its job as the waterer of creation. By convincing the *sapcheeb* to lie on the sheepskin, *Kangeen* breaks the contact between the *sapcheeb* and Earth, from which it emanates, and manages to overpower it, just as Hercules did with Anteus. And all of this is done by using an object belonging to the celestial dimension.[28]

And finally there is the power of the whip *Kangeen* uses to subdue the *sapcheeb*. It comes from the horsehair used to make it, since the Huave (like many other Mesoamerican peoples of the past and present) believe that the hair contains strength. This belief also explains why hair is saved or hidden after cutting and why it must be covered so that lightning cannot strike it, since lightning burns up anything that exhibits 'strength' rivaling its own. Moreover, the horse is considered 'the strongest animal', so horsehair is believed to be particularly forceful.

Although we have devoted a lot of space to the *sapcheeb*, we do not want to detract from the overall positive

---

→ one of the comic tales of the rabbit and the coyote, the rabbit gives the coyote some *ok* seeds and makes the coyote believe that they were obtained by squeezing its testicles with a stone. The greedy coyote is persuaded to imitate the rabbit and thus castrates itself and dies.

28. It is interesting to see how similar this episode is to a Huichol myth in which the hero protects his penis with a magic deer antler and breaks the teeth of women's vaginas. But in extracting his penis after intercourse he must be very careful that it does not touch the ground (Zingg 1982, II: 233-34). For the Huave the hardness of the hero's penis is not due to the antler armor but is inherent in his very name (*Kangeen* 'penis of stone'), and he escapes the castrating vagina of the *sapcheeb* by avoiding contact with the ground.

associations Earth has for the Huave. If we consider all the factors discussed, perhaps we can conclude that, in addition to its boundless generosity in nourishing its creatures, Earth also has a dark, rapacious side, which generally remains latent but may be aroused and become very dangerous in certain space-time circumstances. And it is not surprising that this happens when the Huave feel less protected by the custodians of cosmic order (above all, lightning). In fact, on the Isthmus of Tehuantepec the hot, dry season coincides with Lent, when the statues of the saints in church are covered and the devil prevails: "it's his time, he reigns for the whole time; God can't do anything. That's why they say that during that time the devil goes about."

Earth, however, should not be confused with the forces of evil. Quite the opposite. Nevertheless, under certain critical conditions it is believed that Earth takes advantage of the absence of the guardians of order to transgress and give vent to its negative potential. After long months of no contact with the heavenly life-giving liquid, just a few drops of an unseasonal rain not 'brought' by lightning are enough to unleash its voracious appetites.[29] However, since its femininity is ambiguous and incomplete, Earth cannot satisfy these appetites by itself because it would be a violation of the separateness and complementarity characteristic of both the earthly and heavenly planes. Therefore, Earth directs its desire toward man, the creature

29. Perhaps it is not completely unreasonable to interpret probing the earth with a stick in search of turtle eggs and thus becoming a victim of the *sapcheeb* as another 'sexual provocation' — especially if it occurs when Earth is in a state of 'overexcitement' due to special weather conditions (v. stories 1 and 2). The belief that insufficient rain will have a negative effect on the parched earth is also found elsewhere: in the Sannio area of Benevento, in Italy, for example, if the first rains after a long sunny season are light and do not penetrate deeply into the ground, it is said that 'the earth becomes evil' and produces a prickly weed (personal communication from Patrizia Burdi).

closest to it capable (albeit less satisfactorily) of carrying out the fecundative role of the heavenly forces and thus ending its distressing deprivation. And so it tries to snare him in all possible ways: by invading his spaces (for example, the seashore) and by trying to steal his virility. But a union of this kind, which overturns the natural order by confounding different ontological dominions, must be tragic for the weaker element, in this case, man.

Certainly we can apply to the Huave the symbolism noted more generally by Báez-Jorge (1988: 226) of "contacts with Earth (as woman or serpent) [which might] represent death. Dying is returning to Earth, to Mother, in order to be born again. Man dies when he is devoured (swallowed, bitten) by Earth, by the Earth-Serpent-Woman, a numinous image that brings to mind *Cihuacoatl*".[30] Therefore, Earth's unrestrained, unnatural appetite, where food obviously equals sex, assumes the form of the castrating *sapcheeb*, a creature who belongs by right to the "numinous family of women with toothed vaginas [. . .] monstrous, semi-human creatures, who may possess an animal *alter ego* or animal attributes", and who can only be overcome with magical instruments that belong to the major divinities or evoke them (Báez-Jorge 1988: 319), as, for example, the net or the sheepskin-black cloud.

* * *

Huave beliefs about Earth exemplify how the members of a society express their perception of reality in symbols.

---

30. For an example of 'to die' meaning the same as 'to copulate', see the ancient Nahuatl expression *itech nahci in Tlaltecuhtli* 'to come before the lord of the earth' "to die the sick one" (Molina 1977: II: 42r), composed of a verb (*itech nahci*) which Molina (*ibid.*) translates as 'to have relations with a woman' and of the name of the earth god (cf. Graulich 1988: 96).

Symbols used in iconography, cosmology and mythology vary in form from culture to culture and can be observed in both ritual and non-ritual behavior. We have seen how the representation of the earth divinity changes considerably according to the circumstances and the appropriate registers for them. In rites accompanying birth and healing, when the very existence of the individual is in play, there are self-interested motives for describing the qualities and powers of Earth rather explicitly, emphasizing its positive aspects. But the obscure sides, expressed in more complicated, metaphorical images are presented in narrative, which is more remote from everyday needs and thus permits more freedom of expression.

The rites and the prayers tend to stress the theme of the Earth's immense power and of man's total dependence on it. The stories, instead, reveal traits Mesoamerican earth divinities still retain, despite the radical changes introduced by Christianity. These traits are incompleteness, the lack of self-sufficiency, and the fact that man, though infinitely more fragile, has something that these earth divinities — even if only occasionally — need and desire. This accounts for their rapaciousness towards humans, for their alimentary-sexual hunger of bodies and souls, and thus the recurrent motive of the devouring monster. Elsewhere, this motive has not always been personified with as strong a sexual connotation as it is in the Huave *sapcheeb*; but the castrating beings with toothed vaginas (of which *sapcheeb* is one) clearly have the same symbolic meaning as other voracious and mutilating asexual or zoomorphic representations of Earth (for example, the earth monster that devours a limb of the god Tezcatlipoca [Caso 1973: 45]).

Although elements like those found at San Mateo del Mar are widespread in Mesoamerica, what we should like to stress is that a system of symbols like the one just examined must be understood first of all from within, by considering all its components synchronically. While historical and comparative studies offer indispensable points of departure for interpretation and for filling the voids inevitably produced by today's rapid process of acculturation and secularization, they do not adequately explain this kind of cultural construction. Since these complex representations are symbolic, they are also polysemic. But this does not mean that these representations have an infinite number of meanings. The meanings should be sought exclusively within Huave culture. One need only delve sufficiently in breadth and in depth. This is the only way to appreciate the imaginative and consistent way each group uses, manipulates, and reworks the elements it shares with other groups when it adapts them to its own particular culture and environment.

References

Aramoni Calderón, D., 1992, *Los refugios de lo sagrado. Religiosidad, conflicto y resistencia entre los zoques de Chiapas*, Mexico, Consejo Nacional para la Cultura y las Artes.

Báez-Jorge, F., 1988, *Los oficios de las diosas. Dialéctica de la religiosidad popular en los grupos indios de México*, Xalapa, Universidad Veracruzana.

Caso, A., 1973 (1953), El *pueblo del sol*, México, Fondo de Cultura Económica.

Clastres, P., 1977 (1974), *La società contro lo stato. Ricerche di antropologia politica*, Milano, Feltrinelli.

Correa, G., 1960, "El espíritu del mal en Guatemala. Ensayo de semántica cultural", in M.A.L. Harrison e R. Wauchope (eds.) *Nativism and Syncretism*, New Orleans, Middle American Research Institute, Tulane University, pp. 37-103.

Cuturi, F., 1981, "Osservazioni sulle concezioni anatomiche e fisiologiche dei Huave di San Mateo del Mar, Oaxaca, Messico", *L'Uomo* 5, 1: 99-133.

Cuturi, F., 1990, "Dalla laguna delle sirene al mercato dei gamberi", *La Ricerca Folklorica* 21: 61-68.

Foster, G.M., 1945, *Sierra Popoluca Folklore and Beliefs*, Berkeley, University of California Press.

Gossen, G.H., 1979 (1974), *Los chamulas en el mundo del sol. Tiempo y espacio en una tradición oral maya*, México, Instituto Nacional

Indigenista.

Graulich, M., 1988, *Quetzalcoatl y el espejismo de Tollan*, Antwerpen, Instituut voor Amerikanistiek.

"Historia de los Mexicanos por sus pinturas" 1985 (1533?), in A.M. Garibay (ed.) *Teogonía e historia de los mexicanos. Tres opúsculos del siglo XVI*, México, Porrúa, pp. 22-79.

Hunt, E., 1977, *The Transformation of the Hummingbird. Cultural Roots of a Zinacantecan Mythical Poem* Ithaca, Cornell University Press.

Ichon, A., 1969, *La religion des Totonaques de la Sierra*, Paris, Centre National de la Recherche Scientifique.

Ingham, J.M., 1986, *Mary, Michael, and Lucifer. Folk Catholicism in Central Mexico*, Austin, University of Texas Press.

Kaufman, T.S., 1974, "Meso-American Indian Languages", in *Encyclopaedia Britannica* (XVth edn.), London, Encyclopaedia Britannica Ltd., vol. 11, pp. 956-63.

"Leyenda de los soles", 1975 (1558), in P.F. Velásquez (ed.) *Códice Chimalpopoca. Anales de Cuauhtitlan y Leyenda de los soles*, México, Universidad Nacional Autónoma de México, pp. 119-28.

Lok, R., 1987, "The House as a Microcosm. Some Cosmic Representations in a Mexican Indian Village", in R. de Ridder & J.A.J. Karremans (eds.) *The Leiden Tradition in Structural Anthropology. Essays in Honour of P. E. de Josselin de Jong*, Leiden, E. J. Brill, pp. 211-33.

López Austin, A., 1984 (1980), *Cuerpo humano e ideología. Las concepciones de los antiguos Nahuas*, México, Universidad Nacional Autónoma de México, 2 voll.

López Austin, A., 1990, *Los mitos del tlacuache. Caminos de la mitología mesoamericana*, México, Alianza Editorial.

Lupo, A., 1981, "Conoscenze astronomiche e concezioni cosmologiche dei Huave di San Mateo del Mar (Oaxaca, Messico), L'Uomo 5, 2: 267-313.

Lupo, A., 1991, "La etnoastronomía de los huaves de San Mateo del Mar, Oaxaca", in J. Broda, S. Iwaniszewski & L. Maupomé (eds.) *Arqueoastronomía y Etnoastronomía en Mesoamérica*, México: Universidad Nacional Autónoma de México, pp. 219-234.

Lupo, A., 1993, "The Importance of Prayers in the Study of the Cosmologies and Religious Systems of Native Oral Cultures", in J. Davies & I. Wollaston (eds.) *The sociology of sacred texts*,

Sheffield, Sheffield Academic Press, pp. 83-93.

Lupo, A., n.d. *El modelo residencial de los huaves de San Mateo del Mar (Oaxaca)*, Roma, Quaderni del Dipartimento di Studi Glottoantropologici, in stampa.

Molina, A. de, 1977 (1571), Vocabulario en Lengua Castellana y Mexicana y Mexicana y Castellana, México, Porrúa.

Nicholson, H.B., 1971, "Religion in Pre-Hispanic Central Mexico", in R. Wauchope (ed.) *Handbook of Middle American Indians*, vol. 10, pp. 395-446.

Preuss, K.T., 1982 (1968), *Mitos y cuentos nahuas de la Sierra Madre Occidental*, México, Instituto Nacional Indigenista.

Rita, C.M., 1979, "Concepción y nacimiento", in I. Signorini *Los Huaves de San Mateo del Mar. Ideología e instituciones sociales*, México, Instituto Naciona Indigenista, pp. 263-314.

Sahlins, M., 1985, *Islands of History*, Chicago, The University of Chicago Press.

Signorini, I., 1979, *Los huaves de San Mateo del Mar. Ideología e instituciones sociales*, México, Instituto Nacional Indigenista.

Signorini, I., 1981, *Padrini e compadri. Un'analisi antropologica della parentela spirituale*, Torino, Loescher.

Signorini, I., 1990, "Al Messico con Cardona: riflessioni sulle tassonomie animali degli Huave", *L'Uomo* 3 n.s., 2: 323-338.

Signorini, I., n.d. "Rito y mito como instrumentos de previsión y manipulación del clima entre los Huaves de San Mateo del Mar", ponencia presentada en el *13th International Congress of Anthropological and Ethnological Sciences*, México 29/7 - 4/8/1993.

Signorini, I. & Lupo, A., 1989, *Los tres ejes de la vida. Almas, cuerpo, enfermedad entre los nahuas de la Sierra de Puebla* Xalapa, Universidad Veracruzana.

Signorini, I. & Tranfo, L., 1979, "Enfermedades. Clasificación y terapias", in I. Signorini *Los Huaves de San Mateo del Mar. Ideología e instituciones sociales*, México, Instituto Naciona Indigenista, pp. 215-61.

Stairs, G.A. & Stairs, E.F., 1981, *Diccionario huave de San Mateo del Mar*, México, Instituto Lingüístico de Verano.

Tedlock D., 1985, *Popol Vuh. The Mayan Book of the Dawn of Life*, New York, Touchstone.

Tranfo, L., 1979, "Tono y nagual, in I. Signorini *Los Huaves de San Mateo del Mar. Ideología e instituciones sociales*, México, Instituto

Naciona Indigenista, pp. 177-213.

Ziehm, E., 1982 (1968), " 'El Héroe'. Introducción", in K.T. Preuss *Mitos y cuentos nahuas de la Sierra Madre Occidental*, México, Instituto Nacional Indigenista, pp. 9-72.

Zingg, R.M., 1982, *Los Huicholes. Una tribu de artistas*, México, Instituto Nacional Indigenista, 2 vols.

7

Narratives and Pilgrimages

Ari Rajsbaum Gorodezky

For the Huicholes, as for many other peoples, myth describes something that really happened. It is the history of one's ancestors. Huicholes understand that true facts are independent of the way they are seen by men, or of the way they are transmitted. It is characteristic of myth, as Mircea Eliade said (Eliade, 1972), that it tells of a sacred history that took place at a special time, whose features diverge sharply from those of daily life. Myth deals with time at the moment of creation, when the cosmos was born and organized. And yet this very special condition means that it is always possible to recover it through religious practices. Because it happens continuously it is partially trans-historic. But if myth establishes the beginning, it does not necessarily deal with the beginning of things. It deals, rather, with the ontological basis of things, with something that happened in the distant past and still happens, far from profane reality.

The idea of sacred time, as indicated by Eliade, exists among peoples with very different social characteristics. The aim of this paper is to show how the Huichols' conception of the world is not an exclusively abstract development, nor is it something transmitted only through the chronicle of myths. Indeed, I will try to describe how it derives from individual happenings in which men relate themselves to mythical time, as if they were moving inside such time. I will then show the different degrees of hierarchically ordered human participation that characterize the sacred world of a religious man. Lastly, I will give examples of the different contexts in which these experiences occur.

The Experience of the Sacred

I once heard a Mestizo asking a group of Huicholes how one can learn what happened to the ancestor gods. The Huicholes answered that this can be known through participation in 'the customs' (religion). He who is true to his gods can see through different religious practices how the world was born. This means that men are able to enter the sacred world and, through experience, become acquainted with the founding facts. This capacity is limited and varies from one individual to another, but it is this participation which is the most relevant for men who want to learn about their origins. The Huicholes consider this to be the basis of personal learning, and precedes oral transmission.

The religious experience of a Huichol who is in contact with the sacred world may be defined either as a mystic or a prophetic experience. G. Sholem (1987) defines a mystical individual as "a person who has left an immediate expression of divinity, of ultimate reality, has lived it as real, or at least searches consciously for it" (Sholem, p.4). Sholem says that mystical experience "manifest itself under two aspects. It lacks adequate expression of its own. Deep inside it is amorphous. The clarity of its essence is outlined with little precision, while the 'divine touch.' is experienced with greater intensity and depth; the possibility of a clear and objective definition also becomes very low. . .". Alternatively, this experience may be interpreted in multiple forms: "a great variety of senses may be attributed to it" (*ibid.*, p.7). Communication of a mystic experience is always difficult, because it lacks a form, and because of its *sui generis* character. The categories of subject and object are also abolished in the mystic experience.

In spite of these facts, a mystic person must use his ancestral language and the cultural symbols that precede him, symbols that were not created by his own experience. He must use language so he may communicate with others. He must, from the existing codes, recreate symbolic constructions that confer form on something that, in principle, is amorphous. In that way, poems, chants or other forms of artistic expression produced by myths are translations of sacred manifestations. These translations may be more or less faithful to the original experience. In many cases, the closer they are to the experience, the more incomprehensible the translation may be to the irreligious person. On the contrary, the more understandable the translation is, the further away from the original experience.

The amorphous character of the mystic experience also has other consequences. The experience may be interpreted in multiple ways, which leads the spiritual person generally to consider that his traditions and concepts have been verified by the experience. Communion with the sacred might result in prophecy, the main difference between the prophet and other mystics being that "the prophet listens to an intelligible message that never shows imprecise signs when captured or when sedimented in later memory" (*ibid.* p.10).

The Huicholes consider that the fundamental part of their learning and the center of their religious life is found in the experiences of contact with the sacred world. One can then ask, what are these experiences about? Are they amorphous experiences that confirm the concepts learned by other means, or are they prophetic experiences that have a well structured and clearly transmittable content? For the moment, I will leave these questions aside and start describing the features of those manifestations that Huicholes consider to be a communion with the sacred.

The Huicholes stablish contact with the world of 'Kakauyarirri' (translated as 'ancestors', or 'gods', and sometimes as 'saints') in different ways, often through ceremonies performed by groups, that may be familial or communal.[1] A 'cantor or singer' participates in them. The chant varies in form according to the occasion which is what interest us now. It deals with the conversation between kakauyarirri and kauyumari, their messenger, who speaks through the mouth of *mara'akame* or shaman. A literal translation of the chant would be absolutely incomprehensible for people who are not Huicholes, due to the constant references to mythological situations and personages. The cantor uses a great number of neologisms, that are partially incomprehensible even to Huichol. On the other hand, in the conversation between the *kakauyarirri* there is no explanation of the context, for the conversation occurs as a natural dialogue between people. For this reason, the chant will be very difficult to understand for those who, unlike the cantor, have not penetrated the world of the ancestors and do not 'see' what is going on there (who is talking, who is answering, etc.).

The chant is a direct expression of communion with the sacred world. The Huicholes make a second translation in order to transmit this experience to those far away from being intimate with this world. This is the mythic narrative. Graphic translations may also be done; the modern art of the Huicholes being an example. It is worth underlining that for them, the origin of the mythic narrative is found in the direct manifestation of the sacred to men. Therefore, the mythic narrative is secondary to the direct expressions of

1. I thank Marcela Gleizer Salzman, Leonardo Cohen Shabot, Stephen Shecter and Yuri Escalante Betancourt, for their comments.

the experience of communion, as in the song. The manifestations of the *kakauyarirri* are very diverse, because their world is considered a living world. The great variety of mythological stories or the differences between chanters are thus not strange for Huicholes. To them, myths are not, as some anthropologists have erroneously claimed, immovable and untouchable sacred texts.

Translations of the original experience preserve some of its sacred character, and there too it is a matter of distance. The nearer the expression is to the original experience, the greatest is its sacredness. There are, in addition to ceremonies in which the cantor enters the world of the gods, less direct forms of entering that world, like the rites or ceremonies that the community uses to mimic the heroic deeds of the ancestors, jumbling themselves up with them in the process.

The need to create translations of things learned by experience might indicate a certain degree of similarity between the Huichol holy experience and the mystic experience as defined by Sholem. This does not mean that we should expect a unity to all mystic experience; rather, we can refer to common difficulty in communicating the experience and to the different degrees of oral and ritual expressions. Other experiences the Huichol have may well be part of Sholem's definition of prophetic experiences, like the healing effected by the mara'kame as they transmit clear and defined messages from the kakauyarirri. However, these types of experiences are not relevant for the objectives of this paper, which focuses more on the ways men learn about the cosmos.

Space

There is a distinction the Huicholes make between daily life space and sacred space. According to them, the west end of the world is close to San Blas in the Pacific Ocean. The east end is in Ra'unar, near Real de Catorce in San Luis

Potsí. Some of their versions of the order of the cosmos (those that speak of the first ancestor's pilgrimage) say that the center is Wirikuta, in a place close to Ra'unar. To them it is obvious that the physical distance between Wirikuta and Ra'unar is much shorter than that between Wirikuta and San Blas. Wirikuta is thus not a geometrical center. In fact, the most important center is in the cave of Teacata, in the Sierra of Jalisco. The coexistence of different 'centers' indicates that "center" is a different concept from the one used in our culture. It is difficult to outline the precise meaning that the conception of space holds for the Huicholes, but it is clear that for them, there is something in space that may be revealed to humans, something that cannot be seen at first sight. What might best be called 'virtual space', as we shall discuss later, when we describe their cosmology.

In its manifestations to men, sacred space has the same qualities that the stories of the ancestors do: man can penetrate the sacred space, but he will need to translate his experience into a comprehensible language for those who did not enter it with him. Descriptions of holy spaces, like those of myths, are flexible. One can therefore find direct manifestations of the experience of penetration into the sacred space; in rites, such as pilgrimages or chants, and in translations of these manifestations in their stories explaining the rites or the order of the cosmos. This in turn gives rise to as much variation in cosmological descriptions as in the myths themselves.

Cosmology

Cosmology consists of reference points. A universe with no points has no meaning. According to M. Eliade (Eliade, op. cit.) the symbolic significance of 'center' originates in these points. We deal with a center, because starting from there, all that surrounds it acquires meaning, and not because of its physical position. To understand a cosmology, one has to describe its reference points and how they are related.

In every society, the most important means by which the organization of space is understood is through living experiences or through contextualized descriptions. Abstract pictures, or explanations, of space are secondary to individual experience, and less common than the latter. M. Anguiano and P. Furst were the first to describe how a concrete experience, the ceremony of 'Tatei Neixa', is fundamental to building space for the Huicholes (Anguiano and Furst, 1978).

Among Huicholes, the ordering of reference points occurs in a context where different events develop. Mythic characters move inside this world. When men have certain religious experiences, they can also move inside it. One can choose different ways of going through this 'internal map' (taken from M. Anguiano and Furst, p.24), or of explaining it. But since mythic world has an order, it is not possible to pass through it in a chaotic manner. One has to choose a path. I have heard some Huicholes from Santa Catarina call this path 'the path of knowledge'. When somebody starts getting acquainted with 'the custom', that is, the knowledge and practices that conform to the Huichol religion, he has to do it through a pathway. Only afterwards, he will be able to pass through others. This is the way cosmology is learned. In eveyone of these routes, the form of that part of cosmology as well as a shaded form of the global structure of the universe is reflected.

The term 'path of knowledge' is not exclusively metaphoric. The 'custom' itself becomes a road that people have to cross as they walk through their religious career. For example, in the 'tukipa', the temple of the Cohamiata village, there are persons called *jicareros* who take care of the different god's votive vessels. The Urukuakame conducts the activities of this group. Guadalupe López Carrillo, who is incharge nowadays, describes the ritual cycle of 'jicareros' when he speaks about custom. At the end, he says "I only know abou that. I can only talk about that (about the ritual cycle) because I am the head of jicareros. The cantor may speak about other things (for example, about curing illness), because he says all the gods wishes...". Mr. López knows a lot about the custom, but limits himself to talking about the path that is being traversed at that moment.

Let's take a look now at a description of a fragment of the path of Urukuakame to understand how cosmology appears in it. He first describes the rites that must be done for cultivating during the rainy season, the need to present offerings, kill bulls and hunt deer. Then an offer must be given to 'the whole world'. Here is his description of the cosmos from the point of view of his own religious responsibilities: " . . .we have to give, in the first place, to the sea Aramara (the west), to Chapala Rapawiyeme (to the south), to Tatevarí and Naariwame (caves in the Sierra, patrons of fire and rain). Second, to Haurratema and Ututabita (both in the north). . .One can then go to Wirikuta (to the east, in San Luis Potosí) . . . In Aramara there are only deer and snakes. In Tatevarí are found tigers, lions, deer, snakes, large scorpions, and rattlesnakes. The mara'akme sees all those things. In Ututabi one sees only deer, males and female, and eagles. Many things are seen in Wirikuta. The peyote is like a teacher. Every distance to the sacred places can be seen. The sun shines on everything. Everything comes together in the peyote vision. The animals can be seen as in the craftsmanship we make. The large eagle (representing the sun) can say where the bull, sheep, goat will be killed". (López Carrillo, personal communication)

The description of the Urukuapame contains, not only the annual ceremonial cycle, that is directly the path where he is now, but a reflection of the construction of the universe: There are five cardinal points: the sea to the west; Chapala to the south; Ututabi and Haurratema to the north, Wirikuta to the east, which also functions in this case as the center, because the peyote is there. From there all animals and directions may be seen.

Among rituals, pilgrimages have a great importance, since the Huicholes pass along the roads where the cosmos is built as they move to the sacred places. They serve the gods, doing what they established, repeating their actions and the world they created. Cosmogony and cosmology relate in this way to each other; men enact the gods' actions and get closer to their sacred universe. In these actions, the world was created with its present order. The creation of the world is observed and represented by the rituals, and, as we saw in the example of the Urukuakame, an important part of cosmogony is reproduced by pilgrimages.

It is worth emphasizing some important features of the pilgrimage to Wirikuta. Different aspects of this topic were analyzed previously by Lumholtz (1981), Furst (1972), Myerhoff (1977), Negrin (1985), Zingg (1982), Benítez (1968) and Weigand (1975).

Pilgrimages take place during the dry season, between November and April. The groups involved belong to the same Tukipa, or in some cases, to the same village. The pilgrimage will cover territory stretching from the Tukipa that corresponds to the Sierra up to Wirikuta, a plateau close to Real de Catorce in the state of San Luis Potos. Peyote, the holy plant, grows here. The plant is related to corn and deer. Different preparatory rites exist before a pilgrimage starts, such as public confession of extramarital sexual intercourse. During the journey, other rites take place. For example, the names of everything, are changed, and the pilgrims call people and objects with their new names: desert becomes sea, children are old people, truck is called boat, etc. During the pilgrimage, travellers pass through sacred sites, just as the ancestors did. Most important are the springs, where mothers of water live, the Wirikuta plateau where peyote grows and the Ra'unar hill, where the sun rose for the first time.

The collection of the peyote is done at Wirikuta. For the

Huicholes this means hunting, because the plant is also considered a deer that must be hunted. The night after harvest, the mara'akame sings the birth of the world, the pilgrims, after eating the holy plant, watch their visions and listen to what the gods want to say.

Cosmology, chronicle, imitation of ancestors

Huicholes believe that when time began the gods came out of the sea. According to the version of the town of San Andrés Cohamiata, they came out from Aramara, to the west of the Sierra. They started to walk from there to the east, founding places as they walked. Tatevarí, the grandfather fire appeared during the trip. The ancestors continued their way to the east searching for a light, since everything was dark. The sacrifice of a child who was to be transformed into the sun happened at that time. The ancestors continued their way to Wirikuta, in the east, where they had to wait for the sun's birth, while the gods traveled under the earth. When the sun rose, the goddess Nakawé elevated him, so he would not burn the earth. This was the first pilgrimage of the ancestors. A second one took place afterwards, when the ancestors went to hunt the deer-peyote and to heal their sicknesses.

As mentioned before, the mythic world appears to Huicholes in different contexts. The most relevant is that of direct participation, its manifestations the shaman's chant. Other contexts are the mythological chronicles and rituals which involve imitation of the gods. Pablo Carrillo, from San Andrés Cohamiata told me how the pilgrimage was done in the past.[2] It was a continuous story which lasted about 10 hours, with only one break for eating. Before starting, he had a glass of liquor to prepare his soul for the 'trip' in which

---

2. I recorded the narrative of Pablo Carrilo in 1991. Julio Ramírez de la Cruz, from the University of Guadalajara, translated the fragments that were in Huichol.

he would get closer to his ancestors by means of his memory. No interruption was permitted. The intention to mimic the gods appears clearly at the end of the story: when pilgrims come back from the Sierra, Tsaurírrika (the cantor) says some words of farewell: "Here ends everything, nothing bad happened to us. I know I did not do it as my ancestors. I know I do not have the words of the ones that spoke with open hearts."

The conscious desire to do things like the ancestors gets men closer to the divine world. But what gets them even closer is the effective imitation, reflected in narration in a very particular way. If only the story told by Pablo Carrillo is considered, it is very difficult to know if the narrator is talking about the ancestors' pilgrimage or about that of today's Huicholes. Pablo Carrillo inserts the description of moving from one place to another into his account of what is actually going on. Let's analyze some fragments: "in that place (Xurayemuyeca) they confessed, purified themselves, put their Kipieri (lighted the fire), baptized each other, they confounded their way of speaking... then, they drank water very late, almost at night".

The actions described, are the same that are performed today during the pilgrimage: they confess their extramarital intercourse, they purify themselves throwing knots on the holy fire that symbolize these contacts, they light the sacred fire using the *kipieri* (a beam that serves as the base and seat for the grandfather fire, that points to Wirikuta), they baptize people with specific names for the trip, they change the names of things and do not drink until sunset. So far, it may be thought that this describes the present pilgrimage, but it could also be the ancestors' pilgrimage. That is why Daniel Villa of San Andrés Cohamiata, says, being in Wirikuta: "It is today as if time was still being made, as if the gods were here, as if we were the pilgrims of long ago. That is why we do almost the same today as the gods did, the way the gods wanted it."

Cosmology and the Mara'akame chant

In the mythology and rituals we have mentioned, an east-west axis and a top-down axis appears, which emphasize positively the poles of east and top (Wirikuta, climbing of the sun), (Rajsbaum, 1991). The myth goes on to tell that a whirlwind rose in Wirikuta, and took the story to the four edges of the world. A new opposition then occurs, that of center/periphery. Huicholes learn these aspects of cosmology on the pilgrimage that passes through to the east-west axis, and on the inward journeys around the four cardinal points and the center. At every cardinal point, as was mentioned before, they leave their offerings.

Aside from stories, cosmology appears in one of the most important religious experiences for Huicholes: the shaman's chant. The voice of Kauyumari, the deer messenger of the gods, who tells what he sees and listens, is heard during the mara'akame's chant. The structure of the world is reflected here as well. To take one example: The cantor is Eusebio López Carrillo,[3] from tukipa of San José, from the community of San Andrés Cohamiata. The walk to the desert varies slightly from one group and from one occasion to another. In the case we are dealing with the chant took place the last night of the pilgrimage to Wirikuta. The groups from each community also come to a different place to gather peyote, and to spend the night. People from San Andrés Cohamiata as well as those from Guadalupe Ocotán, deposit their offerings on the hill of Kauyumari. Then they advance about 1 km to gather the peyote. A little group climbs to Ra'unar to deposit offerings for the sun. When they come back at night, the most important rite may start. At sunset, people start eating peyote. Grandfather fire is lighted at night: the *kupieri* is started, each participant

3. I recorded the chant of Eusebio López Carrillo during the pilgrimage to Wirikuta in 1990. The translation to Spanish was done by Julio Ramírez de la Cruz.

Fig. 1: Peyote and deer hunt
(votive panel made of coloured threads of wool. Huichol).

places a stick on the fire and some flower to feed him. They all pray at the same time, and then Tsaurixica, the cantor Eusebio López Carrillo, seated on his Huichol bencn, smokes Tacuachi, the ritual tobacco, and starts singing.

At first he invokes the gods, until they call Kauyumari to ask him to get closer. Kauyumari speaks through the *mara'akames*'s mouth.[4] The ancestors are the only ones who really know the shape of the world because they watched its creation and know how far one thing is from another, they know the 'distances' (geographical relations) that give shape to the cosmos. In the mysterious language of the chant, one hears from afar:

> ..."they did it here...
> Tatitekia, his distance
> the sea, its distance
> They are listening so far away".

At the center, there is(are) a place(s) in the world where all the kakauyaririri can live, and all animals can be seen, even if they also live in other places. It is said, that history lies there, and an ancient goddess Wiriubi, drunk with peyote, got lost there:

> "... Wirikuta, Wiriubi, where the historic lies...
> where it lies...".

Wirikuta receives his name from there. The center liberates:

> "...In Wirikuta will the blue deer liberate,
> will liberate...".

The east-west axis also shows up in the chant. Mara'akame sees how the gods emerged from the sea:

> "...they passed through the sea...they arrived swimming..."

Once the ancestors emerge from the sea, the world starts taking its shape. For example, dew is borne when the water is shaken off from the ancestors bodies:

> "There he shook off the water, for the first time, oh brothers....
> there, covered with dew.."

The gods stopped during their walk and founded the places known at present. The natural elements, as well as places are given shape and direction. The social and religious practices arise, and men show in them their reciprocity. The following passage tells of the most important ancestor emerging from the cave of Teakata: the grandfather fire, Tatevari, after which the religious practice of taking care of fire begins:

"An old man (the fire) went out... not seeing well
...the *kipieli* (the beam where fire seats)
I showed it to him...
he grabbed it
...he was born by Haiteakata
...his followers arrive
and then, washed his face."

Today, the representatives of the followers that place *kipieli* and take care of fire are present in every ritual. At that point in the chant, people, full of excitement, cry out because of their visions and pray to the fire. The mara'akame still sees the road, the sacrifice of the child-sun and its way out to Ra'unari. The ancestors ask Nakawé, the Grandgrandmother Growth to raise the sun. The ancestors speak:

"... our sun comes
until then, they knew him..."
"... our sun moved"
"... he passed so close ...
They said to Nakawé:
because of you, this is being done."

The chant goes on for hours, while people observe, under the effects of peyote, how the gods give a form to the world.

Discussion

We have shown how the Huicholes learn their cosmology from experiences that bring them into contact with sacred matters. These may be direct experiences expressed through the chants or other manifestations of the mythic world, such as stories, or active participation in ceremonies in which men merge with myths, imitating the ancestors. Huicholes consider that learning, is first of all, a living experience. The ethnographic texts frequently give the impression that mythological narrative is central for the endo-culturation of the group. From the present paper's perspective, I would argue that mythological narrative is deeply important, but it must be looked at in relation to the religious experiences that, according to Huicholes, are their origin. Taking this into account, transcriptions of myths in ethnographies should put more emphasis on their contexts and in the way they are told.

The chant of the *mara'akame* is the most interesting of the examples given in this paper, since it deals with aspects pertinent to the theory of religion, that probably require the creation of new typologies. It is clear that the mara'akame's experience is close to Sholem's description of mysticism, since there is clearly a difficulty in transmitting a living experience. I assume that the use of poetic language and neologisms are tools to shape something that is not structured as daily perceptions are. The need for consecutive translations (the chant, the narrative, the explanation) means that it is helpful to manage the chant as a mystic experience. Alternatively, there are concrete ideas during the chant of the mara'akame, happenings, visual and auditory perceptions and clear messages from the mythic character. These imply that the *mara'akame*'s experience is more concrete or has more of a structured form than a typical mystic experience. The existence of a clear structure is related more properly to prophecy. Besides, one can find in the mara'akame's chant an attempt to claim authority that derives from other-worldly messages, and which is typical of prophecy.

Besides the elements already mentioned, the chant presents different aspects that do not exist in the mystic or in the prophetic experience, as described by Sholem. Some of these aspects are discussed in detail in the literature on shamanism (i.e. Eliade). Most important are: the participation of the cantor in a world where different things happen between diverse characters, the cantor's sensorial perceptions, and especially the fact that the experience of the cantor may and should be shared by other members of the group. Thus, there is a basic difference between mystic experience and prophecy, although both are personal experiences. The mythology of monotheist religions also report collective experiences with regard to holy matters (the apparition of saints, miracles, etc.), however, apart from being more present in mythology than in the believer's life, they are always considered as extraordinary cases while for the Huicholes, these are happenings which are part of their ritual calendar.

As for learning cosmology, it is clear that the Huicholes consider that it derives from concrete experiences involved with religious life. These are very diverse, as already said, and exceed by far the examples selected here. The question is, are the experiences the Huicholes consider most important, those in which people directly 'see' the sacred world, greatly structured, or are they, as Sholem says, amorphous? If amorphous, their lack of structure permits individuals to interpret their experiences according to symbols learned since childhood, in a manner that confirms the religious beliefs of the group.

References

Benitez, Fernando, *Los indios de México*, tomo II, ERA, Mex, 1968.

Furst, Peter, Nahmad Salomon, *Mitos y Arte Huicholes*, Sep, Sep-Setenas, Mex, 1972.

Jáuregui, Jesús. "La antropología de Diguet sobre el occidente de México", en: Diguet, L., *Por tierras occidentales, entre sierras y Barrancas*. México 1992.

Lumholtz, Carl.- *El México desconocido* II tomo, Ed. Nacional, Mex, 1972.

El arte simbólico y decorativo de los huicholes, Mex, INI, 1986.

Myerhoff, Barbara.- *Peyote hunt: the sacred journey of the Huichol Indians*, Ithaca and London: Cornell University Press, 1977.

"The deer Maize peyote Symbol complex among the Huichol Indians of México", *Anthropological Quarterly*, 1970, 43, 2, Apr, 64-78, UCLA.

Negrín, Juan.- *Acercamiento y histórico y subjetivo al huichol*, Guadalajara, U. de G.,1985.

Rajsbaum, Ari.- "El fuego, la luna, el sol. Análisis de un mito huichol". *Expresión Antropológica,* Número 6, Toluca, Mex., Octubre-Diciembre 1991.

"El número 5 entre los huicholes". Dahlgren, Barbro (comp.): III *Coloquio de historia de la religión en Mesoamérica y áreas afines.* UNAM, Instituto de Investigaciones Antropológicas, Mex., 1993.

Sholem, Gershom.- *La cábala y su simbolismo.* S. XXI, Mex., 1987.

Weigand, Phil, C.,- "Posible references to La Quemada in Huichol mythology" in: *Ethnohistory* 22/1, winter, 1975.

Zingg, Robert M. - *Los Huicholes, una tribu de artistas,* tomos I y II, INI, MEX, 1982.

8

Páez Cosmology[1]

Hugo Portela[2]
Herinaldy Gomez

The present paper considers some aspects of the cosmology, as a global thought system, which regulates and guarantees the welfare and the ethnicity of the Paez society, expressed in different moments of daily life, as a 'cultural ethic' which rules individual and social conduct and the relationship with the environment. This is a product of the exercise of comprehension and significance which is made of the cosmos, in order to understand, explain and project it in forms of intercultural relationships.

This approximation to the Paez cosmology is achieved from three fundamental points:

Territory: Understood as the semanticization that the

1. The Páez are an ethnic group which in their own language call themselves nasa kiwe, literally 'people of the territory'; it is the most numerous in Colombia with 110,010 Indians (DNP: 1992), distributed en the north-eastern region of the Department of Cauca, in south-western Colombia (See maps No. 1 and 2). Previously it was considered that the language belonged to the Chibcha family, but recent studies have shown that it is an isolated language (NIEVES: 1992:2)

2. Professors and researchers of the University of Cauca, Colombia. Members of the Andean Federation of Social Foundations FAFSO.

group makes of the physical-geographical space where culture unfolds. Seen as a possibility of traversing a path "which leads from the photographic objectivity of a 'human landscape' to the complicated mental and meaningful structures which sustain and make them human". (Garcia: 1976:13).

The relationship human body Paez-Nature: The human being is perceived as intimately bound to nature, identified with it; a conception where the motivations can be found in the interplay of representations of mythical and religious identities. As Bastien observes in reference to the Andean world: "They see systems of nature as the identification of themselves".

Cleansing, renewal and offering rituals: These give evidence of the integral cosmological system carefully regulated and officiated by the *thë 'walas* (wise men) who permanently socialize cultural normativity.

The Paez Territory[3]

The geographic territory of the Paez is composed predominantly of fragile ecosystems of great aquatic wealth, where perpetually snowcapped mountains such as the volcano Nevado del Huila (5,750 m), high altitude barren plains like Las Delicias (3,750 m), Moras (3.670 m) and Guanacas (3,518 m) and the important lagoons like Juan Tama and Paez are found. The deep, narrow banks of rivers in the lower regions (1,500 m) among which the Negro de Narváez, Paez, Plata, Ullucos rivers and the Lucero and Simbola streams and rapid torrents of water, are of great importance to the ethnogeographic conception of the Paez.

3. Special reference is made to the region of "Tierradentro" (inside land) as the center of the gestation of Paez cosmology; this site is located on the eastern slopes of the Central range of the Andes, with a extension of 1, 990 km^2 (CRC: 1984), composed of the municipalities of Paez and Inzá. (See Maps No. 3 and 4)

Research carried out since 1986, shows the correspondence between the geography of Tierradentro with *kwe kiwe* (*kwes*: our, *kiwe*: land or territory), one of the three worlds in which the Paez cosmology is divided: *ëeka*: that which is above, *kwe kiwe*: our land or territory and *kiwe dihu*': that which is below.[4] This cosmography is very similar to that of other ethnic groups of the Colombian and South American Andes region.

For example: In south-western Colombia, the Yanaconas (Cerron: 1990, Lopez: 1991), Totoroes, neighbors of the Páez (Palacios: 1992) and peasants of Indian ancestry in Sotará (Urrutia: 1991), all distinguish in the Universe the same three levels: that of above, this world and that below.

In the high altitude plains of Peru and Bolivia, the Aymará thought of the twentieth century (Bouysse-Cassagne, Harris: 1987), establishes the differentiation between *alax pacha* (above), *aka pacha* (earth) and *mangha pacha* (below), where the term *pacha* has been erroneously translated as universe. Thereby the notions of time and space are included with a western connotation of totality and abundance. This is not the meaning of the term in the Andean Aymará thought neither is that of the term 'worlds', used in the naming of space. South American Andean groups do not conceive the universe as an 'undifferentiated totality which includes everything'.

"The universe is conceived as a composition, an encounter of equal and of opposed elements",[5] as a writing where besides reading an indication and an orientation, the relationship with history, ancestors the ancient and 'gods'

4. This information has been corroborated in workshops with *thë'walas* and members of the community, directed by the Paez ethnolingüist, Marcos Yule, in Mosoco, village of the Vitoncó reservation.

5. Harris, Olivia and Bouysse-Cassagne, Thérese. Pacha en torno al Pensamiento Aymará. En: *Tres Reflexiones sobre el Pensamiento Andino*. Hisbol, La Paz: 1987, p. 18.

are also read. This, based upon concrete reference points which are seen and felt by all individuals and without which there would be no meaning, since they provide primary principles of classification and differentiation which operationalized, guarantee life and ethnicity.

OUR LAND (KWES KIWE)

Our land is composed of sacred territory — savage and uncultivated — inhabited by spiritual beings, and non-sacred — tame and cultivated — where the nasa live.

Sacred Territory: Savage and Uncultivated

Sacred Territory as mentioned by Polia (1988:85) is an interpretation made by westerners of what the Indians think as 'enchanted' and 'powerful' spaces, which in both Spanish and English express literally only partially the meaning which Indians attribute to these terms. These are alternated in their use with 'virtues' and 'spirits' which are "the powers of the tutelary forces of these places; it is incumbent that the *thë' walas* evoke the virtue of these sites and make it become active".[6]

Many sites are denominated savage, fierce and uncultivated in the same way as Yanaconas (Ceron: 1990, Lopez: 1991), Coconucos (Faust: 1989) and Totoroes (Palacios: 1992). These are places inhabited by wild animals, fierce spirits and fierce Indians or 'Pijaos', ancestors who refused to be baptized. Undomesticated spaces which have not been 'entered' by Christians.

In the South American Andean world, these places are also considered to be extremely dangerous and terrible,

> Although they have a positive aspect, for example: The slopes are so savage that they should not be

6. Polia Meconi, Mario. Las Lagunas de los Encantos. Medicina Tradicional Andina del Peru Septentrional. Peru. CEPESER: 1988, p. 85.

> approached except with great precaution; but at the same time it is in these places where people are taught to sing or play . . . they are dangerous but also sources of unmeasurable energy and wealth . . . this character, both fierce and fertile, which so many sacred places have, make people treat them as diabolic . . . they have a genesic power not only as a result of having engendered the present population, but also due to the generative power of the dead, and their essential intervention in agriculture . . . not all sacred sites have such 'savage' conduct. Some are guardians either of family houses or of whole communities, they are generally benevolent, preserving prosperity of those who treat it well and punishing those who do not behave as they should. These exercise not so much a genesic as an ordering power . . . (Bouysee-Cassagne, Harris, pp. 44-45).

The Paez sacred territory is made up essentially of high altitude plains, lagoons, rocks, cliffs, mountains and forests, found in the highest and most distant places. They are considered to have 'great power' and 'spirituality', and in them are found the 'fierce'[7] plants utilized by the *thë'walas*. They are extremely cold and in them 'Christians do not enter', — which signifies the impossibility of establishing permanent housing — although temporary lodging can be achieved after offering and renewal rituals.[8]

---

7. These plants are the most important and are for the exclusive use of the *the'wala* in the practice of ritual; they are recognized because it is not necessary to induce through the use of coca and tobbaco a heightened sense perception to feel in his body the signs which are emanated.

8. The offering is made with *aguardiente*, the bottle is taken in the left hand and a small shot glass is filled and thrown into the air toward the right side; then the same action is carried out but toward the left. For the renewal, the person takes in the left hand portions of sesame plant (*c'a yu'ce*), in the duel and makes a circle around the body from the right foot, upward →

Natural springs, marshes, dense and spiraling forests, not necessarily at high altitudes or far from cultivated land also enter the category of sacred territory.

In the high altitude plains associated with pinnacles and rocks, where water is 'born' and in the lagoons where it is 'detained' and stored, contact with the primeval world, the genesis of the *nasa* world is made. There the ancestors live. In thunder, rainbow, and the 'duende' (dwarf) — three key integrating elements of the cosmovision — are located doctrine, power and wisdom. They gestate cultural heroes who make history with the people, and who later return to the bosom of the lake from where they continue to be fundamental to social life, culture and ethnicity.

The concept of water 'detained' and stored in high lagoons associated with stones, pinnacles, and rocks, as the sources of life, power and wisdom, are found spread throughout the Andean region of south-western Colombia (Paez, Guambianos, Coconucos, Totoroes, Yanaconas and peasants of Indian ancestry). They evoke these places as the origin of human life and of the ethnic group.

The Aymará of the high altitude plains of Peru and Bolivia designate these as primeval places; among them are the Island of Titicaca (today Island of the Sun) or *Tiwanaku* whose Aymará name *Taypi Quala* means the central stone (Bouysse-Cassagne, Harris, 1987:19). For the Incas, *Collasuyo*, one of the four divisions of the earth,[9] located to the south, owed its name to the Colla del Sur Indians; *colla* means 'thing emerging from water' and in this zone many communities have their origin. In this region Lake Titicaca is found; from it *wira cocha* brought the sun, moon and stars.

→ towards the head, down to the left foot, an then puts the plant in the mouth and chews it and then deposits it in the left hand to rub the body in the mentioned direction.

9. Nachter, Nathan, Sociedad e Ideologia, IEP. Lima: 1973.

The thunder, inhabitant of the center of lagoons, is an expression of power, force and wisdom.

The person who has been caught or touched by thunder, "who has been whipped and has survived is seen as having a sign that he may be a *thë'wala*, since he is contaminated with the power of thunder, which if it does not kill, gives power of life. Among the Aymará all the beliefs which accompany those 'touched by lightning' designated them as 'frontier' beings. It is probable that from this liminal situation spring powers to communicate with devils, mountains, lightning, souls and the pachamama. "I am beloved of the gods who did not kill me (lightning) . . . for this reason I began to act as a 'magician'. But first I learned to read the coca." (*Ibid.*, 46).

Lightning is conceived both as the giver of power and wisdom and the guardian of norms through its anthropomorphization in the Duende, which is ever-present in these territories. Since 'the Duende is always there' and 'it has Duende' are common elements of reality, to enter these territories, to travel through them or to extract part of their resources, each Paez must first carry out renewal rites and offerings to the Duende. The purpose of these rituals is to reiterate norms related to the rational use of resources and reciprocal actions. (Portela, Gomez: 1992:12).

Through visions and dreams the Duende guides the individual in the search for power and wisdom, power seen as the capacity to know, and wisdom as the capacity to orient life collectively and in equilibrium with nature.

> When it is announced with a traditional bag full of medicinal plants, this is a sign that the individual who has seen it must go to look for a *thë'wala*—wise man — to lead him in the search of Paez secrets and knowledge related to ecosystems, ethnobotany and cultural tradition.
>
> (*Ibid.*, 13).

The rainbow lives in the river banks and along the banks of the lagoons, but it is displaced throughout the territory wherever water exists: rivers, streams, springs and pools. The rainbow is the bridge between the sacred world and the non-sacred.

> The rainbow molded by the drizzle can cause welts, blemishes and itching to the skin of those who are out during this time. It can also cause miscarriage in pregnant women who do not stay indoors.
>
> (*Ibid.*, 8)

For the Aymará "the most dangerous place is the foot of the rainbow. That is, the region where the colors of the prisma, the earth and the sky become confused". (Bouysee-Cassagne, Harris, 46) The rainbow is an inhabitant of the South American, Andean territories.

Non-Sacred Territories — Tame and Cultivated

These lack power and spirituality as they have been tamed by the permanent presence of human beings who cyclically plow their ground to cultivate. The spaces correspond to warmer or not so cold areas, which can, and should be cultivated.

In the median altitudes, where an equilibrium between cold and warm climate exists, settlements are constructed. Here it is not only permissible for the Paez to live, but also to cultivate beans and corn, basic products in their diet. However, in the hot and cold regions there are also family gardens which are visited temporarily at the time of planting and harvest. Previous rituals assure the maintaining of equilibrium in the environment and their own bodies during these visits. This can be seen as a micro-vertical use of land which is generalized in the Andean regions. (Murra:1975, Oberem:1981, Langeeback:1987, Mejía:1990).

THE WORLD THAT IS ABOVE (*EEKA*)

The world which is above is the aerial world inhabited by the sun, moon, stars, and clouds in their different forms and colors. It is found connected to *kwes kiwe*, in the high frontiers where the earth meets the sky by means of flashes of light from lightning, where water forms drizzle and the rainbow. These are considered meteorological phenomena of the earth but are at the same time heavenly.

There are scarce references about the sun, the moon and the stars in oral traditions. The sun is associated with heat and the moon with cold and with agricultural cycles. The cultural hero Juan Tama was engendered by the stars in the high altitude lake which still carries his name.

Father Castillo Orozco in the Paez-Spanish Dictionary of 1877, refers to concepts about the sun which have not been encountered in the present collective memory:

> *Itaquí*, this word means sun, whom these Paez, similarly to the Incas, considered for some time as god. So far I have not been able to root out from some Indians the habit they still have of saying farewell with the phrase *itaquí pitícá* which means 'go with the sun' or in the company of the sun. . . .
>
> *Itaquí finó*, site or plan of the House of the Sun, which these Paez Indians have as such, there are two sites, one near the village of Tálaga in the peak of Taravira, with a longitude of more than two blocks . . . tradition has it, that these sites gave answers from the sun, it is affirmed that in these places there was dancing, that they went to find themselves in the sun, there they ran . . .

The clouds suspended in the aerial space forebode, watch over and testify. Black clouds signify that there is an accumulation of *pta'z*,[10] which forebodes the threat of intercultural conflicts, social tension, absence or forgetting of norms and prescribed rituals to achieve community welfare. White clouds testify that the rites of cleansing, restoration of equilibrium and the distancing of the threat of *pta'z* have terminated. The clear, blue sky is a good omen, a good sign, there is tranquility, harmony, even if temporarily.

The spirits of the recently dead, who guard the social and cultural dynamics, live in the air and in the clouds. These spirits of the dead are projected on the territory as guardians and as threats. (Portela, Gomez, 1992:10).

THAT WHICH IS BELOW *(KIWE D'IHU')*

It is that which is not seen, which is below the earth and can be acceded to through the curves, indentations or depressions of the earth, at the lowest points of the topography. But it is also in the high altitudes where water springs forth or is born and in lagoons.

This is a world similiar to *kwes kiwe*, inhabited by the 'pijaos'[11] (*pip'hs av'*) who upon the arrival of the Spanish conquerors refused the impositive baptism, preferring to bury themselves alive with all of their belongings. The sites where the remains of these people are found are called 'guacas de pijao', being these the most tangible signs of an earlier age 'before god', which transcends the original time of the Christian world. It reveals itself in the becoming of historic consciousness which the group has of its pre-Christian origin (Uŕrutia, 1991:6), 'and that their existence

10. *pta'z:* important and at the same time complex category of the Paez cosmovision, which indicates that to the environment, the individual, the community is latent in all the territory.

11. The fact that in the world above *(ëeka)* live the *nasa* people and also in our world (*kwes kiwe*) and below (*kiwe d'ihu'*) live the pijaos indicates that the territory is not only of origin but also of exclusive Indian possession, and that as such it is equally guarded in an intercultural-interethnic manner.

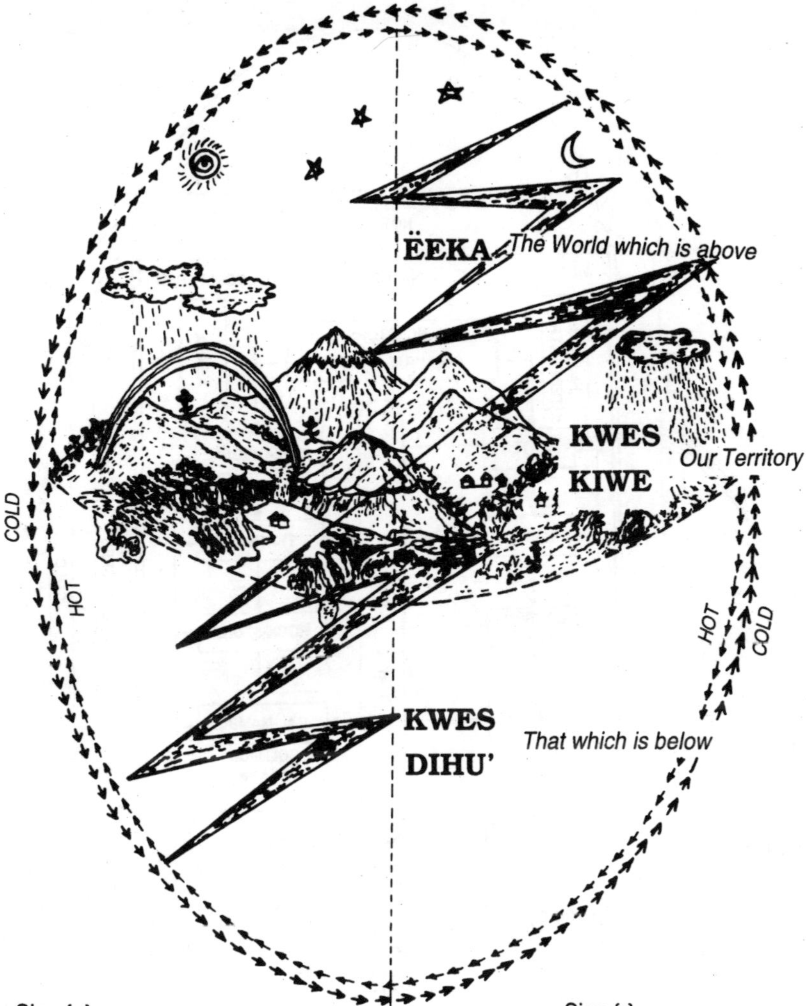

Sign {+}	Sign {-}
left	Right
Sun	Moon
High Altitude Plains	Cold Plants
Wild	"Not Good" Man of Medicine
Ancestors	Excess of the Dirty
Thunder	Negative Energy
Strong Plants	

Fig. 1 : Cosmogram

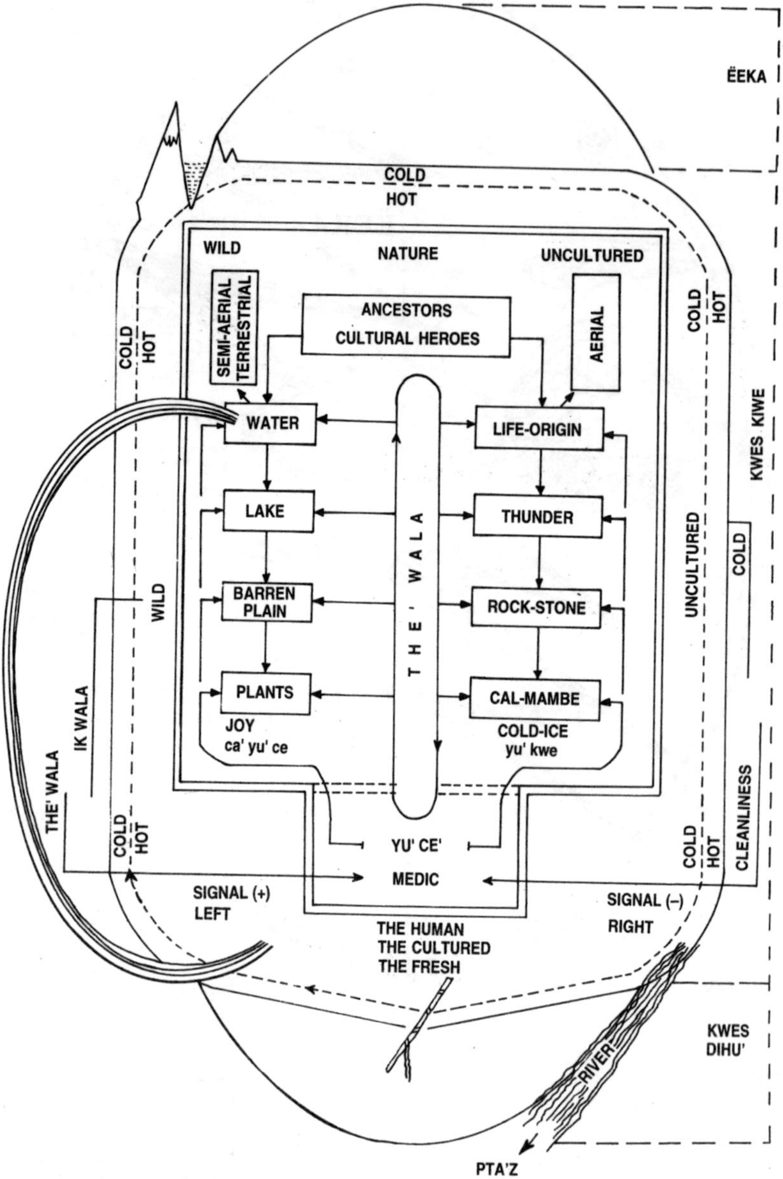

Fig. 2: Diagram of Paez Cosmology

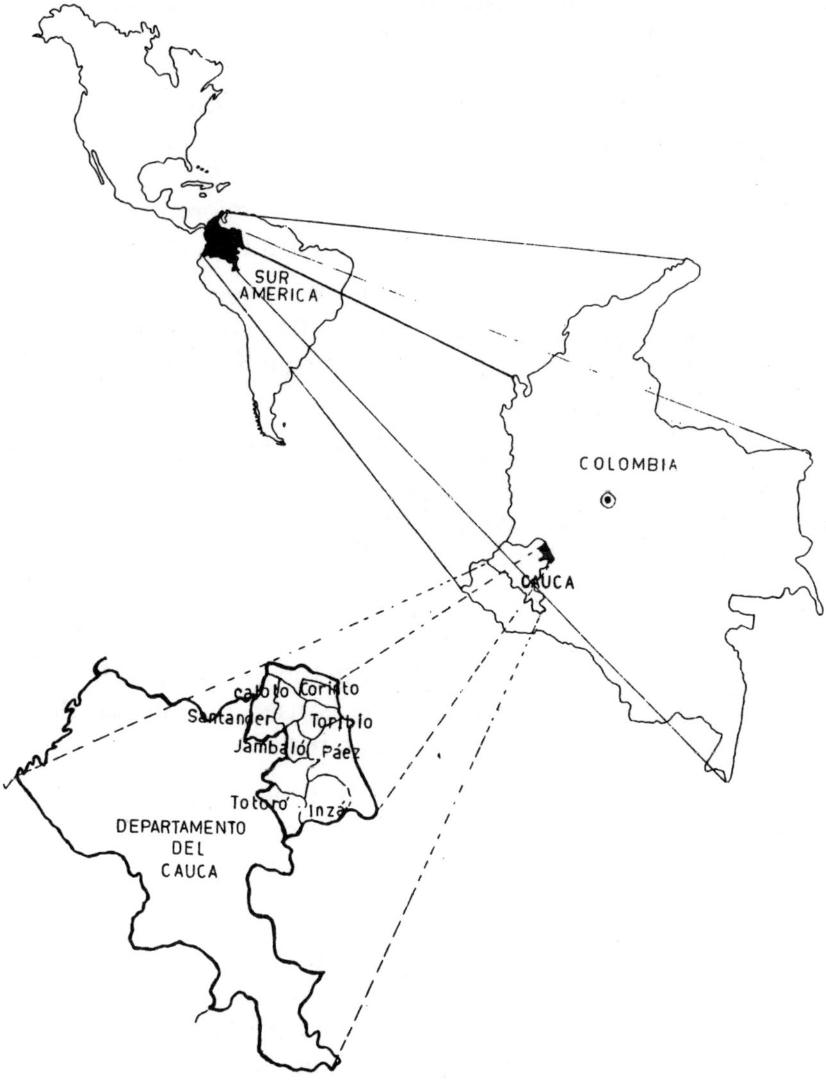

Map: Places of Settlement of Paez Ethnic Group
in the Cauca Department in Colombia

is prior to god, prior to the Christian god'.

These savage ancestors besides inhabiting the world below, live also in the sacred territories, savage and uncultivated, *kwes kiwe*, where human beings do not exist. They share it with the spirits of children who die without baptism, as in the Inca and Aymará worlds. Also sharing with the pijaos the lower world are found the small people, (*nasa lee'kwe*), or people without tail, who 'feed upon the vapor of cooking food'. There are various references to the existence of this concept in the Department of Cauca.

The 'tapanos' exist among the Yanaconas of the high altitudes of the Municipality of Sotará (Hernandez, 1989:37) as well as in the Pancitará reservation in the Municipality of La Vega. (Ceron, 18).

According to M. Eliade (1986:95), for the Dogones "the first mythical inhabitants of the region were little black people who have today disappeared below the earth: indefatigable workers, the sound of their hammers can still be heard".

The lower world appears as a place of origin and life, of genesic power which is manifest in the Colombian Macizo and which according to studies carried out among the Aymará are evident in the Andean region.

Returning to Urrutia (1991:9), the meaning of the lower world is enriched and recreated in the cosmogenic analysis which Augusto Tamayo Vargas makes in the poem of The Ayar Brothers in Peru:

> The vital cycle begins in the seed, in the germ, and ends in the cadaver, in the mummified body, *malki* or *seedbed.* The seed put into the world (*uhjo pacha*) is the beginning of the plant and of life, but the cadaver is also located within the earth and in the *seedbed*, another principle of new life.

The human being also unfolds completely and at death leaves the body, which below the ground, is like a seed, like an *seedbed*.

Below this world, which is here, like beings of the same nature, as peer, germ of the plant and germ of the human being. . . .

The *kay pacha* has in its bosom the living which bubbles in silence. . . .

The world below or within is the residence of the dead or of the germs . . . (Vargas: 1980:575)

The three worlds are found interrelated, articulated; they constitute the territorial unity *nasa kiwe*, existing within its frontiers the spaces of greatest power and spirituality. The highest parts of peaks and mountains constitute the limit between *kwes kiwe* and *ëeka*, while the lagoons, springs and depressions form the liminal spaces between *kwes kiwe* and *kiwe d'ihu'*. In this way the special definition above, middle and below, do not have to be understood in a literal sense.

Worlds which turn around the center of 'production of knowledge' constituted in the relationship 'Thunder-Ancestor-Lagoon', where thunder both, earthly and celestial, from the center of the lagoon is erected as power and wisdom. The ancestors of the bottom of the lagoon — as knowers of the world, as cultural heroes — are in charge of socialization and the lagoons are the source of life. For this reason the *thë'wala*, man of knowledge or wise man, having received power and wisdom from thunder, is active in the three worlds, recovering its unity, he moves permanently through them, both physically and mentally.

Circulating and forming part of the three worlds are cold and heat, whose equilibrium is given more by the social use which the *nasa* makes of territory from its classification and interpretation. In the same way, *pta'z* globalizes the

Paez 'universe' as a category which indicates permanent threat, which reminds, announces or sanctions the rupture of equilibrium.

The three worlds of Paez cosmography are connected and interceded in two sections, one left and the other right. These are related to a central point indicator of equilibrium, harmony and well-being. In the preparation of the elements for cleansing and renewal rituals these sections become evident. At the left side are situated the sun, the high altitude plains, the savage, the ancestors, thunder, strong plants, warm blooded animals, the *thë'wala*, the river running from right to left which is in charge of taking out that which is dirty — bad — from the territory, these are good signs in synthesis, positive energy, and the right side are the moon, cold plants, if the 'médico' does not work well, the sign is not good, the excess of *pta'z* or the negative energy or complementary to the dialectic relationship.

In recent research on the history of the Paez and with the help of ethnolingüists, some aspects which have to do with the sound producing spirit (*ks'a'ws*) have been found.[12] It can be affirmed that this spirit is everywhere — some times intentionally undifferentiated from the Catholic god. "It is the giver of life, everything is born of it and lives for it. It has elder sons thunder, the sun, the moon, the duende, the rainbow, and some younger sons, spirits which voluntarily desired to be what they are, animals, plants and human beings, and also some special grandchildren which are the Paez". (Hernandez, Bernal: 1993:43)

The Paez Body — Nature

Lexical elements of *nasa-yuwe* (Paez language) which

12. Reference has also been made by the CRIC Health Program and by the biologists Hernandez and Bernal in the paper. The Thë'wala and Medicinal Plants: Ethnobotony of Paez Medicine in El Çabuyo-Tierradentro, 1993.

denominate parts of the body or biological states, contribute to clarify the Paez cosmology.

For women, menstruation in *nasa-yuwe* is running water (*cacue yu'vyaa, cacue*: body, *yu*: agua, *vyaa*: appear or run). It is the removal of the 'dirt', as the river which runs from the left, withdrawing that which is dirty from the territory. It is the not-life which guarantees life, it is not the 'detained' water of the lagoons, source of life, genesis of the *nasa* world. In the concrete language of the midwives, "the initiation of life in the maternal womb is informed with the term: the woman is detained, that is water does not continue to run in her body". (Portela, Gomez: 1993:5)

Every *nasa* man and woman, from birth has in the body 'a little heat and a little cold'; the cold circulates from the left and the heat from the right. A central intersection point in the crown marks the equilibrium which should be maintained to regulate the circulation of heat and cold, to avoid excesses which are observed as not-well-being, pain and illness. Given the predominantly cold climate, part of cultural normativity is directed more toward avoiding cold than heat. Therefore, Paez settlements are located at median altitudes, where an equilibrium between cold and heat exists, these are the warm zones.

'Stone' is a mythical element which is very important for the Paez. Throughout the territory stone is distributed in many forms and sizes which remind people of the historic movements of the cultural heroes so as to arrive to the bottom of the lagoons where they reside. *Kwet* means stone and in the vocabulary of the exterior human body appears in composed words like *yükwet* which means 'knee' and in *puka kwet* where *puka* is 'near' or 'around', being then 'around the stone' or 'cheek'.

The voice *vic* is 'point' or 'summit' and refers to those sites where *kwes kiwe* meets the aerial world of *ëeka*, places of great power, where the *thë'walas* go to establish contact with the spiritual world. It is found in composition words like *c'uc'vic* in which *c'uc'* means 'breast'. The meaning of the phrase thereby becomes 'the point of the breast' or 'nipple'.

Kaf denominates external and some internal cavities of the human body. For example: *ickaf*, *ic* is 'nose' and refers to the hollow passages in the nose which permit the relationship between the external and internal. In nature, *Kaf* corresponds to 'hole' and it is precisely by means of these holes or depressions in the earth that access to the interior world is obtained. In the lower world (*kiwe d'ihu'*) contact is established with the *nasa luc'kwe.*

The human body is compared to a tree; *khat'* is 'skin' in humans and 'bark' in the tree. *Wace* in the tree corresponds to the 'roots' and in the human body is equivalent to 'tendon'. *D'i'th* is the human bone and in young corn corresponds to the stem. *Ku'ta* is 'shoulder' or 'arm' in the body and is part of the name of the limb of a tree, *f'tu ku'ta,* where *f'tu* means 'tree' and *ku'ta* means 'arm'.

The declaration which the *nasa* world makes 'I am tree' is as natural as saying 'I am Indian'. The *nasa* simply perceives an intimate link with nature, is identified with it. In this way she/he can be a tree.

Conceiving the body as a tree indicates the intimacy with nature and reinforces the importance of *kiwe d'ihu'* (the lower world), as a place where the vital cycle is initiated for plants, animals and persons. It not only corresponds to the biological process of birth and death, but also to the temporal and cosmological cycle which recollects all originary perpetuatory experiences of the group. The relationship between the Paez human body and nature clearly shows how the lexemes which name the parts of the body have an analogous significance which crosses the body with nature.

Many lexeme show the topological relationship between

the human and the geographical. Human body is a territory composed, among others, by elements like water, stone, summits, depressions, roots, and stems. Similarly, energy circulates in nature in the form of virtue, power, spirituality and in the human body as signs.

The signs, as a code of knowledge, can be perceived by all the *nasa*, but not decoded, as this depends upon shamanic techniques. Signs serve the *thë' walas* especially to interpret what is happening to persons, society, and environment. These signs move throughout the entire body, they are circular and contain two extreme and opposite points: the point of the left foot (which can be the heel, the arch, the toe or the side), and the point of the right foot. Circulation is bidirectional, it can begin on the right side and move toward the left, or *vice-versa*. But the meaning which the sign acquires is according to the circulation it takes; if the direction is toward the right side of the body, this implies that the illness is gaining territory, while the contrary means that there is improvement.

These signs, circulating in the whole body, enter through bare feet in contact with the earth, reconstructing the territory in the Paez body by putting it in contact with the world above (*ëeka*) and the world below (*kiwe d'ihu'*).

Cleansing, Renewal and Offering Rituals

These rituals may be observed in all daily social practices of the community; without exaggerating it may be affirmed that the Paez is a society of rites, officiated by men called *thë'walas*, wise men and/or traditional 'doctors'. They have received power and wisdom from thunder, which is situated at the central point of the production of knowledge, where the three worlds of the Paez cosmography couverge.

Cleansing, renewal and offering rituals can be carried out together, as a ceremony, or separately, depending upon individual, family, and community requirements. In essence these maintain a structure which evidences the cosmological system as a cultural system which sustains Paez ethnicity.

The cleansing rite must be carried out at night and requires preparations which consist of getting toasted coca leaves, *aguardiente* and tobacco which are donated by *cabildos*, "communities" of people. The *thë'wala* receives these and supplies medicinal plants as well as the '*mambe*' and part of the coca. This giving and receiving represents the permanently renovated principle of reciprocity in the double movement between society and nature.

"VOLTEADA DE LA JIGRA"

The *thë'wala* begins the 'mambeo' from the moment in which all the people who are going to participate in the ceremony arrive at the previously indicated place. Before putting the 'mambe' into his mouth the *thë'wala* rotates it over his body from the right foot, up toward the crown and down toward the left foot. He then indicates to each one of the participants how they should put coca, tobacco and *aguardiente* in a different 'jigra' (bag) from the one he uses as traditional 'doctor'. Each one, separately, takes the three ingredients, one by one, in the left hand, and makes the same rotation as that of the *thë'wala* and then puts them into the 'jigra'. This part of the ceremony is over when all have carried out this procedure.

Various aspects can be evidenced in this first phase:

- The *thë'wala* propitiates the initiation of the increase of his sense of perception of the signs.
- The signs are dynamized among the participants. The rotations which are repeated by participants, after the *thë'wala* (right foot—crown—left foot), predispose the human body to the restoration of their proper place of the signs which are lost through the right side.

CHOICE OF THE RITUAL SITE

- The site is indicated in the body of the *thë'wala* by a sign that marks the direction from right to left.
- The site should be located in front of a source of water which runs from right to left (if water sources are impossible, holes are dug to the left of the space occupied by the people.)

DELIMITATION OF THE CEREMONIAL SPACE

- The *Thë'wala* sticks his *chonta*-wood staff into the ground at his left side, marking in this way the sacred territory of power: the lagoon, the *barrenplain*, the savage, the spiritual (geographically) which do not coincide with the real location).
- In his left section of great power, the *thë'wala* is situated. Between the different stages of the ceremony he concentrates, looking for greater sensorial perception (spiritual communication) to guide the process.
- In the right section marked by the body of the *thë'wala*, or better to the right side of the officiant, the persons charged with *pta'z*, who are dirty and require cleansing, are organized side by side in a line.
- The extreme right of the line must be closed by a man, because women are always located in the middle of the group of participants.

THE THREE WORLDS AND THE CARRYING OUT OF THE RITE

The *thë'wala*, after having 'mambeado' a little, gets up and begins to 'voltear la jigra' (spin the bag) patient by patient in the following way: He takes the 'jigra' (bag) together with the *chonta*-wood staff — which comes from the sacred world — in his left hand. Utilizing his right hand he moves the left one making a rotation over the patient from the right foot, passing over the head and returning to the left foot. This cultural exercise recovers the relationship with the three worlds; *kwes kiwe, ëeka, kiwe d'ihu'* and their interconnection with the left and right sections (to simplify the text, this rotation will be referred to as r.f.-c-1.f.). If there are various patients the rite will begin at the extreme right. Each time that the rotation is finished for one patient the *thë'wala* blows strongly toward the left.

When the line is finished, the *thë'wala* makes various rotations r.f. -c-1.f. over his body, blowing each time that he finishes. This is a breath which blows from *kwes kiwe*, our territory, toward the world above, *ëeka*. Then he sits down again to meditate, without suspending the 'mambeo' as this gives knowledge of the ancestors and of the cultural heroes, especially those located in the sacred world. 'Mambe' is also given out to the patients. but before giving it to each one the *thë'wala* always makes a rotation r.f.-c-1.f. around himself.

There is a first instant of diagnosis which is achieved by consulting the signs (reading of the signs given by the thunder which in falling passes through the three worlds). Depending upon the diagnosis and upon the kind of cleansing it is possible to continue on to the following stage which consists on the hunt of the 'candelilla' (sparkle or flash) — enemies or the dirt. Of these, the red ones are the most dangerous.

A cleansing lasts for at least two days. When sufficient 'candelillas' have been hunted, the next stage is of the burial of the dirt on the banks of the river and to the left of the human body. (The dirt or *pta'z* is extracted by the *thë'wala*, a being of the *kwes kiwe*, helped by the knowledge of the ancestors and the power of thunder; that which is dirty must be deposited in the world below).

The next step in the ceremony is the distribution of plants in two sessions. First coca, tobacco, medicinal herbs and *aguardiente* are passed out to '*mambear*' and to blow toward the river. Then comes the bath with medicinal plants. This is carried out by sprinkling water on the right side of the back and the crown of the person, and ending on the left side. When the bath has been finished there is a second session of medicine in which more plants to chew and *aguardiente* are distributed.

References

Bernal Villa, Segundo. "Medicina y Magia entre los Paeces." *Revista Colombiana de Antropologia, Antares*, no. 2. Bogotá: 1954.

———, "Mitología y Cuentos de la Parcialidad de Calderas, Tierradentro." *Revista Colombiana de Antropología. Antares* VII, pp. 117-221, Bogotá: 1953.

———, "Bases para el Estudio de la Organización Social de los Paez." *Revista Colombiana de Antropología. Antares*, VIII, pp. 291-367. Bogotá: 1954.

Bouysee-Cassagne, Therese y Harris, Olivia. "Pacha: En torno al Pensamiento Aymará." In *Tres Reflexiones sobre el Pensamiento Andino*, Hisbol. La Paz: 1987.

Castillo i Orosco, Eujenio (sic) Cura, de Tálaga, *Vocabulario Paez-Castellano*. Catecismo, nociones gramaticales i dos pláticas con adiciones, correcciones i un vocabulario castellano-paez por Ezequiel Uricoechea. Paris, Collection Linguistique américaine, V2, Maisonneuve y C. Libreros — Editores, MDCCCCXXVII.

Ceron, Carmen Patricia, *El Puma y la India de Punturco. Una Mirada al Territorio de la Etnia Pancitará*. Tesis de Grado, Universidad del Cauca. Popayán: 1990.

Faust, Franz, *Sistema Médico entre los Coyaimas y los Natagaimas*. Hohenschäflarn, Ediciones Claus Renner Verlag, 1986.

———, *Etnogeografía y etnologia de Coconuco y Sotará. Revista Colombiana de Antropología*, Volumen XXVIII, Bogotá: 1989-90.

———, "La Cosmovision de los Coconucos y Yanaconas en su Arquitectura." *Novedades Colombianas*. Museo de Historia Natural no. 2. Universidad del Cauca, 1990.

Findji, María Teresa and Rojas, José María, *Territorio, Economía y*

Sociedad Paez. Universidad del Valle. Cali. 1985.

Galvez Abadia, Aida Cecilia, *Tradición y Cambio en el Cabuyo: Una Comunidad Paez en Tierradentro. Cauca*. Popayán 1980.

Garcia, José Luis, *Antropología del Territorio*. Talleres de Ediciones Josefina Betancourt, Madrid: 1976.

Gartner, Martin, "Izquierda y Derecha en el Cosmos. Simetria frente a la Teoría de la Inversión del Tiempo." Biblioteca Científica Salvat, No. 14. Barcelona: 1986.

Gomez, Herinaldy, *Proceso de Campesinización de una Comuidad indígena*. Tesis de Grado. Universidad del Cauca. Popayán: 1981.

Gomez, Herinaldy. "Aportes Antropológicos a la teoría y la práctica de la Antropología Jurídica en Colombia. *Normas Formales: Costumbres legales en Colombia*, Esther Sanchez B. Editor, Compliador. Bogotá: 1988.Gomez, Herinaldy y Portela, Hugo. *Territorio, Cultura y Thë'walas*. Paper presented in the VI National Congress of Anthropology: Symposium on Medical Cultures in the Construction of America. Universidad de Los Andes. Bogotá: 1992.

Gonzalez, David. *Los Paeces o Genocidio y Luchas Indigenas en Colombia*. La Rueda Suelta. Bogotá.

Henman, Anthony, *Mama Coca*. La Oveja Negra. Bogotá: 1980.

Langebaek, Carl Henrik, "Tres Formas de Acceso a Recursos en el Territorio de la Confederación Cocuy." *Museo del Oro*. Boletín No. 18. Ediciones Siglo XXI. Bogotá: 1987.

Lopez. Claudia, *Los Caquiona, Frianos de Sangre Caliente*. Tesis de Grado. Universidad del Cauca. Popayán.

Mejia, Mario, "De la Selva Silvestre a la Colonización Mecanizada en el Caribe Colombiano. *Cuadernos de Geografía*. Universidad Nacional de Colombia. Bogotá: 1990.

Murra, John, *La Organización Económica del Estado Inca*. Siglo XXI. Mexico: 1987.

———, "Los Limites de las Limitaciones del 'Archipiélago Vertical' en los Andes." *Maguaré*. Universidad Nacional de Colombia. Bogotá: Juno, 1987.

Oberen, Udo, "El Acceso a los Recursos Naturales de Diferentes Ecologías en la Sierra Ecuatoriana." *Contribución a la Etnohistoria Ecuatoriana*. Instituto Otavaleño de Antropología, Otavalo: 1981.

Polia, Mario, *Las Lagunas de los Encantos*. Medicina Tradicional Andina del Peru Septentrioal. Cepecer. Piaura: 1988.

Portela, Hugo, "Enfogues Antropológicos sobre la atención primaria de Salud: Integración de la medicina alopática y tradicional," *Revista Palabra.* Nos. 3 and 4. Ed. Universidad del Cauca. Popayán: 1987.

——— and Gomez, Herinaldy, *La Cultura Médica en la Cosmovisión Paez. — La Cosmovisión Paez o Armonia de la Salud.* Paper presented in the VI National Congress of Anthropology: Symposium on Medical Cultures in the Construction of America. Universidad de Los Andes. Bogotá: 1992.

——— and Pardo, Carlos, "Dinámica social actual de la medicina Paez en Tierradentro; proceso de cambio." Memorias del Simposio Medicina Tradicional Curanderismo y Cultura Popular en Colombia Hoy. V National Congress of Anthropology. Villa de Leyva. 1989 and in *Memorias de Eventos Científicos Colombianos.* ICFES ICAN. 1990.

———, "Reflexiones acerca de la Investigación sobre Medicina Tradicional en Comunidades Indigenas, Cauca." PERSPECTIVA: 2:34-39. Universidad Pedagógica y Technológica. Tunja: 1990.

——— and Gonzalez, Omar. et al., *Yo Soy el Arbol o la Identidad Cuerpo Naturaleza.* GLOTTA: 3:8-13. Bogotá: 1988.

——— and Gonzalez, Omar et al., *YU'CE: Atención Primaria en Salud, zona nororiental Indígena del Cauca.* Investigaciones Antropológicas. Ed. Universidad del Cauca. Popayán: 1988.

———, Yu'cesa (Gente que Cura), Video Cassette. Sonoviso of 82 Slides. Popayán, 1992.

Rappaport, Joanne, "Mesianismo y Transformación de Simbolos Mesiánicos en Tierradentro." *Revista Colombiana de Antropoloogía.* Vol. 23, pp. 365-413. Bogotá: 1980-81.

———, "Historia, Mito y Dinámica de Conservación Territorial en Tierradentro, Colombia." *Informes Antropológicos,* No. 3 pp. 47-62. ICAN, Bogotá.

———, "Imágenes Miticas, Pensamiento Histórico y Textos Impresos: Los Paeces y la Palabra Escrita." *Rituales Y Fiestas de las Americas.* Congreso Internacional de Americanists. Ediciones Uniandes. Bogotá: 1988.

Thomas, Louis Vincent, *Antropologia de la Muerte.* Fondo de Cultura Económica. Mexico: 1983.

Villa, Eugenia, "Los Paeces: Un Grupo Humano en Proceso de Suicidio Biológico y Cultura." Universidad del Cauca. Popayán: 1978. Mimeographed.

9

Significance of Order in Music and Dance

A Study in Musical and Dance Cosmology of the Santal Tribe

Onkar Prasad

Order is basic to the existence of both Man and the cosmos. In traditional thought life of the former is regulated by the latter. The daily as well as thc ycarly life activities of Man such as getting up in the morning, eating, sleeping, sowing and harvesting — all are governed by the astronomical cycle. These activities of Man may also find reflection in the artistic behaviour which needs to be studied in the context of the music and dance of the Santals.

In India the Santals are the largest homogeneous tribe of Proto-Australoid origin speaking Austro-Asiatic language. They are spread over almost the entire eastern region of the country having their main concentration in some adjoining areas of Bihar, Orissa and West Bengal. They live primarily on agriculture. Though they have only recently invented their alphabet and have a growing interest in formal education, they still retain the characteristics of a tribal society.

The Santals are characterised as 'pleasure-loving' people and have a number of musical and dance forms, viz, *Baha*[1],

1. This form of music and dance is named after the flower-festival, the *Baha* that is organised in the month of *Chait* (February-March) to celebrate the beginning of the Santali year.

Bir[2], *Chaṭiar*[3], *Dasãe*[4], *Doṅ*[5], *Karam*[6], *Lagṛe*[7], *Mage*[8] and *Sohrae*[9], each named after and associated with certain ceremony of the year. Though each form of music and dance is supposed to be performed on a particular occasion, some are performed on occasions other than their own. For example, *Sohrae* which is specific to the post-harvest festival held in winter is also performed during *Coṛok*[10], the hook-swinging festival of the summer. Similarly the *Doṅ* which is specific to the marriage-ceremony is also performed on the eve of festivals such as the *Baha* (flower festival), *Coṛok'*, *Erok'*[11]

---

2. It is a form of music and dance associated with annual hunt in the forest.
3. It is a form of music and dance associated with ceremonial purification.
4. It is named after the festival, *Dasãe* that is celebrated in the month of *Asin* (September-October) when the Santal boys have completed their course in medicines.
5. It is known after a dance performed during the marriage-ceremony, the *Bapla*.
6. It is known after the festival that is held in the name of a sacred-tree, the *Karam* (*Adina cordifolia*). The festival is organized by an individual Santal with the object of bringing prosperity and pleasure in life. A specialist known as *Karam-guru* is invited to recite the songs of *Karam* on the occasion that deal with the history of world from creation and through ages according to Santal traditions.
7. It is rendered specially on the eve of the *Coṛok'-puja* (hook-swinging festival) but it can also be sung on other festive occasions.
8. It is a form of music and dance associated with the festival of thatching.
9. It is known after the festival, *Sohrae* that is held by the Santals when their harvest-work is over in the month of *Pous* (December-January).
10. The *Coṛok'* is a hook-swinging festival organised during summer.
11. It is an agricultural festival which is held in the month of *Asar* (June-July) before the sowing of the winter paddy starts. The festival is concluded by singing and dancing in the village-street.

(sowing festival), *Hariar*[12] (sprouting festival), *Karam* (a festival of prosperity) and the *Sohrae*. So is the case with the *Lagr̥e*. Though it is specific to the rain-making ceremony, it is also performed during *Baha, Cor̥ok'* and *Sohrae* festivals.

It may be observed from above, there are at least three occasions, namely, the *Baha*, the *Cor̥ok'* and the *Sohrae* on which both the *Doṅ* and the *Lagr̥e* forms of music and dance are performed in a definite order as shown in the following three tables:

Table 1

Name of the Occasion	Form of Music and Dance Presented	Order of Presentation
	Baha	*Baha*
Baha	*Doṅ*	*Lagr̥e*
	Lagr̥e	*Doṅ*

Table 2

Name of the Occasion	Form of Music and Dance Presented	Order of Presentation
	Doṅ	*Sohrae*[13]
	Gilwaḍe	*Gilwaḍe*[14]
Cor̥ok'	*Lagr̥e*	*Lagr̥e*
	Sohrae	*Doṅ*
		Gilwaḍe
		Sohrae

12. It is an agricultural festival which is performed in the month of *San* (July-August) when the paddy seeds have pushed out new shoots. The festival is held before transplantation of the paddy seedlings begins.

13. Customarily on the occasion of the *Cor̥ok'* the villagers enter into the *Akhra* (dancing ground) with the village-priest singing and dancing the *Sohrae*.

14. It is a form of music and dance performed before and after the performance of any type of music and dance outside the village-street 'to bind' and 'to open' the *Akhra* respectively to protect from evil-forces.

Table 3

Name of the Occasion	Form of Music and Dance Presented	Order of Presentation
	Doṅ	*Sohrae*
Sohrae	*Lagr̥e*	*Lagr̥e*
	Sohrae	*Doṅ*

It may be observed further that the performace of the *Lagr̥e*, on all these occasions, precedes the performance of the *Doṅ*. This aspect of musical and dance behaviour raises a number of questions, such as, what do the *Doṅ* and the *Lagr̥e* stand for and why do the Santals follow a definite order in the presentation of these two musical and dance forms. The present paper is an attempt to find out answers to these questions on the basis of data collected through field study among the Santals of Bolpur-Sriniketan block of the Birbhum district, West Bengal during 1991. In addition to this, some data from the secondary sources have also been used.

As music and dance in the Santal society are associated with ceremonies, which in turn are given name and form by myth, it is necessary that they are discussed in mythico-ritual context of performance. But before doing so it is necessary to understand what the *Doṅ* and the *Lagr̥e* symbolize. This could have bearing on our understanding of the meaning of the very order in which they are presented.

The 'Doṅ'

The *Doṅ* form of music and dance, though performed almost throughout the year as said earlier, is specific to marriage which ritually symbolizes 'union'. The theme which the *Doṅ* song deals with is related to the Santal cosmology—such as, the primeval condition of the universe, constitution of human body and union between the male and the female. In a *Doṅ* song, for example, rendered during marriage, the sky is described to have been without water and the earth without soil in the beginning of creation. Later, as described, the air lifted the water up into the sky and the earthworm lifted the soil up the water, which finally resulted in the formation of the cloud and the earth respectively. The song runs as follows:

sermare dak' banu,
dhartire hasa banu,
sange dharti sajaw banu,
hoe doe rakap'keda sermare dak'
lenḍoṅ hasae rakap'ket'
sangi dharti sajaw ena.

There was no water in the sky,
There was no soil on the earth,
Truly the earth was not fully arranged.
The air lifted the water up into the sky,
The female-earthworm lifted the soil up
(the water),
Thus, the earth was properly arranged.

In a different *Doṅ* song rendered at the time of performing the ritual of *Cumaura*[15] (literally meaning 'kissing'), during marriage, the human body is described as being constituted of two basic physical elements of the universe — air and earth. Reference to water, the third basic element, comes in analogical terms, viz., water of the spring of life.

The song is as follows:

hasa hormo hõ hoe jivi,
jian jhardak' do chilkau kana

---

15. It is a rite performed by the bride's mother during the marriage before the new husband and wife enter the house. At the door, the bride's mother waves the winnowing three times over the heads of the couple scattering the articles such as *Dhubighas*, paddy and *Aḍwa coole* (unboiled rice) behind their backs.

jivi bań hilok' do
hasa dhurire measaw abon.
jian jhardak' do mesaw cabak'

The body is soil,
And soul is air,
Where the spring of life flows.
The day the soul goes out,
We turn to soil,
The water of the spring of life also
sinks into the earth.

In yet another *Doń* song sung during the occasion when vermilion is put on the forehead of the bride, reference to union between the groom and the bride through the mediating function of water is clear.

As the song runs:

mõre goṭen ul sakam
mimit' loṭa dak'
chilkaw amkan com bańco
hordom bindi yidin' jonom jonom.

Five mango leaves,
And a potful of water,
I do not know,
If you really sprinkled water over me
I do not know
If you really wetted me or not

On other occasions like the *Erok'* — the sowing festival, the *Doń* songs refer to the relationship among the cosmic elements analogous to male-female paradigm. For example, in a *Doń* song rendered on the occasion of the *Erok'* the paddy seed is decribed as weeping for its wedlock with the earth, which is necessary if the earth that returns to sterility when left to self has to be made reproductive. But this is not possible unless the rain from the sky mixes with the earth and makes her wet. As the song runs:

The paddy is weeping
The paddy is asking.
When will be my wedding?
When the water of the sky
Drenches the earth
Then will be your wedding.
[From Archer 1974: 22]

It is observed further that 'union' as theme also gets reflected through the body movement of the *Doṅ* dance accompanying the song. In this dance the Santal women who form a circle and interlock their hands first advance two steps to the right and then gracefully extend each one's leg forward. This causes the hip and the body movement to become prominent. Mukherjee in this respect observes that the hip and body movements in the *Doṅ* dance suggest only one meaning, viz., recreating in artistic forms the human urge to procreation. The very object of dance associated as it is with marriage-ceremonies was stated by an old Santal to be a form of magic, where the married pair might unite in love and affection and get children so that the Santals might increases in number (Mukherjee 1945: 369).

From the analyses of different songs as well as the dance it is clear that the *Doṅ* symbolizes 'union'.

The 'Lagr̥̃e'

Like *Doṅ*, the *Lagr̥̃e* form of music and dance is performed all through the year but as told earlier, is specific to the rain-making ceremony. When there is no rain during the rainy season, the peak period for agricultural operation, *Lagr̥̃e* songs are rendered in invocation to rain-god to make the skies rain.

swarager hur hur
prithimite dhula chilu urilo
dhaner sisȯ chilo marilo
mansuser chati chilu phaṭilo he

In the sky, clouds rumble, Oh god!
On the earth, dust flies
O god! the ears of corn dry up.
The hearts of men are breaking, O god!
[From Mukherjea 1945: 368]

The *Lagr̥e* dance characterised by waving of the feet forward and swinging to the right, as observed by Hembram (1979), also signifies rain for better crops and fertility and the *Lagr̥e* drum-beats accompanying the song and the dance, as revealed through its phonetic expression, fulfil the same function. The drum-beats cited below testify this:

dharti c-etam ing atang da-ting
da-te tetang lagai iting

On the surface of the earth invoke rain
O Rain! quench our thirst
[From Hembram 1979: 4]

On the basis of the analyses of the song-text, drum-beat vocables and body movements in dance it may be said that *Lagr̥e* symbolizes 'rain'.

As said earlier, there are three occasions; the *Baha*, the *Coṛok'* and the *Sohrae* to which both the *Doṅ* and the *Lagr̥e* forms of music and dance are common. Of these three occasions I would limit my discussion to *Sohrae* only as the order of presentation of the *Lagr̥e* and the *Doṅ* on each occasion remains the same.

The 'Sohrae'

Sohrae is a festival held during December-January when the Santals have brought their paddy home after harvesting from the field. The festival, according to a myth, has been named after Sohrae, the eldest daughter of the first Santal couple, Pilcu Haram and Pilcu Budhi, in whose honour it is observed. As the story goes:

Sohrae was the eldest daughter of the first Santal couple, Pilcu Haram and Pilcu Budhi. They had eight daughters and seven sons in all. One day Pilcu Haram took the sons out hunting while Pilcu Budhi took the daughters for collecting potherbs. As they gathered them they came to a banyan tree and began to eat its fruits. The daughters climbed the tree — the eldest climbing first and the others after her. When they had all climbed, the eldest was at the top and the youngest nearest to the ground. Then the seven brothers came. They saw the girls eating fruits and as they looked Maran Buru in the guise of Lita filled the brothers with desire. So they sent the youngest brother to fetch some fruits for them. He went to the tree and since the youngest was nearest to the ground he asked her to give a fruit to him. The girl said, "I will throw it down" but the boy said "Give it to me with your hand". Then the girl came lower down and as she gave the fruit to the boy, he caught her hand and pulled her from the tree. When he had caught her he made the girl his wife. The next youngest brother asked for fruit. The next youngest sister was nearest to the ground and he made her his wife. In this way the seven brothers took seven of the sisters as their wives. When they had finished the eldest sister was still in the tree and as there was no husband for her, she began to weep bitterly. When the brothers and sisters saw her crying, they said they would never forget her and once a year would offer her a virgin thing. From that time on an egg has been offered in a paddy field and Sohrae has been called the elder sister in memory of her.

[From Archer 1974: 189-99]

The *Sohrae* festival is celebrated for five days. The first day known as *Um*[16] is marked by the performance of ceremonial ablution, the second day known as *Bongan*[17] by the worship of the house-hold spirit, the third day known as *Khunṭau*[18] by setting brief ritual of salutation to the bullocks, the fourth day known as *Jale Hilok'*[19] by catching the fish and crab and the final day known as *Sakrat*[20] by ritual of hunting. Of these five days, celebration of the first day is a must. This day major as well as other minor spirits are remembered and venerated by the village-priest for the welfare of an individual Santal and the community living in the village. Without this no music and dance can follow to celebrate the festival. It is, therefore, necessary that the ritual observed on the first day of the *Sohrae* is described in some detail. On this day the village-priest and the field-priest, after taking bath in a pond, go to a nearby rice-field. The village-priest traces some small circles with the powdered rice there, pours some unboiled rice and puts vermilion marks on each of the circles and places an egg over the first one. He addresses the major spirits, viz, the 'Lady of the Sacred Grove', 'the Great Mountain', 'Five-Six' and a female spirit of the sacred grove known as *Gosãe Era* requesting them to take their care and to protect them from evil spirits or any other unknown calamity. He, in return, makes sacrifices of fowls in their names. Finally he makes a libation of rice-beer.

---

16. It means 'the day of bathing' and refers to the first day of the *Sohrae* festival.
17. It is the second day of the *Sohrae* festival on which every head of the household offers sacrifices to *Abge* (Subclan spirit) *Hapramko* (ancestral spirits) and *Oṛak' Bongas* (household spirits) once a year to ensure their continuing protection.
18. It refers to a ceremony of mock-play with the bullock that is held on the 3rd day of the *Sohrae* festival.
19. It is the fourth day of the *Sohrae* festival on which the Santals move from house to house of the village to collect tolls and perform the act of mimicry.
20. The last day of the *Sohrae* festival is known as *Sakrat'*.

After the village-priest has finished his worship, the field-priest who has already traced a circle at a distance, brings out blood of his thigh, mixes the same with some unboiled rice and lays the same there. He makes sacrifice of a blackfowl in the name of the 'spirit of the outskirt'.

This follows cooking of the sacrificial fowls and eating and drinking of rice-beer. In the meantime, the village headman addressing the people present there, suggests them "to put twelve wads of cotton in their ears and to see and hear nothing for five days". He, then, turning to the young boys tells them to "take the ripe but not the unripe" and at the same time to observe taboo on clan endogamy.

To end up the ritual in the field, the village headman summons the cow-boys asking them to drive their cattle over the circles. The cow or the bullock which has treaded over the egg is declared to have brought fortune to her or his owner.

In the late evening, first the 'songs of awakening the cattle' are sung before every cowshed by the villagers and each family woman standing before the cowshed rubs the horns of the cattle with oil and throws unboiled rice over them.

This is followed by the performance of the music and dance in the village street. The participating girls stand in a line across the village street to dance from one end of the village to the other and all the village boys including the childern and other male members stand in front of them. Some of the male members carry the percussion instruments such as the *Tumdak'*[21] and *Ṭamak'*[22] to play and some to make gestures of various kinds. The performance begins with the singing of the *Sohrae* song which is followed by drumming and dancing with forward movement to reach the other end of the village street. On their way when the

21. It is a cylindrical drum of the Santal.

22. It is a kettle-drum of the Santal.

participants have reached the *Manjhithan,*[23] the girls form a semi-circular row to perform the *Lagr̥e* music and dance. Next to this, the dancers without changing the arrangement, perform the *Doṅ* form of music and dance. When this is over, they break this arrangement to rearrange themselves in a line across the village street to start singing, dancing and drumming of the *Sohrae*. On the other end of the village street they perform *Durumjak'*[24] i.e., singing and dancing by stooping to take the turn. In this way the persons participating in music and dance go on moving from one end of the village to the other until they stop performing it.

Analysis

As said in the beginning, the basic concern in this paper has been to decipher the meaning of the order in which the Santals perform their music and dance on a festive occasion. For this purpose the two specific forms; the *Doṅ* and the *Lagr̥e*, have been studied in mythico-ritual context of performance of the *Sohrae* festival.

From the study of the origin myth of the *Sohrae* festival it becomes clear that this festival is held in honour of *Sohrae*—the eldest daughter of the primeval couple, Pilcu Haram and Pilcu Budhi, who was left unmarried and is remembered on the occasion when the earth is also left barren after the harvest of the paddy crop. Here the *Sohrae*, analogically speaking, is in fact, treated implicitly by the Santals as metaphor of the earth left wild and unproductive or sterile. However, in order to neutralize the dangerous forces contained in the wild untamed natural nature of the

---

23. It is a sacred place in a village street erected in honour of the spirits of the predecessors of the village headman. The place consists of a raised mud platform at the centre of which there is a post with a stone at its base.

24. It is a variety of the *Sohrae* music and dance performed in a stooping posture when the performers reach the end of the village-street.

earth or the woman (here it stands for *Sohrae*), the ritual has to be organized (Bourdieu 1977:137). Thus, the ritual of the murder of the field or the earth (i.e., harvesting) has to be enacted in the sacrifice of the fowls which are both its embodiment and substitute, the invisible forces of the nature have to be appeased to get their protection, the virgin egg offered in the name of *Sohrae* (the virgin woman) has to be trampled over to restore fertility and her wildness has to be negated by providing sexual licence by the village headman in which all unmarried persons may indulge in promiscuous intercourse.

It is observed that during this festival singing and dancing of the *Sohrae* are followed by the *Lagr̥̃e* and then by the *Doṅ* as part of the ritual celebration. As mere performance of the *Sohrae* music and dance could mean announcement of the barrenness of the earth there seems to be some logic inherent in including the other two forms of music and dances and maintaining an order in their presentation.

It is stated earlier that the *Lagr̥̃e* form of music and dance associated with the rain-making ceremony and the *Doṅ* with the marriage symbolize 'rain' and 'union'. Performance of the former during the *Sohrae* may mean announcement of 'rain' and the latter the resurrection of the earth which can come only through the repetition of the primal marriage of the sky and the earth mediated by rain. In this context it may be said that the performance of the *Lagr̥̃e* after the *Sohrae* and subsequently of the *Doṅ* reapply the logic of rain-making and union at a time when for practical purpose, rain is not required and marriage does not take place. These can only serve the purpose of revivifyig the sacred strength of the corn or the field (*ibid.*, 135).

Thus, the ultimate logic behind following a definite order in the presentation of the *Doṅ* and the *Lagr̥̃e* forms of music and dances by the Santals seems to underlie the principle of cosmogony in which both the sky and the earth as basic elements of the cosmos are seen physically related to one another like male and female through the mediating function of water.

References

Archer, W.G., 1974, *The Hill of Flutes : Life, Love and Poetry in Tribal India*, New Delhi, S. Chand & Co. (Pvt.) Ltd.

Bourdieu, P., 1977, *Outline of a Theory of Practice*, Translated by Richard Nice, Cambridge University Press.

Hembram, P.C., 1976, "The Drum-beat in Santal Culture", in *Journal of the Sangeet Natak Akademi*, 39.

Mukherjea, C., 1943, *The Santals*, Calcutta: A. Mukherjee & Co. Pvt. Ltd.

10

Echoes of the Cosmic Play *

Baidyanath Saraswati

Dialogue and Monologue

What is this?
This is One.
Who is this One?
This is He.
Who is He?
He is the Self.
What am I?
I am all this.
Who am I?
I am the Self.
Who are you?
I am you.

Man moves in his thought, and asks another set of questions.

Who sends the mind to wander afar?
Who first drives life to start on its journey?
Who impels us to utter these words?
Who is the Spirit behind the eye and the ear?

— *Kena Upaniṣad*, 1

Soundless Universe

The Vedic seers have described the absolute void as

* The discussion presented here is extracted largely from the author's previous works. Illustrations by Sri Rajender Taragi.

Brahman, the first inconceivable thing in thought. *Brahman* sets the stage for the emergence of self-conscious image. It refers to anything about which man may think. It can be grasped by negation as well as affirmation in such categories of thought as "full and empty", "with and without"; seen in this way, that which provides pre-existing referents to sound is "soundless"[1]. Several Upaniṣads endeavour in various ways to explain the meta sign.

> There are two *Brahmans* to be contemplated: *Brahman* as sound and the soundless *Brahman*. Now, it is by sound that the soundless is revealed. The sound here is *Oṁ*. By the sound *Oṁ* one proceeds upward and attains rest in the soundless. This is the goal, this is immortality, this is union, this is happiness. Just as a spider that climbs up its own thread reaches free space, so also one who meditates rises up by saying *Oṁ* and reaches ultimate freedom. But those who believe in (*Brahman* as) sound proceed differently. They listen to the sound within the space of the heart by placing the thumb on the ear. This is compared to seven things: a river, bells ringing, a copper vessel being struck, the creaking of a wheel, frogs, rain, speaking in a quiet place. Having transcended all characterization, (these sounds) merge into the supreme, soundless, unmanifest *Brahman*. There, they are free from individualizing characters and differentiations, just as different sorts of nectar having blending into honey have lost their individualizing characters.
>
> — *Maitrī Upaniṣad*, VI.22.

Thus, "soundless" is the supreme reality conceived within the Universe of *Brahman*. The difference between sound and soundless is stated further: *Brahman* is that which cannot be heard by the ear but that by which the ear has hearing.

1. Cf. Saraswati, 1999.

Word as World

Tradition tells us in innumerable ways that Word is world.

> The Word is infinite, immense, beyond all this. . . . All the Gods, the celestial spirits, men and animals, live in the Word. In the Word all the worlds find their support. The Word, imperishable, is the Firstborn of Truth, mother of the Veda and hub of immortality.
>
> — *Taittirīya Brāhmaṇa*, II.8.8.

> The Word makes known the Vedas, the ritual, the knowledge of all kinds. It also makes known heaven and earth, wind, space, water, fire, the Gods, men, animals, birds, grass and trees, all animals down to worms, insects, and ants. It also makes known what is right or wrong, truth and untruth, good and evil, what is pleasing and what is unpleasing. The Word makes all this known.
>
> — *Chandogya Upaniṣad*, VII.2.1.

Sound as Elements

Oṁ is the First Word, the First symbol of the Universe. It is the Word before the world. It is the first manifestation, the concentrated reality made word: sound, content, form, matter and spirit. It is the *Śabdabrahman*, the self-affirmation of *Brahman*, the primeval sound of creation.[2]

All objects are made of Five primal Elements, called *bhūta*: Sky, Air, Fire, Water, and Earth. These are universal variable. The five Elements overlap in their formation, each having its own character and property, as shown in Table 1. When it is said that Elements combine in various proportions, it means their characters and properties merge together. For instance, Sound is the physical property not only of the Sky but also of the other four Elements.

2. Cf. Saraswati, 1999.

Sky - Sound
Air - sound, Touch
Fire - sound, touch, Vision
Water - sound, touch, vision, Taste
Earth - sound, touch, vision, taste, Smell.

Table 1
Characters and Properties of Elements

Elements	*Physical property*	*Physical character*	*Sense organ*
Sky	Sound resistence	Absence of	Ear
Air	Touch	Movement	Tectile organ
Fire	Vision	Heat	Eye
Water	Taste	Liquidity	Tongue
Earth	Smell	Roughness	Nose

Thus,Sound is the physical property of all the Five Elements and it is the Earth Element alone in which all the physical properties combine. The basic rules are the same for all other characters and properties.

More esoterically, it is the Sound system that makes life in the Universe communicable. Since the sky is eternal, Sound is also eternal. All beings originate from Sound and to Sound they return. If this theory of Sacred Science is accepted, it goes without saying that life *does* exist elsewhere in the Universe. Precisely because the Sound system (the Sky Element) works beyond the Solar system (the Fire Element).

All contingent beings — men, animals, birds, and insects are attuned to sound. The ear is the source of hearing sound, and throat the source of producing sound.

The organic pattern of sound is complex. There are Five power centres in human body which are awakened for hearing sound:

Forehead	-	Sky (Illuminated *nāda*)
Throat	-	Air (Utterance of sound)
Heart	-	Fire (Solar energy)
Genitals	-	Water (Lunar energy)
Feet	-	Earth (Ground of being)

When physical properties of the body and sense-organs combine with the Five primal Elements the meditator awakens to the sound that pervades the Universe, proceeds upward by the sound *Om*, and attains rest in the soundless.

Creation as Manifestation

The world is formed by the body of *puruṣa*, the cosmic Person. he is immeasurable. Only one quarter of him is visible, three quarters remain concealed. He covers and even overlaps space and time.

A thousand-headed is *puruṣa*
with a thousand eyes, a thousand feet,
encompassing the Earth all sides,
he exceeded it by ten fingers breadth.

Such is the measure of his might
and greatest still than this is Man.
All beings are a fourth of him,
three fourth are the immortal in heaven.

Three fourths of *puruṣa* ascended high,
one fourth took birth again down here.
From this he spread into all directions
into animate and inanimate things.

— *Ṛgveda*, X.90

This uncreated being ascends and descends into every being. From his limb come all things both animate and inanimate: animals of every type, liturgical formulas, hymns and melodies, various meteres, the Four castes of men, the cosmic powers. From his spirit comes the moon, from his eyes the sun, from his mouth Indra (God) and Agni (fire), from his navel the air, from his head the sky, from his feet the earth, from the ears the points of the compass — nothing, nobody is omitted.

What this hymn refers to is the self-manifestation of the world from a cosmological process of creation (without a creator God). *Puruṣa* is not the creator in the Christian sense of God. He did not create out of something other than he himself. His creation is a cosmic manifestation of the temporal reality.

The *Bṛhadāraṇyaka Upaniṣad* (1.4) mentions the creation of the manifold world from the unitary Soul.

> In the beginning this world was Soul (*Ātmā*)
> alone in the form of a Person.
> He created all, whatever pairs there are,
> even down to the ants.
> He knew: I, indeed, am this creation,
> for I emitted it all from myself;
> Thence arose creation.

Space as Brahman

The unitary basis of the world has been told in many ways. Viśvakarma (literally, All-maker), the one God, established all things (*Ṛgveda* X.81) From *puruṣa*, the cosmic Person, all things were formed (*Ṛgveda* X.90). Hiraṇygarbha, the Golden Germ, caused the Earth and the Heaven (*Ṛgveda* X.121). The Upaniṣads make *Brahman* and *ātman* as the two world-grounds, not different and separate, but aspects of the same Great Being. The *Chandogya Upaniṣad* (7.12) makes a more serious attempt to conceive of space.

> In space (*ākāśa*) are both sun and moon, lightning, stars and fire. Through Space one calls out; through

> Space one hears; through Space one answers. In Space one enjoys himself; in Space one does not enjoy himself. In Space one is born; unto Space one is born. Reverence Space.
>
> He who reverences Space as *Brahman* — he, verily, attains spacious, gleaming, unconfined, wide-extending worlds. As far as space goes, so far he has unlimited freedom, he who reverences Space as *Brahman*.

The Upaniṣadic sages were the first to grasp the stupendous idea of "Space as *Brahman*" (*brh* = to expand), the "expanding Universe". They took the word from its cosmological connection to infuse into it a religious meaning.

The sky is divine; the Earth is sacred. Some places on the Earth are more sacred-effective than others.[3] Places associated with cosmic events are especially holy. For instance, when the Gods and demons were fighting to take possession of the Jar of Nectar, which came out from the churning of the Milk Ocean, four drops of split ambrosia fell on the Earth at Haridwar, Prayag, Ujjain and Nasik in India. Once every six or twelve years, on the proper constellation (Table 2), called *kumbha*, hundreds of thousands of people journey to these sacred places to acquire merits and immortality.

Kāśī, another place of Pilgrimage, is visualized as a replica of the paradigmatic Universe. As the name suggests Kāśī (the luminous place) represents Hiraṇyagarbha, (the Golden Germ). Here Brahmā, the progenitor of all creatures and regions, was himself born. Here the Eight directions as well as the Lord of planets, Sun and Moon, had their origin. Situated at the centre of Space and Time, Kāśī is known as *kṣetra*.[4] The word *kṣetra* is so uniquely structured in the

3. Cf. Saraswati, 1991.

4. Cf. Saraswati, 1992.

Table 2
The Occurrence of Kumbha

Place	*Time*	*Position of Planets*
Haridwar	March-April	Jupiter x Aquarius
Prayag	December-January	Jupiter x Aries
		Sun x Capricorn
Nasik	July-September	Jupiter x Leo
Ujjain	May-June	Jupiter x Leo

semantic field that it becomes central to any comprehensive view of man and space. Its meaning flows from the Earth to the astral space (astronomical houses), from the geometric figure to the image panel, from the inner organ (womb) to the outer body, from the product (object, form) to the process (generation, creation) and conversely from macrocosm (*kṣetrajña* Self) to microcosm (*tīrthakṣetra*, place of pilgrimage). The cosmic panorama of Kāśī-kṣetra (*Fig.* 1), as conceived in tradition, is illustrated in the form of a holy circuit, in the radius of Five *kośa* (10 miles, or sheaths) representing Kāśī, the illuminant Universe. Here the conch, the square and Śiva together make a perfect illustration of the symbolic structure of the cosmos. Of this, the circle symbolizes space (*kṣetra*), the quadrangle symbolizes time (*kāla*), the conch symbolizes life (*jīva prāṇa*), and the anthropomorphic Śiva (Mahākāla, the Great Time) symbolizes the universal Self (*kṣetrajña*).

In the somewhat grotesque imagery of the Purāṇas, a pilgrim to Kāśī is recommended to break his legs on a stone, so that they my not run away with him from the sacred space. The central idea is to live there till death. The vow to dwell within the sacred space of a *tīrtha* till death is called *kṣetra-saṁnyāsa*, renouncing the earthly life. To dwell in a *tīrtha* continuously for nine months is called *garbha-vāsa*, living in mother's womb.

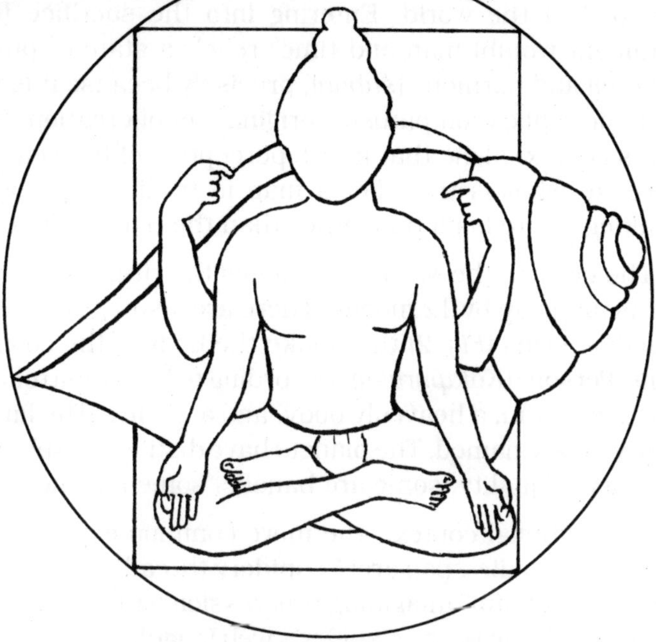

Fig. 1: A round, square, conch and Śiva representing cosmic panorma of Kāśi-*kṣetra*.

From these excellent examples we understand the otherwise incomprehensible conception of "Space as *Brahman*" in the most precise fashion.

Time as Persom

Man's image of the Sky is the same as that of himself. The Sun, the Moon, the Stars and the seasons are the divine manifestations of *puruṣa* — each having name and form, and attributes of Gods, demons, humans and animals. The Sun and Moon have kinship with human beings. Human life is tuned with the Sky. Man's daily routine is organized around the cyle of the Sun, his sustenance by the cycle of the season, his joys (festivals) by the cycle of the Moon.

Man offers sacrifice to God for his well being, as also for the good of the world. Entering into the sacrifice (the illuminant womb) man and time[5] reach a state of purity (*śuddha*) and harmony (*śubha*), precisely because it is the symbolic replication *puruṣa*'s original act of creation. It is in this context alone that man's perception of time can be nearer to what is true. For a man in tradition, properly speaking, there is no time other than the Sacred Time.

The cycle of the Moon determines the ritual time. The year is made up by 12 moons. There are also 12 suns, and 12 zodiac signs (*Fig.* 2) that make the body of the cosmic "Time-Person" (*Kālapuruṣa*). According to Indian astrology, time has a form, a heavenly body, and a quality. The limbs of the year are named. The planets have distinctive spheres and uneven quality; some are banefic, some malefice.

In traditional context, the more common expressions for the human life-span are: "a spidery thread". "a tree", "a river" and "a lamp" imagining progression with occasional sidetracks. Time is like a spider's web (angular), like a tree with branches spread out, like a river with tributaries progressing relatively in relation to the surface of the Earth, or like a lamp flickering, but *not* an arrowlike movement.

In temporal context, there is no universal time covering all ritual events occurring everywhere through every individual. Ritual time is not only discontinuous but also dependent on multiple time orders. Traditions of rituals are varied. Besides there are different systems of time reckoning even within a single tradition. In view of the multiplicity of temporal time-systems, even if the astral time is the same, the ritual time for two observers may be different. Ritual time is marked for event, and the event is dependent on the temporal order (caste, age, sex, place, etc.). The order of ritual changes, therefore, by the change in the social order.

Sacred act, sacred object and sacred time are aspects

5. Cf. Saraswati, 1996

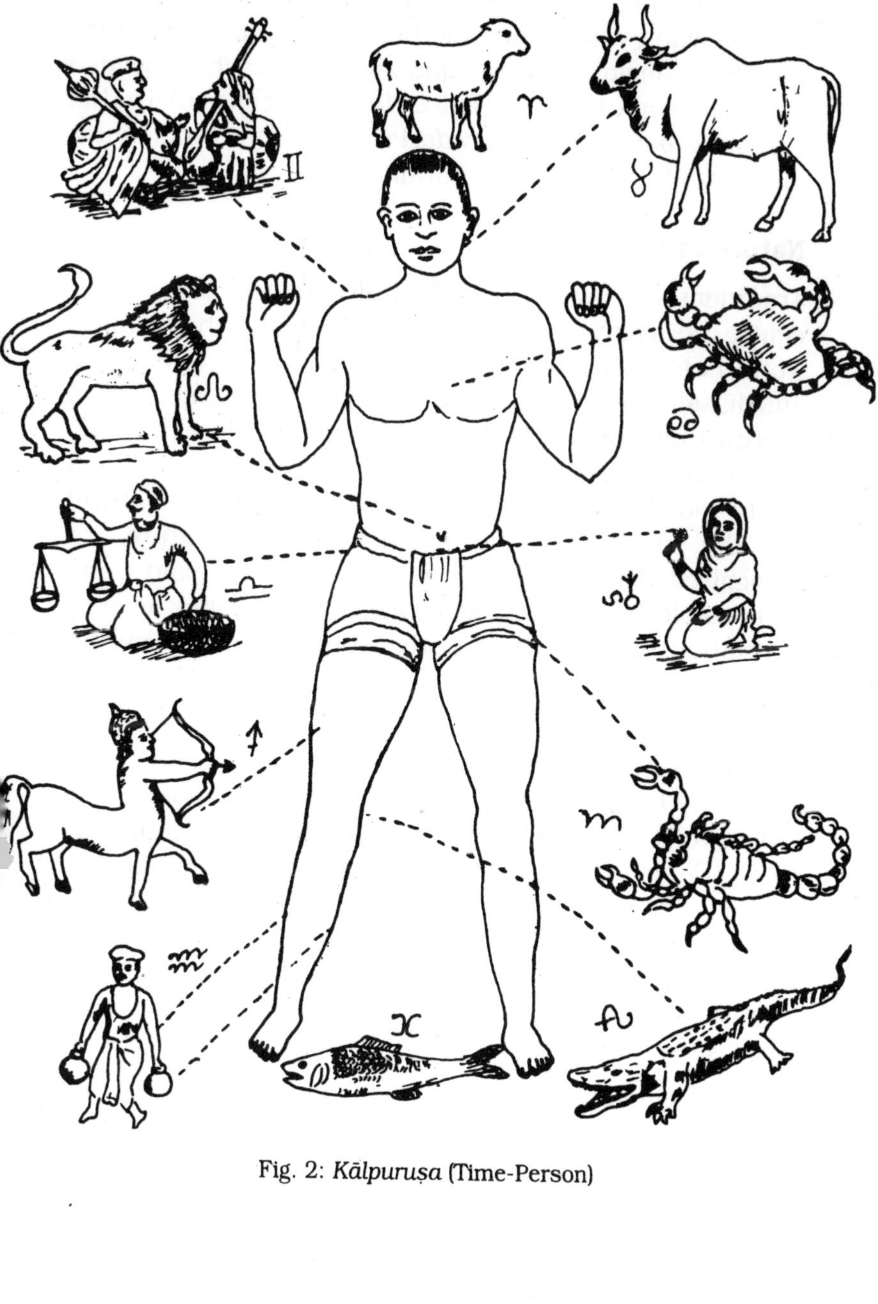

Fig. 2: *Kālpuruṣa* (Time-Person)

of the Great Act (reation of life), the Great Order (maintenance of life), and the Great Time (death and dissolution). They are inconceivable without one another. They can be understood best by the analogy of body, mind, and Spirit, each associated with the cosmic process. Hence Time has been perceived as Person: as *puruṣa* of the *Ṛgveda*, Prajāpati of the *Brāhmaṇas*, and Śiva Mahākāla of the Purāṇas.

Nature as Culture

Traditions look inward upon the Universe. Man is **not** at the centre; he is part of the whole. Like the rest of the material world, he is made of the Elements which at death disintegrate and dissolve into Nature (*prakṛti*)[6]. At the most general level there are nine Elements: Earth, Water, Fire, Air, Sky, Time, Directions, Mind and Soul. Of these the first five are called *bhūta* and the last four *dravya*. The gross (visible Nature) and the subtle (invisible Spirit) aspects of Nature are recognized. The reality of the subtler plane is said to be responsible for the grosser plane. At the higher level of realization the distinction between the gross and the subtle gets obliterated.

Elements of Nature are subject to a fivefold order: (1) *Origination*: from a state of nothingness. (2) *Binding*: Elements constitute human and other forms, both individually and collectively. (3) *Interlocking*: Form and life are cross-linked. (4) *Overlapping*: Elements have both personal (material) and universal (spiritual) attributes. (5) *Transcending*: Life transcends the limits of the form. Death transcends all attributes of Elements, the limits of Temporality. There is no intrinsic disorder in Nature. Dissolution is the integral act of Nature. Transcendence is the order of all orders.

The fivefoldness of nature has a veritable role in the making of a cultural person. Biologically, man is made of five natural Elements: earth, water, fire, air and sky.

6. Cf. Saraswati, 1995.

Pigmentation, formation and function of his body tissues, sense-organs, etc. are associated with natural Elements. psychologically also he is conditioned by attributes of the Element called *guṇa*. Human personality type is determined by biological time, beginning from the birth. Signs of the zodiac which form the body of Time Person affect man's future, the rhythm of life. From securing the conception to the last rite of cremation, a number of body-cleansing rites (*saṁskāra*) are required to be observed. Only then can one become a full member of the society, a culltural being. Purification of body is obligatory for all kinds of worships and ceremonies.

Elements of Nature, in their living state, may appropriately be described as process. They are set into a technical order that causes bio-social types. Like natural forms, the forms of culture are also subject to the fivefold order of origination, binding, interlocking, overlaping and transcending.

Culture as Inverted Tree

The sages have seen the Universe as an organic whole. If man is the microcosm, culture is what makes the human existence cosmic and divine.[7] All creatures emanating from the sacrifice of *puruṣa*'s body are invested with cosmic powers. This act of creation has a religious significance. Since the four castes of men have emanated from *puruṣa*, the sacrifice is essential and efficacious for human affairs. In the Upaniṣads, *Brahman*, the *ātman* (Soul) is postulated as manifest in man's psychical activities. It has various qualities, such as intelligence, truthfulness, endlessness, blissfulness and steadfastness. Man aspires for these qualities, because *Brahman* dwells in his sense-organs and in the mental organ.

The *Taittirīya Upaniṣad* (II.1-5) describes the all-

7. Cf. Saraswati, 1993.

comprehensive *Brahman* of the Universe and the course of the human evolution through Five elements, each called *kośa* (sheath or envelope). Man consists of the essence of food (*anna-maya*). He breathes along with breath (*prāṇa-maya*) together with the mind (*mano-maya*). He consists of understanding (*vijñāna-maya*). And the one that consists of understanding is a self that consists of bliss (*ānanda-maya*). Man consisting of all these Five *kośas* worships *Brahman* as food, as breath, as mind, as understanding, as bliss. He who knows this reaches the *Brahman*-world of bliss.

The universal Self and the individual self become one. The human body is called *kṣetra* (field) and the self who knows this is called *kṣetrajña* (the knower of the field).

Man's relationship with *Brahman* is explained in yet another way. The imagery is complex

> With Root above and Branches below is this
> Primeval Fig Tree. That is indeed the Pure;
> that is *Brahman*; that is termed the Deathless.
> In It are contained all the worlds and none
> ever goes beyond it. This verily is That.
>
> — *Kaṭha Upaniṣad*, 6.1

Admittedly, the tree is the great *prakṛti* (Nature), the primeval Mother. The symbol of the Tree, the Tree of Life, has been known to many ancient peoples. There is, however, one peculiarity of the Indian tradition that is not found elsewhere, namely, the Root of the Tree is said to be above and the Branches beneath, whereas all the other World Trees have their roots in the underworld and their Branches in the Sky.[8]

The symbol of the Inverted Tree goes well with the Indian conception of man and culture.[9] The physical man

8. Cf. Prem, 1982.
9. Cf. Saraswati, 1993.

(made of natural elements) is ritually processed as a social person. The social person (the Four castes of men) undergoes through a transcendent-supernatural-superpsychic process of cultivation of knowlege, and purification of mind and body. This is reflected in the ancient system of the *varṇāśram-dharma* which is structured on a fourfold control mechanism. Life is ordered into four successive stages from learning to performing to gradual indifference and finally to a stage of complete withdrawal from "this worldly" activities.

Human desires are fourfold: the desire to uphold the order of life, the desire connected with wealth and power, pleasure and procreation, and ultimately the desire for transcending all desires — the ultimate freedom to merge into the macrocosm.

The concept of *vasordharā* (shower of wealth), which refers to the cosmic circulation of never-ending food, brings confidence in the higher order of life. The divine ordinance for "act without attraction" keeps man unperturbed in sorrows, free from passion, fear and anger.

> The *Gītā* teaches the way to the "inverted tree" of culture. Lord Śrī Kṛṣṇa said:
>
> With its Root above and Branches below,
> the Fig Tree, they say, is imperishable;
> it has Vedic hymns for leaves;
> he who knows it knows the Vedas
>
> Above and below its branches spread,
> blossoming because of the *guṇas*,
> having for their shoots the sense-objects;
> deep down in the world of men are ramified its roots,
> in the shape of the consequences of action.
>
> Its form as such is not here perceived,
> neither is its end, nor beginning, nor basis.
> Let men first new down this deep rooted Fig Tree
> with the sure weapon of detachment;

Let him pray to win to that heaven from which
there is no return and seek to find refuge
in the Primal Being from whom has emanated
this ancient world of action.

— *Gītā,* XV.1-3

Universe as God's Artefact

If Culture is an Inverted Tree, Art is an Inverted Flute. According to Indian classical music, God delights in the unstruck notes.[10] There is a correspondence between the microtones, the notes and the different deities, colours, time of day, and seasons. The cosmic Person of originative music (s*aṅgītapuruṣa*) and the cosmic Sound of creation (*nādabrahaman*) refer to the originative principle which is rooted in the unknown, the One that breathed forth all from the void.

God Viṣṇu has a thousand names, which refer to immensity. Many of these names refer to the work of art. He is "divine architect". He is the "designer of all". He is the "divine craftsman" who with all the pleasing skill, like a smith, blasted and smelted the Universe together.

God Śiva also has thousand names. He spins the Universe and draws its rotating axis back into timelessness. One of his epithets shows that he is the cosmic Dancer. At the end of Time, he dances the awesome *tāṇḍava*. Another dance, the *ānanda tāṇḍava*, Dance of Bliss in the hall of consciousness, is Śiva's dance within the heart of man. There the Naṭarāja, the Lord of Dancers, shows his fivefold action of creation, maintenance, dissolution, veiling-unveiling, and liberation.

God's epithet as the supreme Artist found the greatest emotional stimulus among the saint poets of medieval India. Kabīr, himself a weaver, used conventional similies to describe God as the weaver of the Universe:

10. Cf. Saraswati, 1999.

No one has understood
The mystery of the Great Weaver,
Who has made the entire world
The frame, and spread his warp.

God is described as potter

The clay is one,
But the Great Designer has designed it
In various shapes, in many forms.
It does not become us to find fault
With the vessels of clay,
Nor with the Potter who shaped them.

God is made a Painter who painted the sky with stars.

Having traced the picture of the Universe
With the brush of spontaneous creativity,
On the surface of His own body,
Having gazed upon It in Himself alone,
Lord Śiva delights.

The Pithora painters of Gujarat[11] have no word for painting. Painting is called "writing". What is painted on the wall is the creation story as "written" by God Pithora. It involves painting, singing, dancing and worship. Everyone present there thinks in terms of the spiritual presence of Pithora. The priest goes into trance and identifies the painted figures one by one. Once the ritual is completed, it is believed, God Pithora stays on the wall of the house and the inhabitants of that house live with Him for ever.

There is another similar thought. Re-creation of the cosmos is a true art. Like painting, dance is also the replication of a primordial act of God. The festival of Lai Harouba[12] (*lai*, God, *harouba*, happiness) begins with songs

---

11. Cf. Shah, 1930.
12. Cf. Vatsyayan, 1987.

of creation by which the deity is awakened. The chief priestess chants the sacred hymns and enters into a state of trance, transforming herself temporarily into a divine messenger. The sequence of dance follows various gestures emerging from the delicate hands of the dancing priestess. The human being is symbolically created. Each limb is described through dance gestures. There are 364 dance gestures through which the cosmos is ritually re-constructed and the entire life-style is ritually played. The choreographical patterns are invariably serpentine, symbolizing the primordial life in waters.

The common elements in the arts of Pithora painting and Lai Harouba dance are conspicuous. Imitation of the primordial act of God, re-creation of the cosmos, revelation of primary patterns in a state of trance, performance of music (original Sound), and making ritual (primordial Sacrifice) the proper context of artistic creation (cosmic Play) are appropriately emphasized.

To conclude, in the traditional context, man's creativity coincides the cosmic play *līlā* — that is not *māyā* (illusion) as such — which at its summit echoes the highest principle of life. It reverberates the divine essence, giving rise to a cosmocentric culture.

References

Gandhi, M.K., *The Bhagvadgītā*, Orient Paperbacks, New Delhi, 1994.

Hume, Robert Ernest, *The Thirteen Principal Upaniṣads*, Oxford University Press, Delhi, 1984.

Kramrisch, Stella, *The Presence of Śiva*, Princeton University Press, 1922.

Panikkar, Raimundo, *The Vedic Experience: Mantramañjari*, Longaman & Todd, London, Darton, 1977.

———, and Bettian Baümer, Time and History in the Tradition of India, *Cultures and Time*, UNESCO, Paris, 1976.

Prem, Sri Krishna, *The Yoga of the Kaṭhopaniṣad*. The New Order Book Co., Ahmedabad, 1982.

Raghavan, V., Viṣṇu-Sahasra-nāmā: The Thousand Names of lord Viṣṇu, *The Power of the Sacred Name*, ed. by William J. Jackson, Sri Satgur Publications, Delhi, 1994.

Saraswati, Baidyanath, 1983, *Tradtions of Tirthas in India: The Anthropology of Hindu Pilgrimage*. N.K. bosė Memorial Foundation, Varanasi.

———, 1991, Ritual Space, *Concepts of Space: Ancient and Modern*, ed. by Kapila Vatsyayan, Indira Gandhi National Centre for the Arts and Abhinav Publication, New Delhi.

———, 1992, Kṣetra, *Kalātattvakośa*, ed. by Bettina Baümer, Indira Gandhi National Centre for the Arts and Motilal Banarsidass, Delhi.

———, 1993, Culture as Inverted Tree, *The Contribution by Religions to the Culture of Peace*. UNESCO, Barcelona.

———, 1995, Elements of Nature and the Order of Culture, *Prakṛti: The Integral Vision*, Vol. 5, ed. by Baidyanath Saraswati, Indira Gandhi National Centre for the Arts and D.K. Printworld, New Delhi.

———, 1995, The Universe as God's Artefact, T*he First International Conference on Religious Art*, Tehran.

———, 1996, Ritual Time, *Concepts of Time: Ancient and Modern*, ed. by Kapila Vatsyayan, Indira Gandhi National Centre for the Arts and Sterling Publishers, New Delhi.

———, 1999, Thinking About Sound, *Dhvani: Nature and Culture of Sound*, ed. by S.C. Malik, Indira Gandhi National Centre for the Arts and D.K. Printworld, New Delhi.

Sethi, V.K. *Kabir: The Weaver of God's Name*, Radha Soami Satsang, Beas, 1984.

Shah, Haku, The Ritual Painting of the God Pithora Baba, Separatum aus *Ezz* (11), 1980.

Vatsyayan, Kapila, *Traditions of Indian Folk Dance*, Clarion Books, New Delhi, 1987.

11

Cosmology, Religion, Ethics, and Philosophy in Republican Rome

Lucretius' Blend of Cultural Constituents

Albert Cook

Lucretius in his Republican poem, written as the State's sense of itself was coming powerfully to head, reflects and — by comparison with his predecessor Ennius — at the same time avoids, the space sense underlying the new Roman Empire. The Romans, it can be said, were integrating peoples as he was integrating perceptions. Now Roman religion was a state religion, and it was, as Dumézil has shown, remarkable for the rudimentariness and the lack of connection, as well as for the 'primitiveness' in its cults.[1] Lucretius, in one synchronic

1. Georges Dumézil, *La Religion romaine archaique*, Paris, Payot, 1974, passim, and esp. 63-65. While underscoring his main thesis that the division of functions in Rome among, Jupiter Mars and Quirinus continues substantially the same tripartite division among all Indo-European peoples, Dumézil (129-130) draws some distinctions between Rome and India that are evocative for the particular qualities of the Roman Lucretius: "The Romans think *historically* while the Indians think *fabulously* . . . The Romans think *nationally* and the Indians *cosmically*. . . . The Romans think *practically* and the Indians *philosophically*. . . . The Romans think *relatively, empirically*, the Indians think *absolutely, dogmatically*. . . . The Romans think *politically*, the Indians think *morally* Romans think

stroke affirms a vast set of cosmological connections, on his simple atomic principle, and at the same time he cuts his auditor loose from allegiance to the religious practices, which would *ipso facto* be a disconnection from the state, though only implicitly.

The cosmology of early cultures is characteristically all-embracing, and this is true both for the Indo-European traditions in Vedic times and for all their later derivatives and analogues. The impulse to full cosmologizing is engrained in perception, it would seem, and beyond the Indo-European traces in Homer, characteristically more faint than those for example in Lithuanian or Norse mythology. Homer's poems can be said to exhibit, as well as a number of details of cosmological myth, at least three full-blown cosmological efforts. These are first, the whole viewpoint of the *Odyssey*; second, in the *Iliad* the Catalogue of the Ships, which provides a census of all the peoples involved; and third, the remarkable Shield of Achilles, where a whole society and its cosmological surround is depicted on an artifact manufactured on Olympus and finding no analogue among the artifacts of this or later Greek culture.

Creation myths, too, in the Indic myths about Brāhma and in Hesiod's *Theogony*, as around the world, explain as well as project a cosmos, something that Lucretius carries through in pure synchrony, oddly, when he had the examples of both mythology and the 'unmoved Mover' of Aristotle before him. But Lucretius remains also distinctly Roman in his syncretic impulse. Rome, shaped from the confluence of many peoples, evolved a syncretic cosmology from many 'native' strains as well as from Greece, and Lucretius'

→ *juridically*, the Indians think *mystically*. If we match Lucretius' characteristics to these oppositions he can be seen to cross the categories, and therefore at once to reflect his Romanness and to transcend it by incorporating 'Indian' features. (Of course with no direct derivation from India other than the remote Indo-European origin.)

integrative effort can be seen in that light as a synchronic recapitulation of an act that for the Romans, of course, took place over some time.

Cosmology in any case is often seen as implicitly synchronic in its systemic coherences, and yet the Rome in which Lucretius grew up drew its religious bases, and their cosmological implications, from a variety of sources layered diachronically through many eras. Yet he synchronizes these, and while he does preserve some Classical gods, he accounts for the creation of everything from celestial bodies, earth, and all living things by the gradual confluence of atoms (5. 94-1028).

In a complex bureaucratic civilization, that of Republican Rome or our own, a ritual system incorporates elements of cosmologically oriented myth to which credence is assigned; and this kind of religion coxists with verbal manipulations of myth and investigations of the nature of myth, sometimes radically, as in Lucretius' case.

Pre-Roman Italy was inhabited by a congeries of disparate peoples and their cults. The range was broad: from the cults of the pre-Roman aborigines, the Ligurians, the Umbrians, the Sabines, the Etruscans, the Falerians, and the crematic Celts — all or most of them providing an inscription of sun and moon, and hence of cosmological intrication, into what we can recover of their myths. At the same time, and at the opposite pole, there were as early as the sixth century BC the sophisticated cosmological and philosophical speculations in the Greek cities of Magna Graecia and Sicily where Pythagoras, Empedocles, and Zeno had been systematizing some of the elements of religion into philosophy.

The Romans, once they became politically dominant, acknowledge the syncretic, layered nature of their cults, distinguishing the *Di novensiles* (imported, innovated gods) from the *Di indigites* (native gods). There were also such adopted gods as the Magna Mater of the Near East, whose introduction was a historic event (204 BC). The Roman religion, in fact, according to Wissowa, was Hellenized in general.[2] And so Lucretius was in a sense following a conventional pattern when he based his anti-religion and cosmology on a major Greek figure, Epicurus, and to a lesser extent on another earlier one who was also, unlike Epicurus, a poet: on Empedocles.

Oddly, as Dumézil has shown, the Roman gods, as distinct from other Indo-European pantheons, stand in curious isolation from one another. Yet the culture was sensitive enough to boundaries to have invented the boundary stone, the famous Roman milestone, and to have enshrined both a God of boundaries, Terminus, and a guardian of threshold states, Janus, in its pantheon. Segal has demonstrated how pervasively Lucretius concerned himself both with the boundaries of the body and with the boundaries of the world, the flaming walls of the universe (*flammantia moenia mundi*) that indicate in the hyperbole of his phrasing the extent of his concern.

Lucretius solved the problem, so to speak, of envisioning a synchronic cosmology by homogenizing it through the system of Epicurus, an atomism in which a uniform structure extended from the microcosmic to the ultra-macrocosmic. To understand this solution was to remove the fear of death and the general religious terror, the *religio*, which, in an emphasis on the 'binding' in the root of religion, gripped those who did not have access to the atomistic solution. His move, going to Epicurus, was an acculturative move, which was pervasive intellectually but not emotionally. Epicurus, in those writings of his which we have, places far less emphasis on controlling fear than does Lucretius, and he is of course far less graphic as well. It can

---

2. Georg Wissowa, *Religion und Kultus der Römer*, Munich, C.H. Beck, 1912.

be said that Lucretius exhibits his own 'binding' in his pervasive insistence on freeing others (and therefore by implication also himself) from that binding. This is a central antithesis governing all the antitheses in his presentation of what he offers as a homogeneous and uncontradictory cosmology.

A cosmological conspectus governs if we take Lucretius' poem as a whole, as can be seen in the very first lines:

> Aeneadum genetrix, hominum divumque voluptas,
> alma Venus, caeli subter labentia signa
> quae mare navigerum, quae terras frugiferentis
> concelebras, per te quoniam genus omne animantum
> concipitur visitque exortum lumina solis:
> te, dea, te fugiunt venti, te nubila caeli
> adventumque tuum, tibi suavis daedala tellus
> summittit flores, tibi rident aequora ponti
> placatumque nitet diffuso lumine caelum.
> nam simul ac species patefactast verna diei
> et reserata viget genitabilis aura favoni,
> aeriae primum volucres te, diva, tuumque
> significant initum perculsae corda tua vi.
> inde ferae pecudes persultant pabula laeta
> et rapidos tranant amnis: ita capta lepore
> te sequitur cupide quo quamque inducere pergis.

> Aeneas' sons' mother, men's and gods' joy,
> fostering Venus, under the sky's gliding signs
> you who make teem the ship-carrying sea
> and the fruit-bearing earth, since through you every race of the living
> is conceived and, arisen, sees the light of the sun:
> you, goddess, you do winds flee, you, clouds of the sky,
> and your arrival; for you does sweet wizard earth
> put forth flowers, for you waves of the deep smile
> and the sky, pacified, shines with diffused light.
> For as soon as the spring face of day opens up
> and the unleashed breeze of fruitful west wind gets strong

at first the birds of the air show, goddess, you
and your beginning, their hearts struck by your
force.
Then do wild herds leap over your joyful pastures
and swim swift streams; so, taken by loveliness,
each
follows you in desire wherever you drive to lead.
(*De Rerum Natura*, 1:1-16)

The census of the creatures of sky, sea and earth in the passage follows a poetic, but not a philosophical convention, exemplified by Alcman (Fragment 89) and Sophocles (*Antigone*, second chorus). Sky, sea and earth are quickly named. Each is given an epithet, as already condensed into the activity, later to be revealed as atomic, which involves them in creative motion: the constellations are gliding in the sky, the sea is bearing ships, the lands of earth are producing fruits. All exhibit the crowding or teeming of the generative force: *concelebras*. Then come the creatures, given a name, *animantum*, that jibes only sketchily with Lucretius' later discussions of *anima* and *animus*. Once conceived and come forth (*exortum*), they exercise a faculty that will have a large role in the poem, the faculty of sight, (*visitque*). The object of sight is here generalized to the light of the sun, *lumina solis*, which in a few lines will be diffused through the sky and subjected to that feeling of peace, the *pax* which is Lucretius' version of Epicurus' *ataraxia*; their sky will be *placatum*.

It is at the point where he is expounding the necessary mixture of various seeds, the 'beginnings' and 'first bodies' (*corpora prima*) on earth as it produces fire, but also streams, leaves, and mountain-ranging animals (2.588-98), that Lucretius shifts to a figure comparable in many ways to his Venus, the Great Mother. The shift of subject does not obviously entail a tonal shift, because he has stayed at the pitch of metrical excitation for his unfolding of scientific data. Lucretius' *Magna Mater* has none of the perversity, the threatening alienation and desperate rapt absorption, in the galliambic meter of Catullus' Poem 63. Instead, she is initially comprehensive, cutting across domains that philosophers, including Epicurus, keep separate: "Wherefore she alone is called the great mother of the gods and mother of the beasts and generator of our body":

> *quare magna deum mater materque ferarum*
> *et nostri genetrix haec dicta est corporis una.*

The 'wherefore' leaps a large logical space, insufficiently buttressed by the 'mountain-ranging kind of beasts' (*montivago generi . . . ferarum*) of the previous line. It is Lucretius' declaration of this principle, retaining the allegorical proposition of a linkage to earth by a varied designation — not *terra* but *tellus* — that introduces the panorama of the car of Cybele and her lion procession. 'Old Greek poets' (and of course Catullus too) have sung this procession, which Lucretius asserts to signify that earth 'hangs in the space of air' (*aeris in spatio . . . pendere*) rather than being based on other earth. And a symbolic reading of the ritual attributes in the Mother's procession follows: the crown on her head indicates cities defended on the heights. She has the castrated priests (*galli*) assigned to her to show that those who have offended her are unworthy to have offspring — a theologizing depersonalization of Catullus' picture of exacerbated sterilization.

Many of the Mother's functions are those of Lucretius' invoked Venus, and the rationale he gives for her rites would seem further to endorse her. But he rejects all this as unreason 'though it is well and illustriously recounted in parts' ('*quae bene et eximie quamvis disposta feruntur*'). The gods really, he says — in one of his clearest endorsements of the Epicurean view of their separation — live separate from men 'in highest peace'. Still Lucretius here permits men to call the sea Neptune, grain Ceres, wine Bacchus, and also the earth 'mother of the gods' — so long as thereby they do not succumb to *religio.*

So the (internal) terrors of spirit and the external 'walls of the universe' (*monia mundi*, 16) are mastered in a way that makes the human situation, with the help of the godlike Epicurus, close in temper to the situation of the gods which the passage immediately describes.[3]

These walls of the universe are real, though infinitely receding. They are caught in the movement of the atoms all the way, and in the poetic afflatus here they yield easily to the metaphorical tinge in the naming of winds, clouds, showers, hoarfrost, white snow, aether, and broadly diffused laughing light (17-30).

In the tonality sustained by Lucretius' verse the 'peace of spirit' that the gods enjoy and that the poem envisions will find a metaphorical anchorage in the invisibility of the temples of Acheron, along with the visibility of all things,

---

3. The 'walls of the universe', *moenia mundi*, come in at strategic points of Lucretius' presentation. In 5.1212-1213 a contemplation of *moenia mundi* wearies the reason and raises the question as to whether the walls themselves will sustain atomic change forever. Epicurus himself is more exclusively mathematical about the edge of the universe, where in Lucretius' invocation he is seen as a hero conquering the *moenia mundi*:

   ergo vivida vis animi pervicit, et extra
   processit longe flammantia moenia mundi
   atque omne immensum peragravit mente animoque,
   unde refert nobis victor quid possit oriri,
   quid nequeat, finita potestas denique cuique,
   quanam sit ratione atque alte terminus haerens

   So the lively force of his mind won through and he passed
   far beyond the flaming walls of the universe
   and in mind and spirit the unbounded whole,
   whence, a victor, he brought back to us what could arise
   and what not, at last the power to anything is fixed,
   and by what reason, and the deeply clinging boundary
   stone. (1:57-75)

unimpeded by earth and by the void underfoot. The poet's consequent reaction, transcending Epicurean pleasure in its complex intensity and poetic excitation, links the combination of perception and reaction to both shrinking (the root meaning of *horror*) and pleasure (*voluptas . . . atque horror*), as Schrijvers points out.[4] The complex feeling is a reaction to an entire state of affairs, *'his rebus'*, when nature lies manifest, covered by the 'force' of Epicurus 'from all angles' (*ex omni parte*).

The gods are caught in the tension of the negative, but the tension persists so that, in the notable introductory case of Venus, Lucretius can affirm them where Epicurus could not have consistently done so. Correspondingly, the impetus towards proof sparks the constructive-affirmative in this poem so forcibly that it can carry its own energy towards a concreteness that is quite un-Epicurean, and also quite distinct from the elegant economy of philosophical presentation in general.[5]

The relation between a universal physical system and imperatives of ethical behavior belongs to the long tradition of earlier Greek philosophy. For Pythagoras this system was mathematical, and it led obscurely to the basis for a quasi-religious cult. For Plato there was also an obscure

---

4. P.H. Schrijvers, *Horror ac Divina Voluptas: Etudes sur la poétique et la poésie de Lucrèce*, Amsterdam, 1970.

5. Erich Ackermann, *Lukrez und der Mythos*, Wiesbaden, Steiner, 1979. "From his own fear before death and before the mythic underworld, man concludes that the eternity of the gods implies their happiness, a false conclusion from Epicurus' point of view". "Aus seiner eigenen Furcht vor dem Tode und vor der mythischen Unterwelt schliesst der Mensch, dass die Ewigkeit der Götter ihr Glück impliziert — ein nach epikureischer Sicht falscher Gedankenschluss"(125).

connection between mathematics and virtue,[6] and Epicurus can be said to follow him, though his atomic system and his psychological ethics, so far as we can tell, have few bridging rationales between them, and all the more because Epicurus departs from both Plato and Aristotle in his view of Being, as well as in his avoidance of politics.[7]

The tonal range at moments takes on an explicit binary opposition, as, first of all, in the repeated distinction btween light and dark. Then there is the contrast between honey and the bitter cup of message, or the early reference to Mars and Venus (1.31), or the use of Paris and Helen (1.470ff.) to instantiate and introduce the deduction of both love and war from atoms. Terror itself, or horror, can even be included in the tonal range because it is the function of Epicurean doctrine to dispel it. At the triumph of reason the 'terrors of spirit disperse', 'diffugiunt animi terrores' (3.18).

As he describes ageing at the end of Book Two the description functions not only for itself but as the last of his preparations for the leap to a direct and prolonged presentation of death in Book Three, which begins as though spirited on by the clarity of its evocation of the Greeks. It is followed by a discourse on its traditional binary opposite, love, in Book Four. In Book Five, expanding to the mortality of the physical universe, he changes his tone as he passes to the beginning of the physical universe,

6. For the connection between mathematics and virtue in Plato, see Joan Kung, "Mathematics and Virtue in Plato's *Timaeus*", in John P. Anton and Anthony Preus, (eds.), *Plato*, Albany: SUNY Press, 1989, 309-40. For Plato's expansion into mathematics after his first trip to Sicily, ***see*** Gregory Vlastos, 'Elenchus and Mathematics' in *Socrates: Ironist and Moral Philosopher*, Cambridge: Cambridge, University Press, 1991, 107-31.

7. "Ourselves must be delivered from that which has to do with the prison of everyday and political affairs", *Sententiae Vaticanae* 58, Bollack, *La Pensée du plaisir*, 522. This is a notion variously repeated in what we have of Epicurus.

and then finally to the beginnings of vegetable, animal, and then human life. Book Six, too, stays in cosmic perspective at first with an account of large-scale celestial and geological phenomena, returning to man with an account of medical phenomena. As though picking up from the other end of his long account of primitivism in Book Five (925-1457), he suddenly takes up the civilization of Athens, putting a legendary peak of human history in the light of a 'worst case' graphic description of the plague at Athens, without any of Thucydides' historical inferences even though he is following Thucydides. This conclusion is the most extreme of his 'worst case' presentations, as though the force of the poem up to this point will stand behind the reader to stomach a contemplation of such devastations.[8]

If we may take our cue from Cicero's description (*Tusculan Disputations*, III), the subject, for Stoics and Epicureans, is *perturbationes*, which for Lucretius are to be rcmoved by a contemplation of the universal atomic system. He does not address directly "the notion [of] the imminence of a great evil . . . such that sorrow is called for".[9] And his complicated evocations around death and anxiety, which

---

8. Book Six, 40-41, repeats two lines from Book One (147-148), as though to buttress by a refrain the strengh of *ratio* against the university of fright.

9. Gisela Striker, '*Ataraxia:* Happiness as Tranquility", in *The Monist*, 73:1 (January 1990), 97-110. As she says, "The conception of happiness that seems to have become popular after the time of Plato and Aristotle . . . seems to come from outside the tradition that began with Plato or Socrates . . . it is the only conception of *eudaimonia* in Greek ethics that identifies happiness with a state of mind and makes it depend entirely on a person's attitude or beliefs" (97). Lucretius, it may be said, living within the assumption, expands it and feels so free in it that he can even invert it, changing the imperturbable tranquillity of Epicurus into a swelled straining towards the triumph of an intellectual clarity.

go beyond Epicurus,[10] are reoriented, subverted, and pacified by the strength of his evocations, though these are so brief as to seem grace notes, of a countervailing peace. The process, indeed, comes to seem a distant foreshadowing of Heidegger's organization around a consciousness of death that explicates a deep 'thrownness' (*Geworfenheit*) towards death. Some such analogy, however anachronistic, is necessary to account for the persisting integral effect of a poem which for the modern reader must begin by being analyzed as composed of discordant elements, a largely discarded scientific theory brought forward to palliate a perennial complex 'care' (Heideger's *Sorge*) over human existence.

So the (internal) terrors of spirit and the (external) 'walls of the universe' (*moenia mundi*, 16) are mastered in a way that makes the human situation, with the help of the godlike Epicurus, close in temper to the situation of the

---

10. **See** Charles Segal, *Lucretius on Death and Anxiety*, Princeton, Princeton University Press, 1990; "Boundaries, Worlds, and Analogical Thinking, or How Lucretius Learned to Love Atomism and Still Write Poetry", in Karl Galinsky, (ed.), *The Interpretation of Roman Poetry: Empiricism or Hermeneutics?* Frankfurt, Peter Lang, 1992, 137-56. Segal expounds forcefully the similarities and differences between Epicurus and Lucretius in their depictions of death, with special emphasis on evocative powers and subliminal implications in Lucretius' presentation. He underscores Lucretius' vivid sense of boundaries of the body and their violation. As he says, "His argument [about the process of dying] is indirect and allusive, perhaps because he is aware that he is dealing with a subject generally avoided by the Master, or perhaps because he realizes that the material takes him into the areas where poetry, with its tendency toward emotional engagement, least comfortably walks the same road as philosophy, with its aim of serene detachment" (26-27).

gods which the passage immediately describes.[11]

The synchronic cosmology functions at once as an explanation of the physical universe and an orienting set of constraints on moral behavior—two functions also combined by the usual, more traditional cosmologies.

[OUT]: "The identification of Natura with Venus", as Anne Amory says, "brings the natural world into close relation with *voluptas*, the center of Epicurean ethics".[12]

---

11. The 'walls of the universe', *moenia mundi*, come in at strategic points of Lucretius' presentation. In 5.1212-1213 a contemplation of *moenia mundi* wearies the reason and raises the question as to whether the walls themselves will sustain atomic change forever. Epicurus himself is more exclusively mathematical about the edge of the universe, where in Lucretius' invocation he is seen as a hero conquering the *moenia mundi:*

    ergo vivida vis animi pervicit, et extra
    processit longe flammantia moenia mundi
    atque omne immensum peragravit mente animoque,
    unde refert nobis victor quid possit oriri,
    quid nequeat, finita potestas denique cuique,
    quanam sit ratione atque alte terminus haerens

    So the lively force of his mind won through and he passed
    far beyond the flaming walls of the universe
    and in mind and spirit the unbounded whole,
    whence, a victor, he brought back to us what could arise
    and what not, at last the power to anything is fixed,
    and by what reason, and the deeply clinging boundary
    stone. (1:57-75)

12. Anne Amory, "*Obscura de re lucidi carmina:* Scenes and Poetry in *De Rerum Natura*", *Yale Classical Studies*, 1969, 143-68. She reads more force into 'honey on the bitter cup' (146-47) than a sceptic might. "He will touch *cuncta* with poetic grace . . . every detail, perhaps for him every word and letter, will have an aroma from the sweet body of the Muses". (153-54). "Lucretius, in spite of his orthodox profession of desire for *ataraxia*, obviously preferred to see things as restless." (168) **See** also John Petersen Elder, "Lucretius 1.1-49", *TAPA* 85 (1954), 88-120. As Elder says (91), "the poem moves with →

However, the tonality of this *voluptas* is quite different in this passage from the posture of Epicurus himself towards erotic pleasure, for which he recommends prudence rather than a creative surging.[13] And Lucretius' own views towards love, as expressed in Book Four, see it Epicurean-wise as a disturbance, much like the religion which in this invocation he would seem to be indulging. This Poem already offers a sort of double contradiction to the overriding argument of the poem, since first, in the general argument of the poem, man should get peace by freeing himself of religion, and not by subjecting himself, as here, to any one god. Second, according to the Epicurean view the gods have no effect on the world, let alone the intimate and forceful effect of this Venus. Rather, they sit off by themselves in a model enjoyment. The phenomena here attributed to the influence of Venus are to be analyzed in the poem as the effects of atomic organization: the winds (1.271-297), the clouds (6.451-534), the creation of life on earth (5.785-636), and the motions of the constellations. (5.509-537). To say that these effects, and love, await the atomic analysis they will get later in the poem does not really diminish the force of the assertions here.[14] In the light of just this passage, Lucretius' tonality towards the gods must be called adaptively responsive and intermittent, whereas Epicurus does not waver in setting them calmly into the perspective of his system.

The emphasis of the formal exposition, as the poem very quickly begins, is all but exclusively on the scientific side of Epicurus, whereas in developing Roman speculation

---

→ unembarrassed ease and rapidity from the physical plane to the . . . mental or spiritual, a movement sanctioned if indeed not required by Epicurean physics, since body and mind are both corporeal, coterminous, and cosensitive". This produces (94) an 'odd dual allegiance'.

13. Diogenes Laertius (10, 18) quotes Epicurus as saying that a wise man should not fall in love, nor is love sent from the gods.

14. This is the line Bailey takes about the *Magna Mater* in commenting on 2.571ff.

it was the ethical side that gathered thought. On the face of it, indeed, one would expect poetry at this date also to be ethical in emphasis, not scientific. Again, the yield of the poem, its effect as well as its message, is a kind of ethics: to produce peace by contemplating the proper scientific view. This peace is a peculiarly Lucretian one, indistinguishable from the pitch of excitement that the invocation plunges into, through the presentation of the affirmative side of his paradox in simultaneously asserting this goddess and denying the gods. Already the meld of poetry and philosophy has got around the paradox in a contradiction that philosophy by itself could not coun-tenance. Only such a poetic strategy will work, or has here worked. In the dimension of fusing poetry and philosophy, Lucretius has found a posture profoundly distinct not only from the prose of his master Epicurus, and all but completely free of the local epic poet Ennius, but also from the earlier masters who couched thir philosophy in verse, from the time of Empedocles, whom he does mention, and Parmenides, whom he does not. Before this Plato skirted the whole problem of philosophy in poetry, with all the complexity of his approach to poetry. But Aristotle attempted to address the problem, oversimply, by characterizing Empedocles as having nothing of poetry except meter (*Poetics*, 1447b).

The first word of the poem, *Aeneadum*, measures Lucretius' depature from Ennius, who is soon mentioned explicitly (1.114-126), honored but left aside, for he sang erroneously of the transmigration of souls, even though he was 'the first who brought down from pleasant Helicon a crown with eternal leaves' (*qui primus amoeno/detulit ex Helicone perenni fronde coronam*). It is quite striking, in view of Lucretius' main theme, that the national begins the poem, as though the poet's point of setting out were not Epicurus but Ennius. We might well think that the Epicurean view was to be presented from an internationalist perspective, and that the start of *Aeneadum genetrix* would be a discordant one, or at least a subsidiary one, even though it is soon effectually picked up by the mention of the dedicate Memmius and his possible embroilment in political affairs (*patriai tempore iniquo*, 41).

The fiction of the noble, lay auditor Memmius undercuts the philosophical schools, setting Lucretius rhetorically into a situation where he must start wholly afresh, whereas in the ideal post-Aristotelian Greece of his master there was a highly developed variety of schools, and the Epicurean Garden was one among many professional communities. And actually, if we reconstruct the situation and climate around the philosophical writings of his contemporary Cicero, there were many philosophical professionals and devotees operating in Lucretius' Rome. But Lucretius writes as though they did not exist, going all out in the strategic advantage of underscoring the essentials and ignoring the qualifications of local controversy. Memmius is not only a pupil but, if the usual identification is correct, a powerful political figure. So he constitutes a departure, more complex in his posture than the addressees of Epicurus' letters, though both Lucretius and his master, who himself is part of the compound addressee of the *De Rerum Natura*, are following the ancient convention, found in Egypt as well as in such construct-figures as Theognis, of setting up a discourse rhetorically in the form of a communication to a younger learner.

There is a particularly Roman twist to Lucretius' Venus, too, if this invocation is compared to the Homeric 'Hymn to Aphrodite'; and Venus was interwoven with Roman life in the first century BC.[15] But we do not again hear of the function celebrated here, and very little directly of Venus, not even in the book devoted to love, Book Four. The emphatic presence of Venus at the beginning carries the sweep that will find its explanation later on in the main

15. For telling details, ***see*** Pierre Grimal, *Love in Ancient Rome*, Norman: University of Oklahoma Press, 1986, 43-44.

exposition of the poem. The invocation fuses the urgency of that explanation, where the *signa* in the sky, and the fact that they are gliding, and the sky itself, will be analyzed as subject to a single structure, a structure only mysteriously connected to Venus—and, again, certainly not for Epicurus, whose gods were causally unconnected to terrestrial life, and who downplayed the force of love here being emphasized.

This *religio*, a 'binding' into religious terror, incapacitates man from getting the pacifying and liberating lesson of the universal Epicurean atomic flux; 'human life is oppressed under heavy religion', ('*humana vita oppressa gravi sub religione*', 1.62-3). *Religio* stands, repeatedly excoriated, as a blind antithesis, similar only in the strength of its emotional tonality to the informed clarity he enjoins. Lucretius brings the heavens to earth, as Cicero said of Socrates,[16] by applying Ionian/Epicurean cosmology to human emotions more extensively than had Epicurus — who is a sort of savior, and even a god (5.19), in Lucretius' presentation.

Both Plato and Aristotle connected their ethical postures to elaborate political imperatives and analyses, buttressing them with physical and psychological analyses which are intermittent but not incidental. Less than half a century later Epicurus' situation distances him from such social considerations, and the ethical part of his writing resembles that of the Stoics in detaching all the ethical speculation from any constructive assessment of social desiderata. The Roman citizen was not the citizen of a free Athens. Lucretius, too, belonged to a society large, complex, and so subjected to large forces that he followed both Epicurus and the Stoics in withdrawing his attention from such problems. His social descriptions, as of the plague, are merely descriptive. They imitate Thucydides but have no connection to an overall process of enchained decisions in the society, which he eschews, as Ennius did not. He reorients Ennius

16. Cicero, *Tusculan Disputations*, V.4.10.

and internationalizes him, but also effectively privatises him.

In keeping with the focus of his absorptions, Lucretius does not deal directly with Plato, Aristotle or the Stoics, even when their discussions bear on the questions he addresses. He confines himself, rather, to Epicurus — and beyond Epicurus, to those who are on a par as predecessors of Plato and Aristotle as well as of Epicurus and himself, the pre-Socratics: with Heraclitus (1.635-705), with Anaxagoras (1.830-951), with Democritus (3.369-379), and with Empedocles (1.716-34). The *carmina* of the cosmologist Empedocles make him 'scarcely human' (*vix humanus*) as a hero (1.730), but his doctrines require a qualification which paradoxically removes him from full parity with the mastery of Epicurus. Yet Epicurus, in turn, wrote no poetry. So for the combination of poetry and correct philosophy Lucretius can stand alone. He does see himself as an originator, 'I cross out-of-the-way places of the Pierides, trod by the sole of none before' ('*avia Pieridum perago, loca nullius ante/trita solo*', 1.926). And he is an originator in poetry while a follower in philosophy: It is the untrod places of the *Pierides* that he crosses.

In the tonality sustained by Lucretius' verse the 'peace of spirit' that the gods enjoy and that the poem envisions will find a metaphorical anchorage in the invisibility of the temples of Acheron, along with the visibility of all things, unimpeded by earth and by the void underfoot. The poet's consequent reaction, transcending Epicurean pleasure in its complex intensity and poetic excitation, links the combination of perception and reaction to both shrinking (the root meaning of *horror*) and pleasure (*voluptas . . . atque horror*), as Schrijvers points out.[17] The complex feeling is a reaction to an entire state of affairs, '*his rebus*', when nature lies manifest, covered by the 'force' of Epicurus 'from all angles' (*ex omni parte*).

17. P.H. Schrijvers 1970.

List of Contributors

Alberto Cook: Departmente of Comparative English and Classics, Box E (Marston Hall), Providence, Rhode Island 02911112, USA.

Ary Reisbaum Godoroski: Seneca 141-802 Col Polanco. México C.P. 11560, México D.F.

Sara Ladrón de Guevara: Secretaría Académica, Edificio A 2do. Piso Lomas del Estadio S/N Universidad De Veracruz, Jalapa, Veracruz. México.

Henryk Karon Kocyba: Escuela Nacional de Estudios Profesionales Acatlán, UNAM. México. D.F.

Alessandro Lupo: Departamento de Estudios Glotoantropológicos, Universitá" La Sapienza", Roma, Italy.

Marie Odile Marion: Escuela Nacional de Antropología, Av. Periférico Sur y Calle Zapote s/n col. Isidro Fabela México 14030 D. F. México.

Hugo Portela and Herinaldy Gómez: Universidad de Cauca, Carrera No. 1 A 22225, Popayan, Colombia.

Onkar Prasad: Pali Characha Kendra, Visva Bharati University, Santiniketan, 731236, W. B., India

Baidynath Saraswati: Unesco Professor. Indira Gandhi National Centre for the Arts, New Delhi.

Yolotl González Torres: DEAS, INAH, Ex Convento del Carmen, Av. Revolución s/n San Angel, México 01000 D. F. México.